Unlocking Practitioner Inquiry

Key components of practitioner inquiry provide an effective approach to lasting educational change. By including narratives of practice from across diverse early childhood settings, this book investigates issues that arise during implementation of inquiry-focussed professional learning cycles. It presents practitioner inquiry as a vehicle for empowering educators and educational systems.

Research-based, this book brings together theory and practice from authors and internationally recognised commentators to inform and inspire early childhood educators. Chapters are thematically grouped in three focus areas. The first centres on background contextual information to set the scene, the second offers real-life stories based on authors' experiences and the third provides insight into broader issues of leadership and professional learning. Voices of educators, teachers and leaders are included to provide multiple points of entry for readers with different interests, backgrounds, and levels of expertise.

As a resource to support ongoing professional practice in the prior-to-school sector, this book is essential reading for early years educators, teachers and leaders of educational change. It is relevant for those investigating how educators in early childhood centres, executive offices and consultancy positions can use data-based, locally relevant investigations of practice to improve educational outcomes.

Katey De Gioia describes herself as first and foremost an early childhood teacher. She has appreciated the opportunity to take on leadership roles across a variety of educational institutions throughout her career. Katey has adopted practitioner inquiry to lead evidence informed change to practice.

Alma Fleet is an experienced teacher and teacher educator who enjoys consultancies with teachers in diverse settings and locations, particularly focusing on practitioner inquiry and pedagogical documentation as vehicles of educational change. She has enjoyed leadership and research roles at Macquarie University and has valued her time with Aboriginal colleagues.

Catherine Patterson has recently retired from working with student teachers at the Institute of Early Childhood, Macquarie University. Her research into practitioner inquiry has enabled her to support experienced educators and leaders in re-thinking their daily practices with children and adults.

Marina Papic is Professor of Early Childhood Education and Mathematics Education at the Australian Catholic University. Marina has worked in the education sector for 35 years and has held various teaching, academic and leadership roles. Her research focuses on teacher professional learning in mathematics curriculum and pedagogy and early numeracy.

Unlocking Practitioner Inquiry

Growing Professionally in Early Years
Education

**Edited by
Katey De Gioia, Alma Fleet, Catherine
Patterson and Marina Papic**

Routledge
Taylor & Francis Group

LONDON AND NEW YORK

Designed cover image: © Getty Images

First published 2023
by Routledge
4 Park Square, Milton Park, Abingdon, Oxon OX14 4RN

and by Routledge
605 Third Avenue, New York, NY 10158

Routledge is an imprint of the Taylor & Francis Group, an informa business

© 2023 selection and editorial matter, Katey De Gioia, Alma Fleet, Catherine Patterson, and Marina Papic; individual chapters, the contributors

British Library Cataloguing-in-Publication Data
A catalogue record for this book is available from the British Library

Library of Congress Cataloging-in-Publication Data
Names: De Gioia, Katey, editor. | Fleet, Alma, editor. |
Patterson, Catherine, editor. | Papic, Marina, editor.
Title: Unlocking practitioner inquiry : growing professionally in early years education / Katey De Gioia, Alma Fleet, Catherine Patterson, Marina Papic.
Description: 1st edition. | New York : Routledge, 2023. |
Includes bibliographical references and index. |
Identifiers: LCCN 2022059740 (print) | LCCN 2022059741 (ebook) |
ISBN 9781032158266 (hbk) | ISBN 9781032158259 (pbk) |
ISBN 9781003245827 (ebk)
Subjects: LCSH: Educational change--Australia. | Action research in education--Australia. | Teachers--In-service training--Australia. |
Professional learning communities--Australia. | Early childhood education--Australia. | Education, Primary--Australia.
Classification: LCC LA2102 .U5 2023 (print) | LCC LA2102 (ebook) |
DDC 372.210994--dc23/eng/20230301
LC record available at https://lccn.loc.gov/2022059740
LC ebook record available at https://lccn.loc.gov/2022059741

ISBN: 978-1-032-15826-6 (hbk)
ISBN: 978-1-032-15825-9 (pbk)
ISBN: 978-1-003-24582-7 (ebk)

DOI: 10.4324/9781003245827

Typeset in Bembo
by Taylor & Francis Books

Contents

Figures

Tables

Contributors

Helen Aitken has been in the early childhood education sector in Aotearoa New Zealand for over 30 years in the capacity of teacher, leader, professional development facilitator, and lecturer in both Auckland and the Waikato regions. She is currently employed as a Teaching Fellow at The University of Waikato and lives in Hamilton with her husband and two young children. Helen has been interested in and engaged with the pedagogical work of Reggio Emilia since 2001, and she has been investigating how early childhood education teachers and settings in Aotearoa New Zealand can be inspired and challenged in ways which complement New Zealand's own cultural context and curriculum. She is a trustee of REANZ (Reggio Emilia Aotearoa New Zealand) and has attended three Study Tours in Reggio Emilia, Italy.

Leanne Armao received the Master of Education from the University of Melbourne (Australia). Her professional interests focus on the Continuity of Early Childhood Learning, Practitioner Inquiry and 'the third teacher': beautiful spaces. Leanne is the Principal of Keysborough Primary School located in Springvale South, Victoria, Australia. Since 2016, professional learning and research has focused on 'Playful Classrooms' and the continuity of early childhood learning. In 2019 the school received the Minister of Education award for innovative practices and transition approaches from kindergarten to school. By the end of 2022, all learning spaces from kindergarten to Year 6 will reflect 'playful classroom' pedagogical practices. Currently Leanne leads a three-year research project focused on oral language and parent engagement through a Community of Practice consisting of four primary schools and five kindergartens. Leanne believes and strongly advocates for shared responsibility in children's learning involving educators, children, and parents.

Chris Celada initially had her pedagogical assumptions challenged when working in diverse early childhood practices in Latin America where she was driven to consider: What is education for ... in a war zone, a peasant village, a meta-city in a third world country? The questions continued while working with recently arrived migrant families in Australia where colliding multiple interpretations of education only acted to complicate the questions. Teaching early childhood education students at college meant that pedagogical perspectives rubbed up against economic and political positions and interests. In her first encounter with ideas from Reggio Emilia in 2000, Chris discovered a way of thinking and practice where questions were welcomed and researched in collaboration with colleagues, children, parents, and community creating new theory, deeper understandings and new, innovative practice. Collaborating since 2004 with fellow questioner Margo Hobba, Chris has come to see practitioner inquiry as a place of research seeking deeper understanding of knowledge-building processes to create new pedagogical practice.

Adam Christie is a passionate early childhood teacher who completed his degree in Early Children Education at Flinders University, South Australia. He is currently studying for a master's degree in educational leadership at the University of South Australia. He has previously worked in non-government and government early childhood services as an educator and leader. Currently, he is an early childhood consultant working alongside leaders and teams with a focus on leadership and pedagogy. His areas of research interest include early childhood ethics, systems leadership, pedagogical documentation and practitioner inquiry. He is the proud Dad of two and an advocate for children.

Maria Cooper is a senior lecturer at the Faculty of Education and Social Work, the University of Auckland, New Zealand. Before beginning her academic career, she worked as a teacher and a leader in a large urban early childhood education centre in Auckland. Her current research and teaching interests include educational leadership from Western and Pacific Indigenous perspectives, early years curriculum, infant-toddler pedagogies, equity-driven initiatives, and qualitative research methodologies. She has received awards for her doctoral research on the collective leadership of teaching teams and her master's research on teacher-family collaboration in assessment. Maria is an experienced mentor for newly qualified teachers and is co-editor of *Ngā Tau Tuatahi The First Years: New Zealand Journal of Infant and Toddler Education*.

Katey De Gioia describes herself as first and foremost a teacher and has worked in the early childhood education and care sector since beginning her teaching career over 30 years ago. She has enjoyed the challenge of leadership roles across educational institutions, including centre director, head of school for a private college, facilitating transition-to-school across local government areas for a state education department, and as a senior lecturer in professional experience at Macquarie University. More recently, Katey worked for a national nonprofit early childhood organisation. She was responsible for leading a program of support for teachers across their career lifecycle. Currently, she has a role in sector engagement and impact within a newly formed national education evidence body. Underpinned by a framework of partnerships, Katey's research work and writing has focused on transitions into educational settings for children from refugee and immigrant backgrounds and engaging in teacher and educator inquiry to effect educational change.

Jessica Dubois leads a team of brilliant early childhood educators in a birth–5 government setting in South Australia. She was a primary school teacher and curriculum leader before becoming an early childhood educator. Her experiences of learning in a remote Indigenous community and currently a community rich in cultural and linguistic diversity drives her passion for intercultural engagement and excellence in practice for all.

Alma Fleet has a long association with Macquarie University, including roles in undergraduate and postgraduate teaching, research and leadership. Her work includes engagement in early literacy, transition to school, professional fieldwork, and educational change. She has also enjoyed working with Aboriginal and/or Torres Strait Islanders to further their educational goals. She is actively involved with educational consultancies, primarily with Semann & Slattery, supporting the team with projects through various Australian state departments of education as well as other groups interested in progressing their professional understanding, particularly through practitioner inquiry and pedagogical documentation. Publications include co-authorship with Janet Robertson, Catherine Patterson, and Katey De Gioia as well as a six-volume early childhood series co-edited with Michael Reed for Routledge. Based in Sydney, Australia, her curiosity takes her to other Australian and international locations to pursue collaborations and investigations with friends and colleagues.

Diti Hill-Denee retired from lecturing in early childhood education at the University of Auckland's Faculty of Education and Social Work in 2014. She continues at the University as an Honorary Academic. For over 40 years, Diti has been actively involved with a wide range of early childhood services and organisations as parent, teacher, and teacher educator. She is currently on the national executive of OMEP Aotearoa New Zealand (World Organisation for Early Childhood) and is a trustee of REANZ (Reggio Emilia Aotearoa New Zealand). She has engaged extensively with the pedagogical work of Reggio Emilia and continues to facilitate professional learning that draws on this work in relation to the New Zealand early childhood curriculum, *Te Whāriki*. She is passionate about inspiring teachers to explore and debate the nature of the teaching-learning process and to reflect on the effect that personal pedagogical practice has on their own lives and the lives of the children they teach.

Margo Hobba is a psychology graduate who went on to work as a teacher-educator with babies, toddlers, pre-schoolers, and adults. Disturbed by traditional pedagogical theories and practices that seem to disregard the baffling nature of human intelligences she has been researching connections between pedagogy and the subjective experiences of knowing and being for many years. Managing the Children's Museum in the State Museum of Victoria offered a unique opportunity to work with the designer Mary Featherston in the conception and production of interactive environments merging children, materials, curiosity, and learning. Discovering Reggio Emilia in the early 1990s presented an opportunity to engage with a long-term project that disrupts traditional assumptions about education and offers an alternative pedagogical reality. For several years now, Margo has been working as a teacher-researcher with her colleague Chris Celada to create professional learning experiences that bring bodies, hearts, and minds together in contexts of research.

Nicole Mockler is Associate Professor of Education, based at the Sydney School of Education and Social Work at the University of Sydney. Her research and writing primarily focuses on education policy and politics, particularly as they frame teachers' work, professional identity and professional learning. She is co-author/editor of 14 books. Her recent scholarly books include *Questioning the language of improvement and reform in education: Reclaiming meaning* (Routledge, 2018, with Susan Groundwater-Smith) and *Constructing teacher identities: How the print media define and represents teachers and their work* (Bloomsbury, 2022). Nicole is currently Editor in Chief of *The Australian Educational Researcher*, a member of the Editorial Board of the *British Educational Research Journal* and the International Advisory Board of *Educational Action Research*.

Linda Newman is currently based at Newcastle University, NSW. She works as a researcher and consultant in the early childhood sector. In recent years her research has focused on participatory work with early childhood educators in Chile, Western Sydney and Newcastle. Linda is currently co-leading (with Christine Woodrow), a practitioner research and professional learning program in the Blue Mountains, NSW Australia. She continues to write papers with colleagues in early childhood practice and in the university sector. She also holds a research grant aimed at investigating children's views about their play and learning environments. This research takes Linda back to an earlier passion for early childhood inclusion. The findings are being used to collaborate with the planners of an innovative, inclusive and environmentally friendly new centre for inclusion in South-Western Sydney. Owners, planners, architects, landscape architects, therapists, researchers, and educators are working collaboratively to fulfil a vision and dream.

Marina Papic is Professor of Early Childhood and Mathematics Education at the Australian Catholic University. She has worked in the education sector for 35 years and has held various teaching, academic and leadership roles including: Head of Department—Institute of Early Childhood, Macquarie University Sydney; Director of the Children and Families Research Centre, Macquarie University Sydney; Goodstart Early Learning NSW/ACT State

Manager; Executive Officer Primary of an independent PreK–12 College; and Manager of Children's Services, Blacktown City Council. Marina has led large research projects focused on mathematics curriculum and practice, early numeracy, and professional development of early childhood teachers. Marina was a member of the ACECQA Ratings Review Panel for two terms and a member of the consortium of early childhood experts contracted to develop the national Early Years Learning Framework. Marina sits on several Advisory Committees including the NSW Department of Education, Early Childhood Education Advisory Group.

Catherine Patterson, recently retired, taught undergraduate and postgraduate students at the Institute of Early Childhood, Macquarie University for over two decades. Her teaching responsibilities centred on facilitating the professional growth of student teachers in professional experience courses. Catherine's research explored the realities of teaching and learning for both novice and experienced early childhood practitioners. Her recent investigations focused on educators using practitioner inquiry to enhance the experience of children in the early years. She used this research to provide professional learning opportunities to support experienced educators and leaders in re-thinking their daily practices with children and adults. Catherine's recent publications were co-edited with colleagues and included explorations of young children's perspectives on pedagogical issues, as well as investigations into processes associated with pedagogical documentation in the early years.

Anthony Semann is one of the founders of Semann & Slattery, a Sydney-based research and consulting firm. Qualified as an early childhood teacher, Anthony spent the first part of his career working in long day care programs eager to learn as much as he could about how to make a difference. It wasn't long after he began his career that he discovered the importance of equity and social justice as being a driving force in social change. He remains committed to naming out inequity, shifting practice towards justice, and living a life that embodies all that he preaches. Twenty-five years on, Semann & Slattery remains his greatest passion and his vehicle for transforming individuals and organisations.

Andrew Stremmel is internationally recognised for his ongoing contributions to teacher education, particularly in the field of teacher inquiry. He has researched and published widely, including Reggio-inspired pedagogies and academic leadership. His research centres on inquiry-based early childhood teacher education and transformation through reflective inquiry. With strengths in collaborative dialogue and narrative inquiry, Professor Stremmel brings extensive experience in his current position as Professor Emeritus in School of Education, Counseling, and Human Sciences at South Dakota State University.

Christine Woodrow is a senior researcher in the *Centre for Educational Research* and Lead Researcher (Early Years) in the *Transforming Early Education (TeEACH) Research Centre*, at Western Sydney University. Christine's research focusses on early childhood education policy, pedagogy and professionalism, with special interests in the ways educators promote family engagement; and enhance equity through culturally responsive pedagogies. Christine's expertise in participative research methodologies underpins her leadership of diverse research projects in Chile and Australia that engage early childhood practitioners as researchers of their own practices and agents of change. These experiences have provided strong insights into the transformative potential of practitioner research and its role in leadership development and sustainable change. Christine is a Chief Investigator on a current Australian Research Council (ARC) grant—*Engaging Families in Early Education* investigating low-income families' participation in early education and the pedagogical, policy and management strategies early childhood services put in place in response to identified challenges.

Acknowledgements

The editors acknowledge that this work has taken place on Aboriginal lands, and we thank the Elders and community members who enable us to share these spaces.

We are grateful to all who have contributed to this work through their presence, writing and openness to learning—the children, families and colleagues who continue to work on behalf of young children and their families, through nurturing practices and professional growth.

In particular, we would like to thank:

- the early childhood professionals and the children who engaged with practitioner inquiry and made this book possible,
- our colleagues who were prepared to share their experiences to create chapters for the book,
- the commentators who contributed their thoughtful responses to provide additional opportunities for reflection,
- the editorial team at Taylor and Francis for their ongoing assistance and encouragement,
- our friends and family who have supported us in this writing and ongoing thinking.

Introduction

Inviting engagement

Alma Fleet, Katey De Gioia, Marina Papic and Catherine Patterson

The task of an Introduction is to welcome participants to an event, invite engagement, and to overview the provocations that are to come. In that spirit, the editors welcome you to this publication investigating practitioner inquiry as a vehicle of educational change. We look forward to hearing from you, perhaps as our thinking provokes yours.

You may choose to dip into the book, finding sections that are most relevant for you (beginners or others wishing to refresh their understanding will benefit from starting at the beginning; others can dive in wherever you are intrigued!). The ideas are offered to invite and continue conversations about practitioner inquiry, as collaborative research, educator investigations, educational leadership tools and opportunities for ongoing consideration and conversation. As a vehicle of educational change, practitioner inquiry is offered here in various forms—including explanations of component strategies, musings about issues that may arise, examples of inquiry in action, and commentaries from three international colleagues, experienced in this domain and curious about ways to extend our thinking. The first part of the book has a particular focus on the rationale and mechanics of practitioner inquiry; the middle part incorporates experiences with practitioner inquiry, particularly in Australia and New Zealand, and the third part steps back to consider some of the larger issues encapsulated in this exploration.

To set the scene, Halbritter and Lindquist (2019, p. 65) offer us a perspective about the relationship between 'learning' and 'knowledge':

> Of course, whenever we are considering pedagogic potentials, it seems wise to begin with a premise about how learning occurs. So here is a premise upon which all that follows is founded: *We learn on the fringe of what we know* [italics in original]. That is, we distrust—as have many researchers and theorists of cognition—that new knowledge is simply added to existing knowledge. Rather, it is assimilated; it is formed.

Interpreting this idea may lead us to understand that "deep learning means collaborative cultures of inquiry, which alter the culture of learning in the organization" (Fullan, 2006, p. 119). This orientation gives us a foundation with which to begin.

DOI: 10.4324/9781003245827-1

Context

Writing from a sociocultural, constructivist frame of reference (Fleer & Kennedy, 2006; Goodfellow & Hedges, 2007), the 13 authors in this publication have pursued practitioner inquiry in a range of ways in various locations, with different degrees of formalised structure or collaborative framing. All are university-qualified teachers with cultural heritage from eight different countries and experience teaching across the early childhood spectrum. Commonalities will become apparent in some of the 'journey' stories shared below, while other things may only be apparent in their writing, such as the influence of John Dewey, or the educators of Reggio Emilia (Edwards et al., 2012), or William Ayers, perhaps Gunilla Dahlberg or Peter Moss, Karen Barad, Henry Giroux or Susan Stacey. More or less pragmatic or philosophical, all are profoundly interested in pedagogy and the intersections of teacher growth and learning alongside children's growth and learning in the context of communities and the environments around them, including interactions with the material and natural world. The teachers who have shared their thinking with us bring further richness to the table. The point being made explicit here is the valuing of the person within the professional persona, recognising the importance of the group around the individual, whether adult or child, and the agency and engagement that sit within a frame of practitioner inquiry.

Journeys Into Practitioner Inquiry

On the third of October 2001, New York was still smothered in the smell of smoldering buildings. Nevertheless, as the Reconceptualising Early Childhood conference organisers had committed to offering the conference despite the collapse of the nearby Twin Towers, a contingent had made the trek from Australia and were present at a pre-conference symposium at Bank Street College. American Jonathon Silin opened the session on Personal and Professional Histories in early childhood followed by Australian Susan Grieshaber who shared stories of her 'ill schooling'. These presentations foregrounded the importance of having personal voice alongside theoretical and practical unpacking of pedagogies. At the same time in Canada, Michael Fullan was writing that, "Twenty-five percent of the solution is having good directional ideas; 75% is figuring out how to get there in one local context after another" (2001, p. 268).

The chapters and commentaries that follow in this book, come from a range of geographical locations and experiential backgrounds. Language being used, therefore, is 'as submitted' by the people who are writing, with some variation across the use of words like 'inquiry' and 'enquiry', 'research' and 'researchers', 'practitioners', 'educators' and 'teachers'. For example, the phrase 'early childhood educators' may encompass all staff with an early childhood qualification, including university and vocational education graduates with degrees, diplomas, advanced diplomas and childcare certificates. In some cases, however, authors have distinguished between these categories for clarity. Labels for different periods of education also vary, with authors defining for their own contexts, for example, whether 'kindergarten' is being used as a label for preschool, or whether, locally, it is referring to the first formal year of schooling. The reader is invited to interpret terms in the contexts in which they are used.

Being open to contextual interpretations, reminds us that journeys rarely have clear-cut origins. Tickets may have been bought for a bus, boat, train or plane, or hiking boots for another kind of expedition, but decisions were made before then and reasons for the decisions happened before that. Other people would have influenced the decisions, whether they were involved directly or not. Contexts would have influenced the decisions, including physical factors and the socio-emotional, socio-political and socio-cultural components of those factors. Timing and mental states come into the mix along with belief systems, values, and philosophical orientations. Lifestyle factors and living conditions may have been relevant, all of which intersects to influence action. The irony is that, when asked to pinpoint the starting point of a journey, only a fraction of these factors become explicit. Those are the elements that have been offered to us in the following section.

As a vehicle to share perspectives across the authoring team, and to help illuminate the ideas which follow, the contributors to this publication were invited to each write a brief piece about their journeys into the worlds of practitioner inquiry. Fifteen authors, including the four co-editors, plus three international commentators, were asked to share their journeys into practitioner inquiry in approximately 300 words each, with the understanding that excerpts or key themes would be included in this Introduction. Although some were not able to contribute, from that invitation have come nine distinctive stories.

'Story' has been a component of human society since the evolution of language. Craig (2020) overviews the terrain with insight from 'scholars who have gone before', referencing Bruner's (1986) acknowledgment of "story as a narrative mode of knowing" (p.725) and Elbaz-Luwisch's (2006) proposal that "giving voice to educators' secret stories is a stated purpose of narrative inquiry" (p. 726). Craig (2020, p. 728) also pays tribute to Connelly and Clandinin's claim that "In essence, 'narrative inquiry is about life and living' (2006, p. 478)." Further, she acknowledges Connelly and Clandinin's (2006) explanation that narrative inquiry as a "research method is also a fluid form of inquiry" (2020, p. 728). Reflecting this fluidity, the 'journey stories' highlighted in this introduction have been combined for this 'production'. The memories and explanations were analysed and compiled to set the scene. Like the program notes accompanying a stage production, the journey stories introduce the players, and engage the reader in the pieces that are to follow.

Consideration of the contributors' 'journey stories' acknowledges that in a word-limited reflection, the points that arise or remain submerged may be arbitrary or dependent on the author's mindset at a particular time.

> [P]erhaps one answer to the question of how stories teach us has to do with time: the time it takes to prepare to tell, the time it takes to tell, the

time it takes to tell again, the time it takes to tell in a different way this time, the time it takes to revise those earlier versions of the story. The time it takes to write the story.

(Robillard & Shane Combs, 2019, p. 4)

It could also be argued, however, that the spotlight falls on things that matter. From personal family memories to 'big picture' concerns, the threads of practitioner inquiry are interwoven across lives and experiences, and foreground the following chapters. For example, in considering her introductions to practitioner inquiry, Nicole★ wrote:

Repositioned to simultaneously understand myself as a teacher and a researcher, I started to question not only my own taken-for-granted practices within and beyond the classroom, but also the taken-for-granted structures and practices of schooling that constrain learning and education for students. This has become an enduring concern of my research in different ways over the years.

Invited to share his personal professional thinking with this group of authors and editors, Andrew mused:

I once heard Vivian Paley say, "it is up to teachers to wonder and write about something that no one else understands – life in classrooms, their experiences with children, their highs and lows, those things that perplex and astonish them." Since 1989, when I began as an assistant professor at Virginia Tech, I have been interested in reflective teaching, which belongs to the inquiry-oriented paradigm of teacher education suggesting that teachers should develop habits of inquiry – that is, to be self-monitoring, adaptive, problem solvers and active decision-makers. Because teaching is a profoundly human activity, part of being a teacher is questioning, seeking answers to seemingly unsolvable problems with an understanding that there may be some questions that we are unable to answer, at least definitively.

My profound interest in the Reggio Emilia approach promoted a deeper understanding of teaching as an inquiry process. By its very nature, teaching young children requires an attitude of seeing things that contain inquiry and investigation. This is an attitude that is relevant to children because of their expressiveness and natural curiosity. Thus, inquiry must be seen as an orientation toward one's practice, a questioning disposition toward the world leading to inquiry conducted within the classroom. And the classroom, therefore, must be seen as the teacher's laboratory. Teachers must think of themselves as generating knowledge, not just using it. Otherwise, we leave it to others to define the knowledge that is of most worth, the questions that are most worth asking, and the knowledge that forms the basis of teaching, a dilemma with which the teaching profession arduously wrestles.

The gift teaching gives is a continual experience of the not-yet-known – even the unknowable – in our students, and in ourselves. As I near the end of my career as an academic, I still have more questions than answers. I believe this sense of curiosity and wonder is the compass we need as we continue to both think and feel our way through the expanse of the unknown, the uncertain, and the unpredictable, especially now during a devastating pandemic.

So, in considering the 'curiosity and wonder' of other contributors to this book, where do their stories begin?

Catherine's recounting begins with "a delightful, mischievous deaf child" who was challenged by the formal expectations for kindergarten children that this beginning teacher was trying to enact. Alma positions her journey "with a mother who was always curious and encouraged me to think". From New Zealand, Maria wrote that, "years ago, I was struck by an early childhood lecturer's message that teachers *choose* to invest in their own transformation by reflecting on their practices and associated values and beliefs, and then interrogating those practices, values and beliefs for positive change".

From a different starting point as an Australian high school teacher, Nicole found herself as "part of a large-scale Commonwealth Government project that involved teachers conducting inquiry into innovative classroom practices". Linda and Katey were both introduced to practitioner inquiry by colleagues who were experienced with the methodology as a core component of professional learning projects with teachers. Margo and Chris offered a video explanation of their journeys with materials to "understand what drives, provokes and motivates teachers to make pedagogical decisions". Two examples taken from their video illustrate their creative imaginings in Figures 0.1 and 0.2.

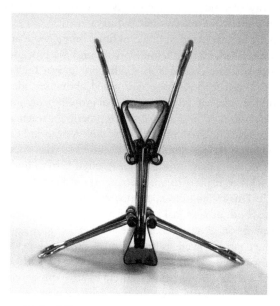

Figure 0.1 Robot with Red Eyes

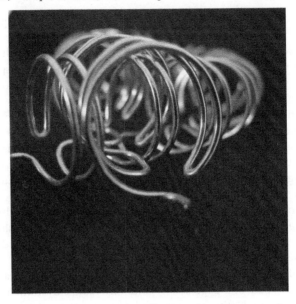

Figure 0.2 Spirals

These 'sharings' remind us that there are varied ways 'into' practitioner inquiry as well as a range of conceptualisations of what the construct conveys. There was no common trajectory; ideas travel, and thinkers acquire them at different points while journeying. Many readers may also find that the seeds of inquiry have been emerging for them in a range of contexts over time, while others may identify specific courses, projects or experiences which introduced them to the components of practitioner inquiry.

Walking onto the inquiry 'stage' at different times brings depth and complexity to the unfolding stories. With a broad framework around the processes of practitioner inquiry, the voices of these contributors, both here and in their shared chapters, invite a thoughtful conversation. Issues are raised about the idea of continuous improvement and the sustainability of professional growth being foregrounded over the limits of single sessions of 'professional development' for teachers. There are also the provocations to read and think more widely, with Margo and Chris realising that "we need to read what Reggio [thinkers] read, not just what they write…starting with Bateson's *Mind and Nature*…so many ideas, often hard to understand. And we began to meet weekly to explore them…moving on to Lenz Taguchi's book about the material turn". This valuing of experiential learning echoes across the chapters. The work is seen as both professional learning and inherently as being research. This is a form of investigation evolving alongside teachers, empowering, and enabling 'the actors' to 'take control'. Then, as Katey writes, "change is evidence-informed".

These 'stepping-back-reflections' invite us also to look thoughtfully at the 'closings', those carefully chosen final sentences in 'considered' writing. Let's 'listen-in' to some of the perspectives from commentators, editors, and authors of the following chapters. As 'research-inquirers', Margo and Chris reflected that, "We are coming to know the difference between knowing something 'in our heads' and the excitement of experiencing theory and practice with the whole being in relation with the material world of which we are part."

In these concluding thoughts to the journey stories, we 'hear' deep thinking, learning, and enthusiasm for the power of practitioner inquiry as a vehicle of educational change through teacher empowerment:

> The sense that I knew 'my children' better than an expert in the education department was a liberating concept, and as a result, I became fascinated by the potential of practitioner inquiry to empower teachers as curriculum decision-makers.
>
> (Catherine)

> Practitioner Inquiry has offered me a passport to learning, a vehicle for joining with those who are learners in the educational domain.
>
> (Alma)

> I am excited to see teachers take control of their own learning and development and reflect on what they want to change! I am inspired by their stories! Through practitioner inquiry I have witnessed their commitment to *continuous* improvement!
>
> (Marina)

> As one teacher shared, 'I have learnt to be more open to challenges, to take opportunities to develop myself; I have learnt to take a deep breath and give things a go!'
>
> (Katey)

> While the work can be challenging, worrying at times and requires time and money, I have no regret.
>
> (Linda)

And, as Maria concluded:

> As the teacher-researchers looked inwards to examine their practices, and outwards to determine how their practices supported or even hindered children's learning, I witnessed learning that was truly transformational. Teachers became more aware of and articulate about their own and children's learning. In turn, children became more confident in themselves, and their families became more knowledgeable about the significance of home-life to their child's learning.

These threads of agency and powerful action are evidenced throughout the chapters that follow, inviting readers to think through (or re-think) their conceptions of practitioner inquiry, while positioning themselves alongside other learners in this landscape. Practitioner inquiry invites all who engage with it to see differently and think more deeply. The engagement enables knowledge-generation and the potential for educational change. Along the way, learning happens, identities are re-formed, and collegiality is strengthened. As Robillard and Shane Combs note,

> Blended scholarship is political; it asks that we understand that values and beliefs are tied up in the personal, that the personal is tied up in the public, that the personal and the public are revealed in our scholarship, and that artificially separating our values from our stories renders us identity-less.
>
> (2019, p. 6)

Reading Highlights

The book is organised into three parts to help you on your journey. The introductory part lays the foundations or invites the experienced reader to revisit inquiry, sharing the learning of the authors. Chapter 1 offers an understanding of practitioner inquiry as a powerful approach to sustainable professional learning. It highlights the importance of a cyclical process that enables practitioners to develop new understandings and practices leading to evidence-informed change. The concepts and strategies introduced in the chapter provide a starting point for the book, particularly for those unfamiliar with practitioner inquiry as a way of working.

Chapters 2 and 3 highlight key components of the inquiry cycle: developing the question, analysing the data and exploring these pieces from the perspectives of teachers and educators who have participated in a cycle of inquiry. 'Useful questions' are those niggles or known questions that we don't have the answer to and are willing to take time to investigate. The cycle of inquiry would not be complete without discussing ways of gathering and analysing data related to the question; Chapter 3 describes what this looks like in context. Processes for analysis are also shared through the lens of teachers undertaking their own inquiry.

The final chapter in this part of the book illustrates with data how inquiry as professional learning can have benefits beyond an individual teacher. The chapter shares how a program of teacher inquiry assisted teachers to maintain their accreditation requirements whilst simultaneously improving classroom practice.

We pause here for the commentary on these four chapters. Nicole Mockler provides her reflection on the 'story' so far, a strong reminder about the transformative nature of practitioner inquiry when time and investment are provided and nurtured.

Part 2 offers authors the opportunity to share with the readers, their stories of experience. The section unfolds with Chapter 5 offering experiences from the author as the facilitator of two inquiry processes that arose in very different ways. What was evident in both experiences was the respect for the facilitator as a determinant of the inquiry process. The author shares the complexities of context as impacting the outcomes of inquiry processes.

Chapter 6 situates inquiry in the classroom context. The authors in Chapter 6 highlight the relevance of 'whole of school', with children as active participants in the change process that enables professional learning for teachers. Multiple data-gathering processes with children are explored, alongside issues of ethics and consent.

The authors in Chapters 7 and 8 are colleagues who share these chapters as companion pieces, looking at the perspectives of professional learning that enable embedding, revisiting, and sustaining over time. Authors note the need to understand and see themselves as teacher-researchers before attempting to facilitate their knowledge with others.

Maria Cooper provides commentary at the conclusion of Part 2, drawing together the threads that are woven throughout. She highlights the importance of shifting mindsets for practitioner inquiry to be successful, to be challenged to move beyond the safe and familiar as it is in the discomfort that we create the greatest learning and change. Maria invites us to share in the 'unique stories' and consider them in terms of personal truths and realities and how this becomes a way of working in services.

The final act, the last stop of this trip—Part 3—provides opportunities to share an exploration of 'big ideas'. The authors of these chapters have had extensive experience in practitioner inquiry or have worked alongside those who have. Looking beyond the embedded cycles of inquiries allows the authors to explore the *other*, the *what else* pieces that arise throughout this form of professional learning. The authors in Chapter 9 share unanticipated outcomes that occurred during their experiences with practitioner inquiry. Teacher confidence in their practice, job satisfaction and ability to articulate decision-making choices are shared, along with teacher experiences of transferring the process of inquiry into other facets of their role.

The authors in Chapter 10 investigate the relationship or intersections between pedagogical documentation and practitioner inquiry. The lead author has been teaching and researching across both processes for many years, and, with co-authors, shares their experiences of these processes and the opportunities to engage with educational change through shared understanding of the philosophical underpinnings of both practitioner inquiry and pedagogical documentation.

Chapter 11 looks at processes and possibilities beyond the individual practitioner inquiry model to effect change in classrooms and educational settings more broadly. The author in this chapter discusses the role of the Educational Leader as pivotal in not only supporting professional learning but also creating learning communities whilst building individuals' knowledge and expertise as leaders.

The final chapter in the book highlights practitioner inquiry as a sustainable way of working towards educational change. The authors bring together the increasing body of literature and their extensive experience both nationally and internationally in working through the lens of inquiry. They share stories from participants, revisiting their experiences and how this process has become part of their ways of working throughout their teaching careers.

Andrew Stremmel provides final reflections in his commentary on this section. Drawing from the authors, he aligns practitioner inquiry with teachers as 'professionals', as opposed to 'technicians' affording an opportunity for creating and sustaining a 'culture of thinking and practice', moving beyond the doing and transmission into meaningful practice constructed with and alongside children and colleagues. He concludes by inviting us to view the teacher as a "critically deep and creative thinker" and to acknowledge the work of teaching as within a "democracy framework…to liberate and humanise education".

The conclusion offers an overview of the ideas that have been presented, from the perspectives of the editors. Key messages are considered in terms of the purposes, the component processes, and potential contexts for practitioner inquiry. Potentials for professional learning are threaded throughout the provocations. As the editors 'think forward', some 'Big Ideas' are presented, inviting readers to consider their own perspectives alongside the concepts being foregrounded.

Whether starting a new journey, revisiting earlier thinking, refreshing your perspective, or looking for an alternative approach to professional learning, this book offers something new for our audience. Whilst this introduction ends our 'program notes'; we now invite you to take the time to read, to question, and to be provoked as we let the production unfold.

Key Messages

- Practitioner inquiry exists in various forms in different contexts and has the potential to generate local knowledge while informing educational change.
- Engagement in practitioner inquiry begins in diverse ways and continues to inform professional practice, research, and collaborative professional growth.

Thinking Points

- As professional collaboration has been identified as a key component of practitioner inquiry, what strategies might be helpful in building that collaboration in your site?
- What opportunities have you had to participate in practitioner inquiry? How will this impact your next steps?

Note

*The quotations from 'journey stories' are from the pieces submitted by invitation, and attributed by first name to the authors, editors, and commentators in this publication.

References

Ayers, W. (2009). *To teach: The journey of a teacher* (3rd ed.). Teachers College Press.

Barad, K. (2017). Troubling time/s and ecologies of nothingness: Re-turning, re-membering, and facing the incalculable. *New Formations: A Journal of Culture/Theory/ Politics*, 92, 56–86. https://doi.org/10.3898/NEWF:92.05.2017.

Bateson, G. (2002). *Mind and nature: A necessary unity.* Hampton Press.

Bruner, J. (1986). *Actual minds, possible worlds.* Harvard University Press.

Connelly, F. M., & Clandinin, D. J. (2006). Narrative inquiry. In L. Green, G. Camilli, & P. Elmore (Eds.), *Handbook of complementary methods in education research* (pp. 177 488). Routledge.

Craig, C. J. (2020). Fish jumps over the dragon gate: An eastern image of a western scholar's career trajectory. *Research Papers in Education*, 35(6), 722–745. https://doi. org/10.1080/02671522.2019.1633556.

Dewey, J. (1986). Experience and education. *The Educational Forum*, 50(3), 241–252. https://doi.org/10.1080/00131728609335764.

Edwards, C., Gandini, L., & Forman, G. (Eds.). (2012). *The hundred languages of children: The Reggio Emilia Experience in transformation.* (3rd ed.). Praeger.

Elbaz-Luwisch, F. (2006). Studying teachers' lives and experiences: Narrative inquiry into K-12 teaching. In D. J. Clandinin (Ed.), *Handbook of narrative inquiry: Mapping a methodology* (pp. 357–382). Sage Publishing.

Fleer, M., & Kennedy, A. (2006). Quality–always unfinished business. In M. Fleer, S. Edwards, M. Hammer, A. Kennedy, A. Ridgeway, J. Robbins, & L. Surman (Eds.), *Early childhood learning communities: Socio-cultural research in practice* (pp. 209–227). Pearson.

Fullan, M. (2001). *The new meaning of educational change.* (3rd ed.). Teachers College Press.

Fullan, M. (2006). The future of educational change: System thinkers in action. *Journal of Educational Change* 7, 113–122. https://doi.org/10.1007/s10833-006-9003-9.

Giroux, H. A. (2010). Rethinking education as the practice of freedom: Paulo Freire and the promise of critical pedagogy. *Policy Futures in Education*, 8(6), 715–721.

Goodfellow, J., & Hedges, H. (2007). Practitioner research 'centre stage': Contexts, contributions and challenges. In L. Keesing-Styles & H. Hedges (Eds.), *Theorising early childhood practice: Emerging dialogues* (pp. 187–210). Pademelon Press.

Halbritter, B., & Lindquist, J. (2019). Collecting and coding synecdochic selves: Identi-fying learning across life-writing texts. In A. E. Robillard & D. Shane Combs (Eds.), *How stories teach us: Composition, life writing, and blended scholarship* (pp. 47–75). Peter Lang.

Lenz Taguchi, H. (2009). *Going beyond the theory/practice divide in early childhood education: Introducing an intra-active pedagogy.* Routledge.

Moss, P., & Dahlberg, G. (2008). Beyond quality in early childhood education and care: Languages of evaluation. *New Zealand Journal of Teachers' Work*, 5(1), 3–12.

Robillard, A. E., & Shane Combs, D. (2019). Introduction. In A. E. Robillard & D. Shane Combs (Eds.), *How stories teach us: Composition, life writing, and blended scholarship* (pp. 2–8). Peter Lang.

Stacey, S. (2015). *Pedagogical documentation in early childhood: Sharing children's learning and teachers' thinking.* Redleaf Press.

Stacey, S. (2018). *Inquiry-based early learning environments: Creating, supporting, and colla-borating.* Redleaf Press.

Part 1
Setting the Scene

1 Practitioner Inquiry

Processes, Potentials and Purposes

Catherine Patterson

As an experienced early childhood practitioner, Yasmin is starting a new job as a room leader. She knows she will be working with staff who have agreed to join a local practitioner inquiry project. Her colleagues seem to be interested in the possibilities of the project, and open to changing their practices. Yasmin is looking forward to the project with a mixture of excitement and nervousness. She wonders what will happen next and she wants to find out more about this way of professional learning…

Practitioners working in early childhood settings are keenly aware that their professional role is characterised by uncertainty, inconsistency, and ambiguity. They often experience these characteristics in their daily interactions with children, families, and colleagues, and are mindful of the challenges in these professional exchanges. Educating young children is not a simple, straight-forward series of skills to be learnt through imitation. Rather, professional practitioners thoughtfully analyse and justify their decisions, carefully considering and reconsidering their beliefs and practices. Over the past decade, an increasing number of publications have encouraged early childhood practitioners to take active control of their own learning through reflection and inquiry. Authors such as Castle (2012), Fleet et al. (2016), Kroll and Meier (2018), Newman and Woodrow (2015), Perry et al. (2012), Reed and Canning (2010), and Stacey (2019) have written specifically on inquiry for an early childhood audience.

Fundamentally, practitioner inquiry comes from a long line of pedagogical approaches that view teachers or educators as intentional practitioners systematically studying their own practice. Kroll (2018, p. 5) draws on the work of Cochran-Smith and Lytle to explain that teacher research is "systematic, intentional inquiry by teachers". She goes on to note that it is 'systematic' because "teachers develop ordered ways of recollecting, thinking about, and analyzing events". It is 'intentional' "in that the inquiry is planned by the teacher" and it is 'inquiry' "because the teacher research comes from questions and generates questions … [reflecting] the teachers' desire to make sense of their experiences." These moves towards an inquiry-orientation have emerged from various educational research descriptors, such as teacher-as-researcher (Stenhouse, 1975), action research (Mills, 2017; Mertler, 2020), and teacher inquiry (Cochran-Smith & Lytle, 2009). Rather than using 'teacher inquiry' or 'teacher

DOI: 10.4324/9781003245827-3

research', the term '*practitioner inquiry*' has been deliberately chosen for use in this book. This approach reflects that of Leggett and Newman (2019, p. 138), as "it expands the possibilities for a wider array of participants", to include directors, teachers, educators, and parents. Thus, practitioner inquiry is an inclusive term, embracing the diverse backgrounds, experiences, and qualifications of those working in early childhood while recognising them as powerful competent learners.

This shift towards practitioner inquiry in the early years has been influenced by provocations from the educators of Reggio Emilia. Their challenge is for practitioners to re-consider an outdated image of the child as weak and needy, and instead to see a child who is "strong, powerful and rich in potential and resources" (Rinaldi, 2006, p. 123). This has led to a similar re-consideration of the traditional practitioner's role (Robertson, 2006, p. 52), toward an image of a capable and resourceful adult learner engaged with professional inquiry in a meaningful and authentic way. This re-thinking of the image of early childhood practitioners is also linked to an increased understanding of the limitations of traditional 'one-off' or single session professional development events (Fleet & Patterson, 2001). As a result, sustained, site-based approaches (including practitioner inquiry) are seen as more likely to promote continuous professional growth.

The appeal of practitioner inquiry is strengthened by its strong relationship with elements of adult learning. Merriam (2001) explains how influential researcher Malcolm Knowles distinguished between adult learning (andragogy) and the learning of children (pedagogy). As a foundational concept, andragogy provided a foundation for a range of studies building on Knowles's original assumptions of the adult learner. While concerns and questions remain about the value of andragogy (see for example Grace, 2006; Hartree, 1984; Loeng, 2018), the original characteristics provide a framework for considering practitioner inquiry as embedded in adult learning principles. Merriam (2001, p. 4) summarizes Knowles's assumptions of adult learners who (1) are self-directed in their learning; (2) have "life experiences" to bring to their learning; (3) are relevancy-oriented insofar as their learning should be applicable to their work; (4) are "problem-centered and interested in immediate application of knowledge", and (5) are "motivated to learn by internal rather than external factors".

The first assumption that views adults as self-directed learners is catered for by the highly personal nature of practitioner inquiry which enables individuals to focus on their own practice. They decide "which elements of their practice they want to study, what questions they want to answer, and how they will collect data and analyze data to find information that makes sense in their immediate surroundings" (Hatch, 2012, p. vii). This provides an environment where educators have agency over their own learning through engagement in a meaningful inquiry.

The second assumption related to the accumulation of experience and knowledge is acknowledgement that practitioners bring "considerable professional knowledge and practical experiences" to professional learning contexts (Fleet et al., 2016, p. 20). Building on this knowledge through site-based investigations creates significant professional growth opportunities for staff. It also develops local capacity as staff work together to discuss critical issues, share knowledge and experience, and reflect on pedagogical beliefs and practices.

Another assumption identifies how adult learners appreciate learning that is relevant to their life situations. This relates to motivation in changing work roles and expectations of early childhood educators. These changes may be due to circumstances such as the release of new pedagogical requirements from government authorities, an increased focus on the professionalism of the field, or the changing use of technology in children's lives. The open nature of practitioner inquiry enables educators to respond to "what is new, inspiring and informative" in professional growth, while being "critical thinkers" reflecting upon new perspectives (Stacey, 2019, p. 88).

Related to this focus on work roles, adults tend to be problem-centred in their learning. They are more likely to be motivated when their learning supports their professional roles, and they can respond to real-life problems in their own context. This pragmatic view of adult learners is reflected in the essential nature of practitioner inquiry as a problem-solving process. It is, however, important to note that problem-solving is not always the outcome of practitioner inquiry. Indeed, it may lead to more questions than solutions. The cyclic nature of inquiry, nevertheless, provides opportunities for educators to clarify their particular concerns and refine their questions to lead to new investigations (Castle, 2012).

Finally, it is generally accepted that adults are motivated to learn by internal (intrinsic) rather than external (extrinsic) factors, although usually a combination of both are present. Within a practitioner inquiry cycle, particular processes such as the identification of a personally relevant question can lead to greater intrinsic motivation. Furthermore, Hall (2009) suggested that the "celebration of one's own intrinsic value as a participant leads to a feeling of being able to reflect upon and challenge accustomed roles" (p. 676). Similarly, Newman and Mowbray (2012) found that engagement in a practitioner inquiry project "facilitated teachers' professional development, enhanced intrinsic personal and professional motivations and enabled teachers to intentionally challenge and extend their knowledge and practice" (p. 465). Extrinsic factors may be seen in appropriate incentives to promote and maintain engagement in practitioner inquiry. Long-lasting sustainable change, however, relies on the internal motivation of adult learners.

Framing key aspects of adult learning in association with practitioner inquiry has revealed the suitability of this approach for professional learning in early childhood contexts. Based on principles of adult learning and featuring a continuous spiral of input, action and reflection, practitioner inquiry contributes to a cycle of reflection and adaptation enabling professional engagement and improvement. The following section will highlight specific processes associated with practitioner inquiry.

Practitioner Inquiry Processes

While practitioner inquiry may have had multiple names and been actualised in diverse ways over the years, its essential nature is based on "a disposition, a way of thinking, reflected in a series of actions that are embedded as an approach to our professional practice and identity" (Gilchrist, 2018, p. 7). That is, it is *part of*, rather than something that's additional to everyday life with children, families and colleagues. Gilchrist continues his explanation by noting that practitioner inquiry should not be seen as "another of the many 'things' we are asked ... to do" in our professional lives, rather it is about continuous inquiry contributing to our own and others' understanding of teaching and learning.

Continuous engagement in inquiry over time is a powerful model for professional learning. It is powerful, in that cycles of investigation can support participants with diverse backgrounds to become aware of quality issues present in professional practice and develop skills to address those concerns. As Tobin (2015, p. x) notes: "What makes working with young children so fascinating is their endless capacity to surprise and sometimes confound even experienced practitioners." The unpredictable nature of early childhood education creates professional opportunities to investigate elements of interest to practitioners in an ongoing spiral of input, action, and reflection. A focus on professional learning "is an essential component of effective practice in any profession" (Hadley et al., 2015, p. 187), and research on professional learning in early childhood "clearly shows the benefit of engaging in continuous learning for the educator as well as children, families and the organisation that employs the educator" (p. 189). This is supported by researchers such as Melasalmi and Husu (2019) who argue "the key to improved learning for children is continuous, job-embedded learning for educators" (p. 91).

The processes involved in practitioner inquiry are often portrayed as a cycle of key points as Figure 1.1 illustrates.

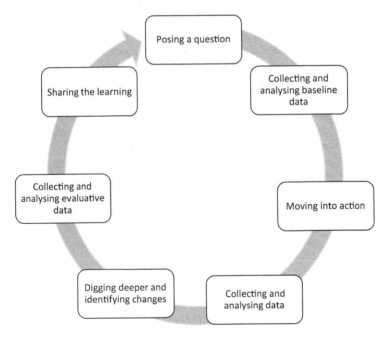

Figure 1.1 Practitioner Inquiry Cycle

Posing a Question

Practitioner inquiry needs to begin somewhere and that is usually with a "burning question about practice" (Dana, 2015, p. 163) which may be developed from a 'niggle' about current practices in a room or across a site, a wondering about children's (or adults') observed behaviours, a dilemma in building relationships with families, or a professional interaction with a colleague that stimulates inquiry or concern. When practitioners "pose questions worth asking, they do so from an attitude—a stance—of inquiry, and they see their classrooms as laboratories for wonder and discovery" (Stremmel, 2018, p. 3). This 'laboratory' of wonder and discovery may be a place of inquiry for both children and adults (Stacey, 2019); a place where "children's questions are expected and valued by their teachers", while at the same time teachers "consider their own questions as well as those that come from the children" (p. 2).

An inquiry question may be focused for example, on an individual child, 'How can I support Ivana's language learning?' Or maybe regular observations of a group of children may provoke questions such as, 'What would create a more enriching and engaging outdoor space for our nursery children?' or 'How can I promote a sense of agency for children in my room?' The question may be content-focused such as, 'What do we need to do to promote a music-rich environment in our room?' Or it may be a question about a dilemma with a colleague(s), such as, 'How can I support educators to facilitate transition times in a more interactive and relaxed fashion?' Engagement with families may be a concern in a question like, 'What opportunities can be provided to engage the hard-to-reach families in our program?'

The most important point is to relate the question to professional practice. The questions provided as examples in this chapter are heavily influenced by advice from Henderson and Meier (2012, p. 96) who suggest educators new to practitioner inquiry find it helpful to use "an action research frame, beginning questions with 'How can I ...?'" Inquiry questions, however, do not have to begin with this phrase, and this advice should not be seen as a constraint. Just as there are a wide range of possibilities for an inquiry, so there are many ways to compose a question that may direct the investigation. Often this initial question may be re-focused over time as more data is collected and analysed. (See Chapter 2 for further information about designing a useful question.)

Collecting and Analysing Baseline Data

At this early stage of the inquiry, along with designing the question, it is necessary to gather more information on what is really happening to ensure the focus of the investigation is accurate and the initial ideas are confirmed by data. This early stage of information gathering is known as 'baseline data' and describes the current situation that is causing concern. Information may be drawn from various sources, including observation notes, photographs or drawings, professional reading, reflective journal entries or notes of discussions with colleagues or families. Baseline data is important at critical points of the cycle. First, it helps establish a direction for the investigation, and second, it provides comparative information for evaluating changes that have been put in place.

Moving into Action

Once the data has been analysed, the inquiry cycle is likely to move to an action phase where practitioners try out potential solutions to the identified concern. Sometimes it is tempting to rush straight from identifying a 'niggle' into immediate action, but it's important not to move too quickly into action. Rather, time should be spent consulting with stakeholders, finding sources of information to support decision-making, working out possible approaches to action, reflecting on alternatives, and deciding how to gather information to keep track of the investigation. Consideration should also be given to the evaluation of the investigation and how to share this information with others. These planning decisions provide a framework for the investigation.

Collecting and Analysing Data

As the investigation develops and practitioners try out their theories, ideas and strategies, data needs to be gathered about the successful (or not-so-successful) aspects of the inquiry. This data gathering and analysis is ongoing throughout the practitioner inquiry process. Data may be gathered in many ways, and ideally should take place as part of regular professional practice, rather than being a separate add-on task. Familiar data gathering techniques such as classroom observations, examples of children's creative work, photographs, video recordings, discussions and surveys with children and adults may provide valuable information. It is also useful to consider the types of data already existing in the setting. As Castle (2012) notes, "There is no limit to the amount and type of data that can be found in an early childhood setting" (p. 69).

The analysis of this information is a critical element in practitioner inquiry, as data only becomes useful when it informs decision-making about practice. Many early childhood teachers are familiar with the 'interpretation' of classroom observations; data analysis shares many features with this concept. Analysis in practitioner inquiry does not have to involve formal research processes such as statistical analysis. Instead, key questions may guide analysis processes, such as: What is the data saying about the investigation? What patterns can be seen in the information? Castle (2012) draws on advice from Phillips and Carr (2010) for questions the educator can ask when reflecting on the data. These include,

What seems to be happening in the data? What is not happening here? What is repeated in the data (words, behaviours, attitudes)? What is surprising, perplexing or disturbing in the data? What information seems to be missing from the data?

(p. 100)

These kinds of reflective questions can be answered in professional journal entries that record the investigation. As teacher researchers gain more experience with practitioner inquiry, more sophisticated data analysis methods may be chosen. (See Chapter 3 for more information about data gathering and analysis.)

Digging Deeper and Identifying Changes

On-going data collection and analysis provides evidence of the inquiry's progress and offers a foundation for the consideration of potential changes and adjustments. A data-based approach enables teacher-researchers to make decisions based on the evidence of their pedagogical practices. Changes may range from a major re-direction of the inquiry to a relatively minor adaptation of daily interactions with children or colleagues. Critical reflection of the data may prompt further reading and thoughtful consideration of alternative approaches. As Stacey (2019) reminds us: "We can revisit, think again and repeat" (p. 3) as often as necessary.

Collecting and Analysing Evaluative Data

Having gathered and analysed data as on-going elements of the investigation and made changes to practice, it may be time to draw the inquiry to a close. This decision may be influenced by diverse circumstances: children moving on to a new environment, project funding ending, the dilemma driving the inquiry seems to be resolved, or maybe there doesn't seem to be any further improvement to be gained by moving in this direction. There is, however, no reason to assume that any of these factors may bring an inquiry to a close. A question may still be relevant with a new group of children; funding may be found elsewhere; the 'resolved' issue may prompt new questions, and maybe a new direction will add depth to the original inquiry.

Whatever the reason for concluding the inquiry, the data gathering and analysis process may move into the evaluative phase of the inquiry. The quality of this data may depend on the initial baseline data processes, as evaluating the significance of the inquiry often entails repeating the initial data gathering to illustrate progress. This provides a direct comparison with the initial situation that prompted the inquiry. This is, however, not likely to be the only source of evaluative data, as the information gathered throughout the inquiry may add depth and new knowledge to the evaluation. As well as personal reflection on existing data, "discussion and collaboration with colleagues is very useful" (Gilchrist, 2018, p. 39) to provide alternative perspectives on progress.

Sharing the Learning

Often it is appropriate to share the learning from an inquiry. This may be quite an informal arrangement such as a small group of co-workers getting together to share their work, or it may be more formal with educators from several centres gathering to present their findings. Families may also be interested in the opportunity to learn about the inquiry. Beyond these informal possibilities, a presentation may be made at a conference in front of a larger audience. Other than spoken presentations of this kind, learning can be shared in newsletters or professional magazines and journals.

Limitations of this Image of Practitioner Inquiry

While elements in practitioner inquiry have been described here in a logical sequence, this may misrepresent the continuing nature of the process. Dana (2015) explains that presenting practitioner inquiry as a series of steps may result in "teachers experiencing a feeling of finality, like they have come to the end of a long journey after they have completed 'the last step'." As a result, "teachers may begin to view inquiry as a linear process and focus on the outcome, the ending of one project, one exploration, one wondering", then return to their previous ways of working. She emphasises that practitioner inquiry should be seen as "a continual cycle that all educators spiral through throughout their professional lifetimes", and improving their practice becomes a "natural part of their work" (p. 163).

In a related concern, the presentation of series of 'steps' possibly over-simplifies the potential for the "messy practice" (Stacey, 2019, p. 2) that is the reality of practitioner inquiry. Dealing with this unexpected complexity means encountering points where it may be necessary to retrace steps and refocus attention. A sequence of steps tends to suggest a straightforward linear progression, but as Stacey advises "we can expect to sometimes be unsure, to take a step forward without really knowing where it will lead us, and, in time, become comfortable with the disequilibrium that this may cause" (p. 3).

Collaborative Approaches in Practitioner Inquiry

Not all practitioner inquiry is an individual effort. A collaborative approach, for example, is evident in some descriptions of inquiry-orientations. These include 'collaborative action research' (Gordon, 2008), 'professional learning communities', (Harris et al., 2017), 'learning circles', (Collay et al., 1998), 'co-inquiry' (Abramson, 2012) and 'communities of practice' (Wenger, 1991). Regardless of the name, this collaborative approach is seen as an effective way to provide meaningful professional learning through shared inquiry into everyday pedagogical practices.

Cochran-Smith and Lytle (2009) explain that practitioner inquiry communities

> often involve joint participation by teachers, researchers, school leaders and others who are differently positioned from one another and who bring

distinctive kinds of knowledge and experiences to bear on the collective enterprise. The key, however, is that all participants in these groups … function as fellow learners and researchers.

(p. 142)

This is particularly evident in examples of practitioner inquiry conducted in early childhood contexts. Staff may have a wide range of qualifications, and as a result distinctions in roles and status may exist; yet when involved in practitioner inquiry, all participants are viewed as educators who can make a valued contribution to the learning community. Abramson (2012) explains that "this sense of joint endeavour … helps create a culture of professional growth in which teachers learn to accept differences of opinion, articulate their thoughts and plan constructive action to improve teaching and learning" (p. 156).

A collaborative approach may be encouraged through a 'buddy system' where a small group of practitioners work together to encourage each other through the inquiry processes. Sometimes members of a buddy group may be interested in the same topic, but as Dana and Yendal-Hoppey (2014) explain, they can be investigating "different questions and wonderings about that topic. When this happens, inquiries potentially intersect, and collaboration can occur at the juncture of that intersection" (p. 82). A collaborative approach may be a partnership of staff within one room, or a group of staff from across rooms. A sole practitioner may identify a 'critical friend' who is an off-site educator or a leader in similar circumstances. A collaborative buddy system may also be developed by using digital tools such as video meetings, shared file systems and text messaging to support practitioner research (Husbye et al., 2019).

The diverse knowledge and experience practitioners bring to a collaborative group may enhance reflective skills and help overcome hurdles associated with lack of self-confidence (Cole, 2020). Sharing experiences in a group can build a sense of trust and empowerment as participants gain confidence in their own decision-making. Albrecht and Engel (2007) explain that "trust grows in an atmosphere of acceptance and when risk taking and making mistakes are seen as natural by-products of innovation and learning" (p. 20). Nevertheless, tensions and challenges may also be present within the group. Early childhood educators, (like all educators and teachers), often hold strong beliefs about their professional practices and these existing beliefs may influence the effectiveness of the inquiry process (Avalos, 2011). Working together in collaborative ways, listening to each other, discussing differences and challenging current practices may encourage practitioners to be both open-minded and persistent in their inquiries.

Ethical Considerations

The daily work of early childhood practitioners is guided by Codes of Ethics published by national professional associations such as British Association of Early Childhood Education (UK), Early Childhood Australia (Australia), Canadian Child Care Federation (Canada) and the National Association for the

Education of Young Children (US). When planning practitioner inquiry, however, it is also advisable to consult ethical guidelines for research, especially if the results are intended for publication. The following organisations publish relevant guidelines on their websites: British Education Research Association, European Early Childhood Education Research Association, American Educational Research Association, Australian Association for Research in Education.

Castle (2012, pp. 62–63) outlines the following ethical guidelines for early childhood teacher researchers:

- Do not coerce or harm research participants physically, emotionally, academically or in any way.
- The early childhood teacher researchers' primary responsibility is to their students.
- Obtain informed consent of parents and children.
- Maintain confidentiality and anonymity.
- Treat children and colleagues with respect and care.
- Establish ownership of the data before beginning the research.

These guidelines should be seen as providing a starting place for conversations about ethical issues in practitioner inquiry rather than barriers to an investigation (Harcourt et al., 2011).

Voluntary Informed Consent

Castle's (2012) ethical guidelines (listed above) recommend obtaining the 'informed consent' of parents and children. This may be a thorny issue for teacher-researchers. Generally, if the inquiry is part of 'regular teaching practice' including observations of children, the use of photographs, and examples of children's work, *and* the purpose of the inquiry is solely to improve professional practice *and* the data will only be used by the practitioner, then voluntary informed consent may not be required. It is still ethically appropriate, however, to inform parents, children, and colleagues of the inquiry by explaining details such as what data will be gathered and how the information will be used.

If, however, the inquiry involves gathering, recording, or analysing more data than usual and/or the findings will be made public beyond the direct environment, ethical protocols would indicate that voluntary informed consent should be sought from all stakeholders, including colleagues, children, and parents. 'Informed consent' can be interpreted as gaining permission from those involved to gather information about them and make that information public. This is usually a more formal process and often involves written permission from participants after they have been informed of the purpose of the research, the data gathering processes, the confidentiality protections, and their right to withdraw at any time without penalty. Parents may sign permission for children's involvement although preschoolers can also consent for themselves. (See Gaches, 2021, and Harcourt & Conroy, 2011, for more details on children's consent in the research process.)

Nurturing Inquiry

Practitioner inquiry is difficult to maintain without appropriate support. Early childhood educators may come as novice researchers to practitioner inquiry, and initial support may focus on the development of practical skills required for the inquiry cycle. These capacities may be developed by working in partnership with more experienced teacher-researchers. To scaffold practitioner research, facilitators may provide workshops over time as academic partners or mentors to support leaders and staff in overcoming the busyness of their daily work.

Leaders have an important responsibility in nurturing a culture of inquiry and professional dialogue in the workplace. As role models, leaders should participate in the collaborative process by investigating their own questions. This enables them to relate to issues encountered by staff and to provide authentic acknowledgment of progress. Beyond this personal level of support, leaders need to consider the financial costs involved in sponsoring practitioner inquiry. Kummen and Hodgins (2019, p. 112) cite Vandenbroeck and colleagues (2016) who identified "the provision of enabling working conditions, such as the availability of paid hours for non-contact time and the presence of a mentor or coach who facilitate[s] practitioners' reflection" as factors in successful professional learning. Although these costs represent a serious commitment for early childhood services, with a supportive, collaborative culture, strong leadership, and a commitment to continuing professional learning, the long-term benefits of practitioner inquiry can outweigh the costs.

In Conclusion

Finally, as Kroll (2014, pp. 8–9) reminds us:

> Although the outside world promotes a myth of certainty that a quality education is made up of the *right* curriculum and the *right* teaching methods, in reality, questions, puzzles, and required instant decision-making make the act of teaching one of disequilibrium and imbalance. Unlike some professions where one can learn to solve problems by following a set of guidelines or procedures, the road map for teaching is strewn with byroads, boulders, lane changes, dead ends, and other unexpected events.

Early childhood educators may chart a path through this complex and uncertain road map by engaging with practitioner inquiry as a powerful and effective approach towards sustainable professional growth.

Key Messages

- Practitioner inquiry is embedded in pedagogical practice enabling educators to investigate their own professional work.
- Practitioner inquiry provides early childhood educators with a flexible structure to improve pedagogical decision-making.

- Continuous cycles of practitioner inquiry provide multiple opportunities to deepen professional growth and empowerment.

Thinking Points

- What do you see as two or three *opportunities* for professional growth at your workplace?
- How might you take advantage of these?
- What do see as two or three possible professional *challenges* at your workplace?
- How might you deal with these?

References

Abramson, S. (2012). Co-inquiry: Documentation, communication, action. In G. Perry, B. Henderson, & D. Meier (Eds.), *Our inquiry, our practice: Undertaking, supporting, and learning from early childhood teacher research(ers)* (pp. 147–157). NAEYC.

Albrecht, K., & Engel, B. (2007). Moving away from a quick-fix mentality to systematic professional development. *Young Children*, 62(4), 18–25.

Avalos, B. (2011). Teacher professional development in 'Teaching and Teacher Education' over ten years. *Teaching and Teacher Education*, 27(1), 10–20. https://doi.org/10.1016/j.tate.2010.08.007.

Castle, K. (2012). *Early childhood teacher research: From questions to results.* Routledge.

Cochran-Smith, M., & Lytle, S. (2009). *Inquiry as stance: Practitioner research for the next generation.* Teachers College Press.

Cole, A. M. (2020). Encouraging practitioner research engagement: Overcoming barriers. *Journal of Practitioner Research*, 5(2), https://doi.org/10.5038/2379-9951.5.2.1165.

Collay, M., Dunlap, D., Enloe, W., & Gagnon, G. (1998). *Learning circles: Creating conditions for professional development.* Corwin Press.

Dana, N. F. (2015). Understanding inquiry as stance: Illustration and analysis of one teacher researcher's work. *LEARNing Landscapes*, 8(2), 161–171. https://doi.org/10.36510/learnland.v8i2.702.

Dana, N.F., & Yendol-Hoppey, D. (2014). *The reflective educator's guide to classroom research: Learning to teach and teaching to learn through practitioner inquiry.* (3rd ed.). Corwin Press.

Fleet, A., De Gioia, K., & Patterson, C. (Eds.). (2016). *Engaging with educational change: Voices of practitioner inquiry.* Bloomsbury.

Fleet, A., & Patterson, C. (2001). Professional growth reconceptualized: Early childhood staff searching for meaning. *Early Childhood Research and Practice*, 3(2). https://ecrp.illinois.edu/index-2.html.

Gaches, S. (2021). Can I share your ideas with the world? Young children's consent in the research process. *Journal of Childhood Studies*, 46(2), 20–33.

Gilchrist, G. (2018). *Practitioner enquiry: Professional development with impact for teachers, schools and systems.* Routledge.

Gordon, S. (Ed.). (2008). *Collaborative action research: Developing professional learning communities.* Teachers College Press.

Grace, A. (2006). Striking a critical pose: Andragogy – missing links, missing values. *International Journal of Lifelong Learning*, 15(5), 382–392.

Hadley, F., Waniganayake, M., & Shepherd, W. (2015). Contemporary practice in professional learning and development of early childhood educators in Australia: Reflections on what works and why. *Professional Development in Education*, 41(2), 187–202. https://doi.org/10.1080/19415257.2014.986818.

Hall, E. (2009). Engaging in and engaging with research: Teacher inquiry and development. *Teachers and Teaching: Theory and Practice*, 15(6), 669–681. https://doi.org/10.1080/13540600903356985.

Harcourt, D., & Conroy, H. (2011). Informed consent: Processes and procedures seeking research partnerships with young children. In D. Harcourt, B. Perry, & T. Waller (Eds.), *Researching young children's perspectives: Debating the ethics and dilemmas of educational research with children* (pp. 38–51). Routledge.

Harcourt, D., Perry, B., & Waller, T. (Eds.). (2011). *Researching young children's perspectives: Debating the ethics and dilemmas of educational research with children*. Routledge.

Harris, A., Jones, M., & Huffman, J. B. (2017). *Teachers leading educational reform: The power of professional learning communities*. Routledge.

Hartree, A. (1984). Malcom Knowles: Theory of andragogy. A critique. *International Journal of Lifelong Learning*, 3(3), 203–210.

Hatch, J. A. (2012). Teacher research in early childhood settings: Needed now more than ever. In G. Perry, B. Henderson, & D. R. Meier (Eds.), *Our inquiry, our practice: Undertaking, supporting, and learning from early childhood teacher research(ers)* (pp. viii–ix). NAEYC.

Henderson, B., & Meier, D. (2012). Getting started and moving into teacher research. In G. Perry, B. Henderson, & D. Meier (Eds.), *Our inquiry, our practice: Undertaking, supporting, and learning from early childhood teacher research(ers)* (pp. 93–101). NAEYC.

Husbye, N. E., Rust, J., Wessel Powell, C., Vander Zanden, S., & Buchholz, B. (2019). Networking practitioner research: Leveraging digital tools as conduits for collaborative work. *Journal of Practitioner Research*, 4(1). https://doi.org/10.5038/2379-9951.4.1.1099.

Kroll, L. (2014). Inquiry and reflection to promote social justice and international understanding. In L. Kroll & D. Meier (Eds.), *Educational change in international early childhood contexts: Crossing borders of reflection* (pp. 7–20). Routledge.

Kroll, L. (2018). Teacher inquiry, research, and pedagogical documentation. In L. Kroll & D. Meier (Eds.), *Documentation and inquiry in the early learning classroom: Research stories from urban centers and schools* (pp. 3–18). Routledge.

Kroll, L., & Meier, D. (Eds.). (2018). *Documentation and inquiry in the early learning classroom: Research stories from urban centers and schools*. Routledge.

Kummen, K. & Hodgins, B. D. (2019). Learning collectives with/in sites of practice: Beyond training and professional development. *Journal of Childhood Studies*, 44(1), 111–122. https://doi.org/10.18357/jcs.v44i1.18785.

Leggett, N., & Newman, L. (2019). Owning it: Educators' engagement in researching their own practice. *European Early Childhood Education Research Journal*, 27(1), 138–150. https://doi.org/10.1080/1350293X.2018.1556539.

Loeng, S. (2018). Various ways of understanding the concept of andragogy. *Cogent Education*, 5(1), 1496643. https://doi.org/10.1080/2331186X.2018.1496643.

Melasalmi, A., & Husu, J. (2019). Shared professional agency in early childhood education: An in-depth study of three teams. *Teaching and Teacher Education*, 84, 83–94. https://doi.org/10.1016/j.tate.2019.05.002.

Merriam, S. B. (2001). Andragogy and self-directed learning: Pillars of adult learning theory. *New Directions for Adult and Continuing Education* (89), 3–12. https://doi.org/10.1002/ace.3.

Mertler, C. (2020). *Action research: Improving schools and empowering educators.* (6th ed.). SAGE.

Mills, G. (2017). *Action research: A guide for the teacher researcher.* (6th ed.). Pearson.

Newman, L., & Mowbray, C. (2012) 'We were expected to be equal': Teachers and academics sharing professional learning through practitioner inquiry. *Teachers and Teaching*, 18(4), 455–468. https://doi.org/10.1080/13540602.2012.696046.

Newman, L., & Woodrow, C. (Eds.). (2015). *Practitioner research in early childhood: International issues and perspectives.* SAGE.

Perry, G., Henderson, B., & Meier, D. (Eds.). (2012). *Our inquiry, our practice: Undertaking, supporting and learning from early childhood teacher research(ers).* NAEYC.

Phillips, D. K., & Carr, K. (2010). *Becoming a teacher through action research.* (2nd ed.). Routledge.

Reed, M., & Canning, N. (Eds.). (2010). *Reflective practice in the early years.* SAGE.

Rinaldi, C. (2006). *In dialogue with Reggio Emilia: Listening researching and learning.* Routledge.

Robertson, J. (2006). Reconsidering our image of children: What shapes our educational thinking? In A. Fleet, C. Patterson, & J. Robertson (Eds.), *Insights: Behind early childhood pedagogical documentation* (pp. 37–54). Pademelon Press.

Stacey, S. (2019). *Inquiry-based early learning environments: Creating, supporting and collaborating.* Redleaf Press.

Stenhouse, L. (1975). *An introduction to curriculum research and development.* Heinemann.

Stremmel A. J. (2018). Posing a researchable question. *Voices of practitioners*, 13(1). https://www.naeyc.org/resources/pubs/vop/dec2018/posing-researchable-question.

Tobin, J. (2015) Foreword. In L. Kroll, & D. Meier (Eds.), *Educational change in international early childhood contexts: Crossing borders of reflection.* Routledge.

Vandenbroeck, M., Peeters, J., Urban, M. & Lazzari, A. (2016). Introduction. In M. Vandenbroeck, M. Urban, & J. Peeters (Eds.), *Pathways to professionalism in early childhood education and care* (pp. 1–14). Routledge.

Wenger, E. (1991). *Communities of practice: Learning, meaning, and identity.* Cambridge University Press.

2 What is a Useful Question?

Marina Papic

Early childhood professionals are using practitioner inquiry as a tool for examining their contexts, taking control of their own learning and development, and improving their practice! How do early childhood teachers, educators and leaders decide what to focus on, what informs their decision and what question of inquiry is most useful?

This chapter will explore 'what is a useful question to be researched?' showcasing scenarios from the early childhood sector. The chapter provides insights into teachers' framing and reframing of their question and how a deep understanding of the children in their care and the wider context they work in, professional learning, the support of an experienced colleague, and the development of their content and pedagogical content knowledge supported them to select a useful question to be researched.

Opening Thoughts

Early childhood teachers, educators and leaders are committed to high quality practice to deliver better outcomes for children. To deliver high quality practice in an environment of accreditation, accountability and regulation, teachers are required to regularly reflect on their contexts and their pedagogical practice.

> As the early childhood education field becomes a target area for quality improvement initiatives, it is important to design professional development practices that have reflection as the core element so that practitioners have intentionally designed time and space to build community, to recognize their own voices and identities, to define what is valuable professional knowledge, to take meaningful action based on their own practice, and to think about the growth of their dispositions.
>
> (Isik-Ercan & Perkins, 2017, p. 351)

Selecting an Area of Inquiry

Teachers regularly consider and reflect on what in their classroom context and environment they feel could be improved or is concerning them as it is not

DOI: 10.4324/9781003245827-4

quite giving them the outcome they desire or the impact they are striving for. This often occurs in collaboration with other colleagues and creates an opportunity to reflect on one's own practice and ways to improve it (McLaughlin, et al., 2004). Finding that focus and developing a question to shape investigation around a challenging area are critical parts of the practitioner inquiry process. While this sounds straightforward, researchers working with early childhood teachers have found that for some teachers this is a difficult experience (e.g., Fleet et al., 2016; Johnston, 2019).

Fleet, De Gioia and Patterson (2016) in their study with teachers in the Sydney Catholic Education Office, looked at issues around identifying a question of inquiry including selecting questions that are too broad to be practicable, and leaders in services or the wider organisation determining the questions of inquiry for teachers. It is also clear that questions evolve over time, going through transformations to target a particular aspect of teacher intent more clearly. Selecting an area of inquiry focus is most successful when it engages the individual teacher, educator, or leader in exploring an area of inquiry that is relevant to them and is self-selected "in a professionally supported environment" (Fleet et al., 2016, p. 18).

What is a Researchable Question?

Although questions worth asking "come from the real-world obstacles and dilemmas" (Stremmel, 2018, p. 3), of everyday teaching, not all day-to-day teaching questions are worthwhile inquiry-based questions. Researchable questions are not "aimed at quick-fix solutions", rather they are "problems of meaning that develop gradually after careful observation and deliberation about why certain things are happening in the classroom" (Stremmel, 2018, p. 3). Researchable questions have the power to profoundly change practice; they evoke wonder and investigation and are a vehicle for embedding new ideas, theories and research into the classroom. Stremmel (2018, p. 3) acknowledges the work of Hubbard and Power (2003) in his explanation that worthwhile inquiry questions "engage the mind and the passion of the teacher; [they] encourage wonder about the space between what is known and what is knowable". They are questions of 'Why', 'How' and 'What'—allowing for multiple investigations and multiple solutions.

Scenario One: Preservice Teachers Framing an Inquiry Question

Research is a powerful tool for reflection, accountability, and improvement in practice. University pre-service teachers frequently engage in inquiry projects towards the end of their degree to develop skills in the practice of researching topics of interest to them. Having a sense of ownership of the question is "a key aspect in the formation of researcher identity" (Robson, 2022, p. 702). As the example below shows, however, while preservice teachers can select an area of inquiry that is of interest or relevance to them, the next step is often not straightforward.

University student teachers in their final year of undergraduate study at one Australian university engaged in an inquiry project as part of their internship in an early childhood service. The tutor shares her experience in working with the students on framing a question:

> Some student teachers had difficulty in framing a researchable question. For example, the following question is almost impossible to answer in a few weeks: "Is the quality of an infant relationship with their educator/s an important influence in the success and quality of an infant's peer relationships?" Similarly, a question like: "Can children have a sense of agency within a Montessori setting?" could be re-phrased as "How can I encourage the development of a sense of agency for children in my room?" This also avoids the problem of asking a question with a yes/no answer.
>
> Other student teachers encountered the problem of directing their question in a more focused way in their attempts to be more 'research-y'. The first question from one student in her workplace was "How can I improve my teaching in respect to the programming; taking into account the wealth of knowledge and experience of the staff, whilst being staff-and family-friendly to understand what is being planned and followed up without interrupting interactions?" Given guidance in re-thinking this focus, her final question was: "How can I support educators in the nursery room to improve our approach to programming?" This re-phrased question enabled her to address her concerns in a more focused way while including her original wishes to acknowledge the "knowledge and experience of the staff" and "to be staff-and family-friendly".

It takes time, reflection, support from a mentor (within or external to the workplace) as well as the willingness to rework the question to identify the 'final' version. Even then, once you start collecting data, you may find that you need to reframe the question again or even ask a different question as you found something more interesting and more important to research.

Consider your researchable question

- Is your question relevant to you and your practice?
- Is your question open-ended, that is, it moves beyond a yes/no response?
- Is it framed in a way to allow you to address your concerns in a more focused way or is it too general or vague?

Teachers' Wonderings

Focuses of inquiry and "teachers' wonderings" according to Hubbard and Power (1993) come from "real-world observations and dilemmas" (p. 2). Dana and Yendol-Hoppey (2020) identify five elements central to teachers' reflection on their practice and their wonderings:

1   The context,
2   The content,
3   The children,
4   The teacher's own beliefs or dispositions, and
5   The acts of teaching.

These elements "provide the foundation for identifying felt difficulties or teaching dilemmas that prompt the development of inquiry questions" (p. 27).

   In my experience working with thousands of teachers, educators and leaders through professional development, their focus of wonderings and then inquiry is quite often a combination of these elements with initial observations, conversations, professional learning, research and/or data informing the direction of that inquiry. The following scenarios exemplify how inquiry questions can come about from multiple experiences and wonderings and can evolve over time.

Scenario Two: Teams Coming Together for Professional Learning and Deep Reflection

Goodstart Bathurst, in regional NSW, is embedded in a community rich in Aboriginal culture. The Director, Emma Kentwell and her team, continually strive to be more inclusive of Aboriginal cultures and embrace Aboriginal perspectives into all aspects of their practice. Emma shares the service's journey of inquiry, how strong professional learning and deep reflection assisted them in identifying the focus of their inquiry:

> At Goodstart Bathurst we value the philosophy of the environment as a third teacher. We pondered on how we could change the trajectory on children's relationship with nature and people for the rest of their lives. This led to a team of educators travelling to Melbourne with myself to engage in a professional development session with the founder of Bush Kinder, Doug Fargher. This professional development opportunity led to deep reflection on how this approach to spending regular time in nature and using the natural space for exploring and learning could look for our children, our community, and our team of educators. As part of our reflection, we engaged in thoughtful conversations, unpacking the benefits of a Bush Kindy program. We reflected on the research of the social, emotional, and learning benefits for children who spent more time outside

in nature. This wondering, our conversations and research led to our focus of inquiry: *How can Bush Kindy allow children to challenge their developing physical skills and contribute to the way they take appropriate risks?*

The team engaged in deep reflection as both a collective team and as individuals establishing a space for conversations in which all educators can learn from one another.

> **Consider your researchable question**
>
> - Can you establish a space for deep conversations in which all educators in your team can learn and grow?
> - What opportunities can you create for deep reflection at both a personal and team level?
> - What community partnerships do you currently have that could lead to useful and relevant questions of inquiry?

Scenario Three: Collaborative Research between University Researchers and Practitioners

Collaborative research between university researchers and practitioners narrows the gap between research and practice (Bruce et al., 2011). Practitioners gain valuable professional learning and support from the researcher; while the researcher has an opportunity to gather data on real-life theory and practice, building new knowledge for the sector (Catelli et al., 2000).

Kelly Johnston, in her PhD study with educators working in a long day care service, aimed to gain insights into how educators can use technology as a tool to extend learning interests and investigations through a practitioner inquiry project (Johnston, 2019). Throughout the project, educators were supported to develop new understandings of how technology could be integrated into scientific learning in the early learning curriculum. Kelly recounts the process of working with the educators in identifying their question of inquiry.

Background Interest in Space

The interest in space in the centre was child-led. The educators said that it emerged from some of the children being involved with the Young Astronomers' program that was held at the nearby university at the time. Educators said that the space theme came up every year and was also influenced by popular culture/ media (such as Star Wars and children's cartoons that included space).

Formulating an inquiry question – the background

Because the practitioner inquiry projects needed to have a technology focus, the educators initially wanted to focus on how engines in rocket ships worked. I provided them with journal articles that illustrated how technology could be integrated as a tool or resource in early learning curricula to support children's investigations on an area of interest. I also provided a summary of the key ideas from the articles in dot point so educators could access them quickly as time allocated for educators to engage with readings was limited (the importance of leadership and leadership support in the practitioner inquiry process is critical and will be discussed further in Chapter 9).

There was a lot of going backwards and forwards as the educators tried to decide on a research question. At this time, a colleague suggested professional development delivered by a science expert, particularly focused on astronomy curriculum and pedagogy in the early years. This was a turning point as everyone had a shared knowledge base. Staff and children alike were so interested, and we had complete buy in! The educators enhanced their content knowledge of astronomy and pedagogical approaches to teaching the content.

Professional Learning and Support from the Researcher

From talking with educators, it became apparent that they were not confident in their own knowledge of space and the solar system. However, the professional development built their content and pedagogical content knowledge so they could create learning environments, implement relevant experiences, model scientific language, and engage in conversations with children through a lens of scientific inquiry. At times educators expressed complete surprise that the children knew so much.

Educators were unsure of how to extend children's interest in space and the solar system due to limited knowledge on the topic and a lack of access to resources that supported exploration in an early learning curriculum. It is common for adults, teachers, and educators to not have accurate understandings of science-related topics. I was able to draw on the summary of information provided to them during the professional development sessions to help shape the practitioner inquiry research questions. The educators decided on the question: *"How can technology support children's exploration of space and the solar system?"*

Kelly's example highlights not only the importance of professional development to shape inquiry questions but also the importance of an experienced colleague, in this case the researcher, to provide support and mentoring. Hewes and colleagues (2019) highlighted that improving curriculum requires "an initial period of intensive, responsive, sustained pedagogical mentorship provided by well-educated, experienced mentors with expertise in early childhood pedagogy" (p. 50).

Consider your researchable question

- Is there an experienced colleague who can mentor and support you in identifying an inquiry focus and question?

Scenario Four: Building Content and Pedagogical Content Knowledge of the Discipline Area that Is at the Centre of the Inquiry

An analysis of questions from 107 teachers working within a large Australian early childhood organisation has shown that teachers (at least in this context) selected questions around four main areas of inquiry: inclusion, reconciliation, learning environments, and documenting children's learning (see Chapter 3 for more details). The four areas related to their practice could clearly be identified as an area that required attention. In this group of 107, only one inquiry question focused on the curriculum area of mathematics and no questions focused on the area of science. A lack of content knowledge in mathematics and science for early childhood teachers, coupled with a fear and anxiety in these subject areas, leads to questions in these important areas of the curriculum not being self-chosen areas of inquiry. The one inquiry question related to mathematics was: *How do I teach mathematics more effectively?* This was a very broad question that could be narrowed and reshaped to support a specific change in practice.

Areas of the curriculum such as science and mathematics are important for children's learning and development. Science and mathematics knowledge, concepts and skills build on children's interests, needs and strengths and are therefore important elements of practice, however, they require teachers to have content and pedagogical content knowledge to identify what needs to change or what needs to be developed. As the saying goes, "you don't know what you don't know". Consider, for example, your practice in a mathematics classroom; to be able to identify your strengths and the areas you would like to develop, you need mathematical pedagogical content knowledge: "knowledge about ways to create and modify mathematical learning environments for young children, knowledge about ways to analyse mathematical development, and knowledge about ways to give, sometimes spontaneously, adaptive support in natural learning settings" (Gasteiger et al., 2020, p. 195).

I share my own experience of how developing teachers' and educators' mathematical content and pedagogical content knowledge supported them to identify useful questions of inquiry:

> Working with teachers in many communities across Australia, I have heard repeatedly: "I wasn't good at maths at school"; "I don't like maths"; "I don't know how to teach maths". This belief and disposition towards mathematics affects a teacher's ability to see, hear and engage their children effectively in mathematics in their classroom.
>
> Delivering professional development to 40 early childhood teachers and educators in a remote community in north-western NSW provided them with the confidence to consider mathematics in their classroom—the capabilities of their children, the specific content that could be explored and the teaching strategies and approaches that enhance mathematical thinking

and reasoning. By addressing their concerns and fears about mathematics and then supporting them to consider their practice through practical hands-on experiences that build mathematical content and pedagogical content knowledge, have conversations, and engage in reflection, they were able to identify questions of inquiry related to mathematics for the first time in their teaching careers:

TEACHER A: "Engaging in hands-on activities and talking about the maths made me reflect on my classroom and how I was teaching, what materials I was putting out and how my spaces were set up … Being provided with ideas of different activities and resources that can develop basic mathematical concepts for younger children really opened up the possibilities of what I can do with my children".

Therefore, the inquiry question became: *How do I provision the environment to encourage children to explore maths concepts?*

TEACHER B: "Engaging in the practical workshop I learnt how useful questioning children in maths experiences can be. It is useful for me as a teacher to know what they are thinking but also help them to, as Marina said, justify and reason. I would like to explore this further, consider what I currently do, where I could engage with children to ask good questions, to build their maths understanding. I need to read more about this and think about how I set up my space for opportunities for children to not only explore maths but talk about their experience".

Therefore, the inquiry question became: *How can I include more questions and conversations into my teaching to develop children's mathematics learning?*

TEACHER C: "The ideas and resources shared are so practical and simple. I was always scared of maths, and this has excited me and made me feel more confident. I want to make my experiences more culturally appropriate for the children I work with and use more culturally relevant materials".

Therefore, the inquiry question became: *How do I embed culturally appropriate maths experiences in my classroom?*

Consider your researchable question

- Have you considered an area of inquiry that will challenge your thinking, that isn't a comfortable space for you?
- Do you need to read more or engage with some professional learning to develop your content knowledge and pedagogical content knowledge in this area (such as mathematics or science) so you can identify a suitable inquiry question?

Scenario Five: Wonderings and Learnings on Current Practice and Available Data Can Inform Questions of Inquiry

Susan Perks, a Mathematics Coordinator at St Anthony's Primary School, Victoria, shares her wonderings which were informed by wanting to make changes that would benefit students. She reflected on what needed change and what was working well that could support change, and she analysed current school data. Susan wanted her focus of research/inquiry to result in action and change in teaching and learning practice more widely across the school. Susan shares below her journey in deciding what to focus her research on:

> When considering what to research, I wanted to focus on what was relevant at our school and what would benefit our students. I had an interest in how we could improve outcomes in maths in our school as our data around number sense concepts were showing little improvement over time, with some students in Years 3–6 continuing to struggle with some basic foundational maths concepts. This made it increasingly difficult for these students to unpack more complex understandings. I also felt that educators in this context had more confidence in teaching Literacy and were more open to discussions around continuing to improve learning and teaching in Literacy. However, I felt there was a great need in maths to improve teacher pedagogy and student outcomes.
>
> I started to explore our student data, have conversations with staff around what challenges they have in the maths classroom and what support they give to students struggling with foundational maths concepts. Over the past 12 months, I had been working closely with the Prep (Kindergarten) teachers, working through professional development focusing on number sense concepts and increasing fluency around the Learning Number in Framework (LFIN) (Wright & Ellemor-Collins, 2018). In the Prep classroom context, student data was improving, and students were showing pleasing improvements in these foundational skills. Additionally, the staff's pedagogical understanding was increasing, with greater collaboration around student data and how to effectively teach these concepts in the classroom.
>
> From this, I began to wonder if these learnings could be transferred to an intervention for students in other year levels that were showing significant mathematics difficulties and had gaps in their learning around these number sense concepts and fluency. I began reading research around maths interventions and noted that maths is seen as an indicator for academic success, and as students enter the middle years of primary school, the gap for students displaying maths difficulties continues to grow. Therefore, intervention seems imperative in Year 2 to support students with these concepts before entering the middle years of primary. Successful literacy intervention is based on daily, small group sessions with a repeated focus and opportunity for explicit teaching, scaffolded practice, and individual

mastery. I believed this research and knowledge should be able to be transferred into mathematics. Our school has had success using the Breakspear model of 'teaching sprints', where teachers focus on one concept intensively with a group of students to improve practice and support student outcomes (Breakspear & Jones, 2021).

I began to bring these pieces together that seemed to be working in our context and could possibly support a wider range of our students. This led me to think about the use of the LFIN framework as a learning progression and assessment-support combined with daily teaching sprints in small needs-based groups taken outside of the classroom for 10 minutes daily. My wonderings included: Would this improve student outcomes for Year 2 students struggling in maths? Would this promote a growth of self-confidence in mathematical ability within the classroom? From further reading, analysis of student data and discussions with the staff I developed my question over time, before deciding on: *What impact does daily, targeted intervention have on student achievement in mathematics?*

I am excited to collect data around my question of inquiry and to see if these ideas come together to form the basis of successful intervention for our students.

Susan's example highlights that it takes time to decide on a research question or question of inquiry. Reflecting on practice involves looking at multiple facets which could include reviewing any existing data. The key purpose of data in educational settings is to improve teaching and learning. Using data to inform a question of inquiry that addresses a problem will improve practice and lead to improved student outcomes.

Consider your researchable question

- Do you have existing data that could inform your inquiry question?
- What aspects of your practice are effective that could lead to further inquiry to address a related challenge?

Scenario Six: Putting Children at the Centre of your Inquiry

Children are curious; they wonder; they ask questions. Observing children, listening to their wonderings, and engaging with them in conversations leads to teachers reflecting on their practice and how they can change their practice to enhance their children's knowledge, build their understandings, cater for individual children's strengths, needs and interests and decide how they can make a difference in that child's learning.

Camilla Gordon shares an example of an idea that came from a child she was teaching during her postgraduate research project, that ultimately led to an inquiry question to enhance her pedagogy around science.

A child asked me where the moon was in the daytime sky. She had noticed the moon in the day, but on this occasion, she couldn't find it. As her teacher, I began a project of learning myself. It began with gathering information about the phases of the moon. When was the moon visible in the daytime? Sometimes it was there, sometimes it wasn't. Why was this so? I asked myself questions because of a child's wondering! *How could I engage children with the idea of finding where the moon was, day and night?* This question delivered for the children a project spanning one whole year and began the development of knowledge for us all—educators and children alike, that literally changed lives.

Science—particularly physics—is in everything that we do, but it requires acute listening and observation by practitioners. Often declaring, "We never did science at school and never understood physics; it makes us feel unable to 'do science'." In the above case, it was a child who stimulated the journey for me. If we look at best practice, we can see teachers reflecting on the learning of children. We can learn a great deal if we look at the teachers in Reggio schools and the way they instill wonder and curiosity in their classrooms, and in turn, the way they practice the art of wondering themselves so they can more completely understand their children. *How can I intervene in children's play to clarify their thinking and wonderings so I can build on their knowledge?*

In the outdoor space we have so many examples of physics—shade and light, warm and cool, still and breezy, hard and soft, noisy and quiet, natural and artificial. All of these are aspects of children's exploration of their environment, but none are keys to a child's learning unless the practitioner listens and observes, and then follows up with questions of his/her own about their own practice.

We are surrounded by ideas and opportunities to stimulate learning if we listen to children and consider their wonderings. These can then inform our own wonderings and opportunities to enhance our practice to support children's learning, understandings, and further wonderings!

Final Comments

Teachers, educators, and leaders should be agents in their own inquiry and research, not merely observers (Kemmis, 2010). They should select questions of inquiry or research that are relevant to them and where they have ownership. As the examples in this chapter highlight, deciding on a research or inquiry question can come about from a combination of elements.

The concept of research literacies is predicated on the importance of ongoing professional learning, where teachers and educators, teacher educators and education researchers, and system leaders know how to identify problems related to their practice, and to students' learning and education more generally, and who can harness skills and knowledge to investigate solutions and implement change.

(White et al., 2020, p. 9)

However, professionals need time to deeply reflect and ponder. They need time to talk to their colleagues about their thinking and wonderings. They need time to frame and reframe their questions of inquiry!

So now that you have your question, what's next? Chapter 3 provides insights into gathering and analysing data in relation to the question posed. What is data? How do I gather it? What do I do with it—how do I analyse it?

Key Messages

- Questions worth asking are those that are meaningful to the practitioner and come from real world problems and challenges in their practice.
- Collaboration with other colleagues and opportunities to deeply reflect on one's own practice support the development of an intentional inquiry question.
- Not all questions are inquiry focused. Some are just reflections on practice that lead to a quick action rather than a commitment to understanding and profoundly improving teaching and learning.
- Framing an inquiry question takes time and is quite often reframed throughout the inquiry process.
- Selecting a useful inquiry question involves a combination of several elements, including an understanding of the children in your care; the context you work in; professional learning; the support of an experienced colleague; and the development of content and pedagogical content knowledge.

Thinking Points

- Consider the scenarios presented in this chapter. Which elements that informed the varied inquiry questions resonated with you? Why?
- What learnings can you take away from the scenarios that would assist you in framing a useful question?
- Consider the wonderings and ponderings you have recently had about your practice. Make time to talk to your colleagues or a mentor about your reflections and consider how your reflections and wonderings could be framed into an inquiry focus or question.

References

Breakspear, S., & Jones, B. (2021). *Teaching Sprints. How overloaded educators can keep getting better.* Corwin.

Bruce, C. D., Flynn, T., & Stagg-Peterson, S. (2011). Examining what we mean by collaborative action research: A cross-case analysis. *Educational Action Research*, 19(4), 433–452.

Catelli, L., Padovano, K., & Costello, J. (2000). Action research in the context of a school-university partnership: Its value, problems, issues and benefits. *Educational Action Research,* 8(2), 225–242.

Dana, N. F., & Yendol-Hoppey, D. (2020). *The reflective educator's guide to classroom research: Learning to teach and teaching to learn through practitioner inquiry* (4th ed.). Corwin Press.

Fleet, A., De Gioia, K., & Patterson, C. (Eds.) (2016). *Engaging with educational change: Voices of practitioner inquiry.* Bloomsbury Publishing.

Gasteiger, H., Bruns, J., Benz, C., Brunner, E., & Sprenger, P. (2020). Mathematical pedagogical content knowledge of early childhood teachers: A standardized situation-related measurement approach. *ZDM Mathematics Education,* 52, 193–205. https://doi.org/10.1007/s11858-019-01103-2.

Hewes, J., Lirette, T., Makovichuk, L., & McCarron, R. (2019). Animating a curriculum framework through educator co-inquiry: Co-learning, co-researching, and co-imagining possibilities. *Journal of Childhood Studies,* 44(1), 37–53. https://doi.org/10.18357/jcs.v44i1.18776.

Hubbard, R. S., & Power, B. M. (1993). *The art of classroom inquiry: A handbook for teacher researchers.* Heinemann.

Hubbard, R. S., & Power, B. M. (2003). *The art of classroom inquiry: A handbook for teacher researchers.* (Rev.ed.). Heinemann.

Isik-Ercan, Z., & Perkins, K. (2017). Reflection for meaning and action as an engine for professional development across multiple early childhood teacher education contexts. *Journal of Early Childhood Teacher Education,* 38(4), 338–350.

Johnston, K. (2019). Digital technology as a tool to support children and educators as co-learners. *Global Studies of Childhood,* 9(4), 306–317.

Kemmis, S. (2010). What is to be done? The place of action research. *Educational Action Research,* 18(4), 417–427.

McLaughlin, C., Black-Hawkins, K., & McIntyre, D. (2004). *Researching teachers, researching schools, researching networks: A review of the literature.* Cambridge University Press.

Robson, J. V. K. (2022). An Action Research Inquiry: Facilitating early childhood studies undergraduate researcher development through Group Supervision. *Educational Action Research,* 30(5), 689–706. https://doi.org/10.1080/09650792.2021.1872395.

Stremmel, A. (2018). Posing a researchable question. *Voices of Practitioners,* 13(1). https://www.naeyc.org/resources/pubs/vop/dec2018/posing-researchable-question.

White, S., Down, B., Mills, M., Shore, S., & Woods, A. (2020). Strengthening a research-rich teaching profession: An Australian study. *Teaching Education,* 1–15.

Wright, R., & Ellemor-Collins, D. (2018). *The Learning Framework in Number. Pedagogical tools for assessment and instruction.* Sage Publications.

3 Evidence for Change

Finding and Analysing Data

Katey De Gioia

Moving Beyond "Knee Jerk" Reactions to a Problem

Practitioner inquiry requires data gathering and analysis to drive and inform professional decision-making. Whilst early childhood practitioners already have multiple points of data collection, associating the process with practitioner inquiry often creates a stumbling block that leads to overthinking what data is or could be. To ensure the inquiry question will be addressed, it is essential to take time to understand data-gathering in relation to (i) the question posed, (ii) the existing data that can be utilised, and (iii) the collection of new data. Further, identification of who should be included to gather data from—for example: children, families, the local community, peers, leadership—is dependent on the question and opportunities that may arise.

Analysis of data may be equally confronting for some novices in the practitioner inquiry process. Too much, too little, feeling that the question is not being answered or not knowing how to analyse can impact the process. This chapter will explore data and analysis, framed through experiences of teachers involved in a large-scale inquiry process. It will highlight both success stories and stories in growth and understanding of the purpose of data and analyses to address the question being investigated.

The Challenges of Data

Interestingly, the word 'data' can incite feelings of worry, enhanced by exposure to peer-reviewed journal articles through university study that demand certain layers of rigour (as should be expected). Recently, a cohort of 107 early childhood teachers from the same organisation were brought together in 16 groups across New South Wales, Australia. They agreed to participate in teacher inquiry as a new way of approaching professional development. There were four meetings in a 12 month cycle to engage with the process, with a series of ongoing assigned tasks between meetings. Teachers were asked to commit to the full 12 months and if missing a session, they would 'catch up' prior to their next meeting.

In the initial meeting, as the facilitator, I provided an overview of teacher inquiry and unpacked the process. I gave reasons why this was a way to view

DOI: 10.4324/9781003245827-5

professional learning as sustainable, that would build on their strengths and, at the same time, engage them deeply in change that mattered to them, their community and context (Fleet et al., 2016; Menter et al., 2011). Part of the first presentation invited the teachers to identify areas of concern and then to engage with the notion of data to understand why the particular area was of concern. My researcher notes (2018), after meeting with half the cohort groups, highlighted the initial response to data-gathering,

> I can feel the apprehension in the room, with each new cohort group I meet. I am new to them and they to me. We don't know each other, and they start off looking expectantly at me—as if I had the answers for them or was going to provide standardised professional development, but I didn't. I held a new way of working, one that I was hoping would empower them to be leading their own professional learning. I have started to note a pattern, they appear eager, then I mentioned data ... facial expressions change ever so slightly, a few shift in their seats and one or two rifle through the notes they have been given for the PowerPoint presentation ...

Data provides the facts that, when collected, enable opportunity for analysis and therefore, address the question posed. It is really interesting to note that early childhood education and care relies heavily on data and early childhood teachers collect data in a myriad of ways, but in this instance, they can be challenged by the word and how it is perceived. Of note, the teachers who agreed to be involved in this teacher inquiry cycle had not participated in teacher inquiry before. All experiences with professional development had been via a one-size-fits-all transmission method; same content delivered in the same manner, so this was quite a new way of working. It also involved moving from *being told*, to taking responsibility and driving practice-change relative to personal and professional growth. Contemporary research shows that, when professional learning is situated in a social context, with the provision of ongoing support through mentoring and facilitation, there is more likelihood of sustainable, engaged change in practice (Nolan & Molla, 2018; Hadley et al., 2015). For teachers, this meant that they were being asked to unlearn their understanding of professional development.

Feeling Confident in the Process – "Is This Right?"

As with all the meetings I facilitated, the initial meeting involved setting the scene—which included an opportunity to define the group as a 'community of practice', drawing on the work of Wenger-Trayner and Wenger-Trayner (2015), to acknowledge the strengths of the collective group of teachers:

- commitment to each other and the group,
- existing and developing relationships,

- competence,
- joint activities and discussions, and
- commitment to help each other and share information.

We also took time to establish group expectations, which included expectations of each member; mine of them and theirs of me. One of the key expectations that was set and agreed to by all members was to "come to our meetings prepared, having completed the work in between sessions, and willing to contribute about the question of inquiry" (Area XA Meeting Notes, 2018). Interestingly, being explicit about this commitment resulted in only rare instances where teachers turned up unprepared; however, this could be contested and reframed to teachers being so highly engaged in their question of inquiry that they were prepared because they were invested in the process.

In between meetings, I would offer opportunities for teachers to connect with each other via online posting, and/or directly to me through a phone or email conversation. One such conversation involved a teacher who had initially expressed doubt over the process of inquiry in the first meeting. She was keen to check in and we had chatted over the phone and via email about her question of choice and data-gathering processes. I had promised to visit her area, but unfortunately needed to cancel due to unforeseen circumstances.

This teacher, Agata, was working with four-year-old children and had chosen a question of inquiry around outdoor environments. She felt she had not gained any traction in the area to date as the outdoor space was often left unprogrammed. Children were not very engaged in the space, and it was not a great place for children or teachers to be. It seemed to be disowned and learning was not evident.

For Agata, the initial foray into data collection for this particular purpose was foreign to her, as was the process of inquiry. She later shared with me:

> I was so scared to bring back my data to the [second] meeting. I wanted you to come visit so I could talk you through what I had done, I wanted it to be right, I wanted to get it right, I didn't want it to be wrong.
>
> (Meeting Notes, 2018)

In the early stages of the cycle of inquiry, data-gathering is critical to understanding the question and determining the direction of a potential change. During the practitioner inquiry project, we discussed examples of this early data-gathering to help participants understand that data or information is essential for the process of analysis. Successful data-gathering also involves engaging in critical reflection to ensure that perspectives beyond oneself are taken into consideration (Miller, 2011). Data analysis serves the following purposes as part of the cycle of inquiry (Fleet et al., 2016):

- provides a process for understanding a problem,
- supports decision-making that is evidence-informed,

- assists in understanding what the question of inquiry *should* be. Initial data, when analysed may identify that the question of concern is not the actual concern.

It is important to spend time reassuring participants that data is not a new concept in early childhood education and care. There is a plethora of data in existence in services, collected and created every day!

Using evidence to carefully inform next steps ensures a clear understanding of the problem i.e., the question of focus, and how to address this. So, the key message from the first meeting was "Don't go back and change anything; ask yourself, what do you see, not what do you want to see. Go back to your centre and collect information *about* your question. This is the first data set for analysis."

Agata's data-gathering and analysis at the early stage of her inquiry were thoughtful and considered. There was some reshaping of the question in moving forward; however, the greatest learning here wasn't for Agata and her outdoor environment, but rather in my understanding of the process for this teacher. Agata was *unlearning* prior experiences and expectations of the delivery of professional learning and development, but to an extent, also the purpose of data collection and analyses. Her *relearning* (Cooper & Klepp, 2017) was framed in an appreciation for her role in professional learning; her confidence visibly shifted after her opportunity for sharing and gaining an understanding of data-gathering and analysis that was fit for their particular purpose.

Determining Data that Will Address the Question

Analysis of question themes suggested that teachers' concerns could be grouped into five broad areas as indicated in Table 3.1. To gain greater understanding of their question topic, the teachers involved in this large-scale inquiry chose three categories of data. The teachers:

- used existing data sources in the service,
- extended on existing data sources,
- created new data sources.

Each of these are explored below.

Category 1: Existing Data Sources in the Centre

Existing data tends to be used when inquiry questions are interrogating current practice. For example, questions around *documentation, indoor and outdoor learning environments* and *inclusion* predominantly drew on an analysis of a variety of existing data. Table 3.1 shows the broad *Question* themes (with examples of specific areas of concern) and data used to address the question. Existing data was not the only data source used, but rather, teachers with these types of

Table 3.1 Question Theme and Data Used to Address the Question

Question theme	Existing data used	Extending on existing data
Questions about documentation • observation tools • overuse of photos • who is it for?	Recent documentation—count of type and focus Number of photos taken in a period of time vs number used to document learning meaningfully Questionnaires/surveys with key stakeholders—Centre Director/Assistant Director/colleagues Source documents: National Regulations, Early Years Learning Framework Photographs taken vs those in the program	Recording of small group experience Targeted photographs Feedback at staff meetings
Questions about involving children in inquiry/project work • open ended questions	Revisiting representation in Quality Improvement Plan Identification of opportunities in programming to pursue inquiry	Assessment of questioning techniques used during small group times Staff meeting conversation Conversation with children
Questions about learning environments • book area • moving from activity-led to support learning • STEM • maths • book area • group time Specific to outdoor environments • intentional teaching • programming • responsibility Specific to infants and toddlers • documentation • independence and agency • environments Schemas to foster learning	Minutes from curriculum meetings Review of past two months of program Reflection of current classroom environment Review of daily routine Running records of children's behaviour Photos of children reflecting engagement Event samples Photos and written observations of children engaging in different areas Review of outdoor incidents and comparison to indoors Thematic analysis of staff meeting minutes for 12 months to identify discussions re: outdoors Review of programming for the outdoor environment to determine accountability Review of program—current and past Revisiting photo documentation Observation of educators during routines	Small group discussion with children that reflects question of inquiry Targeted observations of children in learning areas Targeted photographs in areas Observations for one child (nursery) Observation of specific area in the nursery space Analysis of reflective questions for toddler team

Question theme	Existing data used	Extending on existing data
Questions about inclusion • understanding key concepts of inclusion • embedding inclusion in the program • guiding behaviour to support inclusion in the program	Observation in rooms Analysis of success of strategies used to date Time sample Event sample Anecdotal observations Running records Analysis of room routine and possible behaviour triggers	
Questions about sustainability • is this evident? • why isn't it sustainable?	Audit of posts on Storypark Audit of room practices Survey to families and educators	

questions built on from this by gathering further data throughout the inquiry cycle for two reasons: (1) they felt they didn't have a strong understanding of their question or (2) they felt they didn't have stakeholder perspectives represented adequately to understand the issue.

For example, one teacher, Joelene, had identified her question as: "How can I make the book area more engaging for boys?" She had a classroom of four-year-old children and had shared her ongoing issues about a small group of four boys who felt that the best use for the book area was rough and tumble play (particularly with the large cushions that became great chest plates to ram into their friends!)

Joelene chose the following initial existing data to understand her question:

- Review of the program: Interrogation of the room program from the past two months to identify when there had been a focus on book area and identification of children's observations or planning implications that directly related to either those boys or to the book area.
- Room layout: Reflection of the current classroom environment layout as it currently is and making note of any changes in past two months.
- Review of the daily routine to understand opportunities for access to the book area.

Having analysed her data, Joelene was surprised at the results, she felt that it might just be a case of [gendered] 'boy behaviour' that needed to be 'managed' in those few months before going to school. Key pieces of information that became evident to her were that:

- There had not been any mention of book area in the program, beyond that it was available.

- Book area had been situated right next to the door to the external playground. A floating program was offered for a significant part of the day with constant movement in and out by children and educators, directly past book area.
- There were points throughout the routine of the day where children were asked to gather in book area to read whilst the teacher and co-educators were completing daily duties i.e., setting out beds, finalising settings lunch prior to eating and after lunch whilst cleaning was happening.

As in this example, analysis of existing data enabled teachers to gain perspectives on their questions quite quickly. For some teachers, whilst they had hypothesised what the analysis would show them, the clear evidence confirmed or refuted their hypothesis and in turn, their question. Of note here was the dedicated time that was given to this process of analysis that confirmed the issues. One teacher noted, "I need to take the time to review, this needs to become part of my regular practice", whilst another identified that "I may have been able to solve this problem earlier if I had focused on what I had available to me."

Category 2: Extending Existing Data Sources

The second category of data that became evident involved extending on existing data sources. This was mainly seen as an addition to the data gathered above. It did not require developing or designing a new process for data-gathering, but rather practices or processes that could be used as points for gathering data were manipulated to support new data for analysis. The data-gathering methods outlined in Table 3.1, column three, identify instances whereby it was not a new process of data-gathering or practice for data-gathering, but was conducted in a more structured and/or targeted manner. These types of data-gathering included reflection specific to a question, observation or photo-taking of a specific area, targeted observations and seeking feedback related to a specific area at a staff meeting.

In another site, Divya identified her question of inquiry as, "How can I include open-ended questions throughout the day to support sustained shared thinking with the children in my group?" Divya was the teacher in a room with 3–5-year-old children. She had felt that she was not confident in using open-ended questions and that her conversations with children did not offer opportunities for children to think deeply and engage further. Divya had started with existing data in her room to help her understand her question of inquiry, conducting an analysis of both her reflective journal and the room programming over the past month. Neither of these provided any guidance about when she had used open-ended questioning or when she had engaged deeply in conversation with a child or group of children. She shared that the absence of related data confirmed her thinking that she needed to address her chosen question.

To gain insight into her conversations with children, Divya voice-recorded her interactions with children at key times over a day. She targeted a small group experience, during transition to lunch, in the dramatic play area indoors and the sandpit outdoors. Divya analysed her data, looking for patterns in her conversations and questions asked of children and for potential opportunities to extend the conversation. She reported back to the group that gathering data through this method did not require any additional planning, "as long as the recording app was activated on the phone at the correct time!" but did provide her with the greatest insights when she went back over her recordings to ana-lyse the data. Divya bravely shared with her teacher colleagues that she had learnt a lot about herself when she analysed this data including:

- the transactional nature of her conversations with children,
- that she had missed key opportunities to engage in sustained shared thinking with children,
- that she had favoured closed questions.

Opportunities to interrogate current practice may require moving beyond existing data-gathering methods. As this cohort of teachers discovered, how-ever, rather than moving into totally new data-gathering processes, it may be an extension or modification of existing sources of data that assists in addressing the question.

Category 3: Creation of New Processes for Data-gathering

Meanwhile, the creation of new data-gathering processes was strongly con-nected to questions involving a range of stakeholders, children, families, co-educators, or the broader centre team and/or key representatives from the local community. These new processes usually involved either surveys/ques-tionnaires or interviews. Table 3.2: *Question theme and data used, including new data-gathering methods to address the question* shows the areas of newly developed data-gathering methods to complement or use in place of existing/extending data-gathering processes.

Sally, a teacher and recently appointed Educational Leader[1] in her centre, explained that her question of inquiry focused on how she could engage co-educators across the centre in professional readings. She wanted to establish a *Culture of professional learning and sharing* that she felt, in consultation with the leadership team, was missing from the centre. She developed a questionnaire and shared it amongst her team. They responded positively and agreed with the direction Sally believed they should be heading. Sally was delighted and returned to the second meeting with huge plans for readings she would like them to complete and how they would be unpacking these at follow-up staff meetings. Between meeting two and three (approximately three months apart), Sally and I had many conversations as she felt that the analysis of the ques-tionnaires and her planned next steps were not aligning.

Table 3.2 Question Theme and Data Used, Including New Data-Gathering Methods to Address the Question

Question theme	Existing and extending data	New data-gathering methods
Culture of professional learning • reflection/critical reflection • increase knowledge • engagement	Reflection rooms in Storypark	Questionnaires for educators Individual semi-structured interviews with all the team Trial and error of materials
Leadership • self-doubt • increase effectiveness	Self-reflection: series of specific questions to determine when anxiety appears	Online survey about personal leadership Questionnaires—one for team leaders, one for educators
Reconciliation • understanding • embedding • avoiding tokenism	Assessment of where existing references to Reconciliation occur in the centre Small group discussion with children Analysis of curriculum for past month Audit of current children's books and resources Identification of connections to local community and nature of relationships	Mind map in staff room for educator contributions Interview questions for educators Survey to educators to gauge knowledge and confidence levels Questionnaire about current RAP Personal reflection and same questions posed to team and families
Routines and transitions • sense of belonging • small groups of children • meaningful, authentic experiences • processes of moving environments	Mapping room set up Analysis of routine against room practice Observation of specific routine events (e.g., morning tea) and transitions in and out Small group conversation with children	Questionnaire for educators Questionnaire for families

Sally told me that her data analysis showed that all the team:

- had agreed to be involved in further professional reading,
- wanted to extend their own knowledge particularly around practice, and
- were eager to engage in conversations about what they had read.

Then she explained that she had provided them with a chapter from a book and given them some reflective questions to go along with this. Not one person, besides the centre director, had completed the reading. When asked why, there were some embarrassed looks and brief excuses of 'lack of time' offered. There was an agreed commitment to completing the reading before the next staff meeting.

Sally's frustrations were further exacerbated at the next staff meeting with a repetition of what had previously happened. We chatted—about her questionnaire, about the educators in the centre, about what they were reading during the day—to try to understand what was happening. Sally decided to build on her data-gathering by observing practice across a few weeks of the following:

- reading materials available in the centre,
- time/opportunities to engage in reading (beyond that which happened directly with children), and
- preferred materials to read/browse.

The learning Sally took away from this experience was that there had been social desirability bias (Bergen & Labonté, 2019) in the responses she received in the questionnaire. It can happen that a data set does not fully reflect what is actually happening; opportunities to triangulate data through other means are needed to support decision-making for change. So, in this instance, the first attempt at gathering data through newly developed methods had not worked for Sally and she needed to revisit data-gathering methods to address her question.

Meanwhile, having begun with an 'environmental' concern, Joelene's critical reflection also encouraged her to use new data-gathering methods. Whilst she had acknowledged more structural changes to the book area and to the daily routines as a result of her analysis, she also wanted to directly involve the boys to increase their engagement in reading. She developed two new data-gathering tools:

- checklist of books in the area and tally of times they were requested to be read, noting names of children,
- small group discussion with the boys about their areas of interest, followed up with their engagement with books that aligned to the conversation.

Through tailoring the data-gathering processes more directly to understanding the boys' perspectives, Joelene was able to add a further dimension to her response that called for action. She shared that she had learnt much about herself through the process: change with evidence and purpose had resulted in positive outcomes, not only for that group of boys but more broadly in her understanding in the importance of an inquiry process to enact considered decisions.

Trust In the Data ...

A wise colleague once said to me as I was in the early stages of learning about practitioner inquiry, "Trust in the data". Too often teachers make changes in their daily pedagogy and practice in an attempt to resolve a problem or issue that more often than not, is only providing at best, a short-term solution, and at worst, no change at all but an increase to the already existing frustration. Data are critical in the inquiry process. The cyclical layers of data analysis to support understanding of the question and decision for change, with data analysis to investigate the effectiveness of the change, places the data as central to the success of the inquiry process.

Teachers in this year-long inquiry program were asked to share their thoughts on the inquiry process and specifically on the data-gathering process. Teachers showed courage in not holding all the answers, "it's OK not to know", and "I have become more confident in being OK to find out …" and growth in their practice, "we can always strive to do better …" "I finally feel a sense of achievement; I have solved a longstanding problem I thought I needed to live with in our room." Teachers identified that they felt they now had a method for intimately examining an issue or concern, that data and analyses were the key, alongside perseverance to work through possibilities using practitioner inquiry as the vehicle for change.

Key Messages

- Opportunities for discussing data within teams will create a shared understanding and determine current data available in the setting.
- Depending on the question, a need may arise to develop methods to gather data that is more structured and targeted.
- A question may require data triangulation whereby analysis of data gathered through a variety of means may confirm or dispel existing findings.
- Analysing data is key to determining next steps towards answering the identified question.

Thinking Points

- What does the word 'data' mean to me? How is it already part of my everyday work?
- What processes can I use to interpret my data?
- What might I do if my data is telling me something different to what I think might be the problem?

Note

1 Under the Australian National Regulations, the Educational Leader is responsible for leading the development and implementation of the educational program and the assessment and planning cycle (see Guide to the National Quality Framework https://www.acecqa.gov.au/nqf/about/guide).

References

Bergen, N., & Labonté, R. (2019). "Everything is perfect, and we have no problems": Detecting and limiting social desirability bias in qualitative research. *Qualitative Health Research*, 30(5),783–792. https://doi.org/10.1177/1049732319889354.

Cooper, J., & Klepp, S. (2017). The courage of critical reflection: How unlearning is essential to learning. *eEarly Learning: Thinking on early learning*. Australian Centre for Educational Leadership.

Fleet, A., De Gioia, K., & Patterson, C. (2016). *Engaging with educational change: Voices of practitioner inquiry*. Bloomsbury.

Hadley, F., Waniganayake, M., & Shepherd, W. (2015). Contemporary practice in professional learning and development of early childhood educators in Australia: Reflections on what works and why. In J. Waters, J. Payler, & K. Jones (Eds.), *The professional development of early years educators* (pp. 29–44). Routledge.

Menter, I., Elliott, D., Hulme, M., Lewin, J., & Lowden K (2011) *A guide to practitioner research in education*. SAGE.

Miller, M. (2011). Critical reflection. *Reflections Gowrie Australia*, 4. https://eprints.qut.edu.au/79260/1/Critical_Reflection_-_Gowrie_Article.pdf.

Nolan, A., & Molla, T. (2018). Teacher professional learning as a social practice: An Australian case. *International Studies in Sociology of Education*, 27 (4), 352–374. https://doi.org/10.1080/09620214.2017.1321968.

Wenger-Trayner, E., & Wenger-Trayner, B. (2015). Communities of practice: A brief introduction. https://wenger-trayner.com/introduction-to-communities-of-practice/.

4 Practitioner Inquiry as a Tool for Meeting and Moving Beyond Regulatory Requirements for Teachers

Katey De Gioia

This chapter outlines how one organisation used teacher inquiry to support the maintenance of teacher accreditation. The organisation developed and delivered a professional learning teacher inquiry program with approved NESA hours, that was held over the period of 12 months. The chapter shares findings from a survey conducted at the completion of the program to elicit teacher perspectives on their involvement. Findings show how teacher engagement in the program resulted in unanticipated outcomes in their professional growth, beyond the need for approved hours to meet teacher accreditation requirements.

Internationally, professional standards for teachers have been deemed as the benchmark for quality teaching and learning in many contexts. Whilst the process of teacher registration varies across countries, the focus is on showing evidence against approved standards. Australian teacher registration was agreed to by all Education Ministers in 2011. It is underpinned by the National Framework for Teacher Registration which embeds the Australian Professional Standards for Teachers (APST) in the requirements for registration, known in New South Wales as accreditation (Australian Institute for Teaching and School Leadership (AITSL), 2018). It was not until 2015 that teacher accreditation was established for early childhood teachers in New South Wales (NSW), Australia.

The aim of this chapter is not to provide a critique of, or debate for or against teacher accreditation (see for example: Fenech & King, 2020; Call, 2018; Toledo-Figueroa et al., 2017), but rather to highlight how one organisation used teacher inquiry as a method to support the maintenance of teacher accreditation. This chapter will share the findings from survey data gathered to understand teachers' perspectives of their involvement in this professional learning program. Data analysis shows their engagement was not only about meeting the required hours of professional development, but it led to unanticipated outcomes in their own professional growth that extended beyond accreditation requirements. It afforded

DOI: 10.4324/9781003245827-6

opportunity for them to understand themselves, their practice, and the relationship to outcomes for children, whilst at the same time, aligning to the APST and meeting part of their requirements to maintain their proficient teacher accreditation status.

In a recent review of early childhood professional development literature, Hamre et al. (2017) explained that teachers engaged in high quality, intentionally designed professional development can make effective changes to their practice which, in turn, can improve outcomes for children. Furthermore, opportunities for meaningful professional learning may enhance job satisfaction and teacher retention (Jones et al., 2017).

Setting the Scene: Teacher Accreditation in New South Wales

AITSL states that, "Registration [accreditation] … is one of the most important mechanisms to assure the safety, competency, and quality of a profession. Its design is underpinned by a clear intent to set and uphold high standards of professional practice" (2018, p. iii). The APST encompass seven standards describing what teachers should know and be able to do across four career stages. Each standard details focus areas that provide further information related to the three teaching domains: professional knowledge, practice, and engagement (AITSL, 2017a). Requirements to move through the career stages are the responsibility of teacher regulatory authorities in state/territory jurisdictions.

The 2013, New South Wales (NSW) Government paper, "Great Teaching, Inspired Learning – A Blueprint for Action", identified the measures for improving both student outcomes and teacher quality in NSW schools. This paper also included a recommendation that early childhood teachers be considered for inclusion within the scope of the Institute of Teachers Act 2004 (now known as the Teacher Accreditation Act 2004). Amendments were made to the Act in 2014 to enable teachers working in NSW early childhood education and care services to be accredited alongside NSW primary and secondary teachers (New South Wales Education Standards Authority (NESA), 2015).

Transition arrangements for early childhood teachers commenced in July 2016, with all current teachers working in early childhood education and care services transitioning to 'proficient' teacher accreditation on submission and approval of relevant documentation. From 1 October 2016, those teachers who commenced or returned to teaching (after a period of absence of more than five years), were to be provisionally accredited (NESA, 2015).

The overarching requirements for attaining or maintaining accreditation in NSW are outlined below:

Table 4.1 Proficient Teacher Accreditation Requirements

Moving to Proficient Teacher Accreditation	Maintaining Proficient Teacher Accreditation
• Period to achieve proficient accreditation: 3 years teaching full time or 5 years part time • Must complete a minimum of 160 days of teaching prior to submission • Accreditation Supervisor (trained by NESA) to provide advice and feedback, observe teaching, assist with appropriate evidence against Standards and submit report • Annual fee to be paid	• Period of maintenance: 5 years teaching full time, 7 years part time • Professional development (PD) requirement: 100 hours in total. 20 hours of NESA-endorsed PD (in first cycle of accreditation 2016–2021, this has since increased to 50 hours) and 80 hours (decreased to 50 hours as per above) of elective professional development • Demonstrate practice continues to meet all Standards for proficient level • Annual fee to be paid • Hold current Working with Children Check clearance

Note. This table is based on information from NESA (2021).

Professional Development Requirements for Teachers to Maintain their Accreditation[1]

A component of the requirements to maintain teacher accreditation is that teachers must undertake a total of 100 hours of professional development over the term of their maintenance period. A portion of these hours are to be NESA-endorsed. (When the inquiry program was being offered in 2017–2018, teachers were required to complete one fifth of their total hours, i.e., 20 hours, in NESA-endorsed courses.)

According to the NESA *Accreditation of Professional Development Courses Policy* (NESA, 2021), providers who meet the identified criteria can submit courses for accreditation to be NESA endorsed and applications are assessed for suitability. The aim of this process is to ensure that all teachers have access to "quality PD [professional development] … to improve their practice and improve student learning outcomes and meet their ongoing teacher accreditation requirements."

The remaining professional development hours are attributed to 'Elective Professional Development'. These are events that contribute to professional learning/development for individual teachers and may include, for example, courses not accredited, educational leadership, relevant further study, legislative requirements, mentoring, coaching and professional dialogue that supports teaching practices (NESA, 2022). Whilst elective professional development is not a focus of this chapter, it is helpful to understand the greater picture of professional development requirements for early childhood teachers during their maintenance cycle.

The Teacher Inquiry Program

Teachers at all levels of education are aware of and seek out relevant professional learning and development to meet their teacher accreditation maintenance cycle. Participants in this chapter were involved in a large-scale practitioner inquiry program offered to teachers in a non-profit early childhood organisation. At their final meeting which was a coming-together to celebrate and share their learning, several teachers explained that although they had originally committed to the program to gain the hours to meet regulatory requirements for maintaining their teaching status, they had ended up gaining so much more.

The teacher inquiry program comprised of four meetings across 12 months. A cohort of 107 teachers were brought together in 16 clusters across NSW to meet and share their learning. Each meeting ran for two hours and included both content knowledge about the process of teacher inquiry, and time for participants to address their question of inquiry. In this way, participants were involved in a dual process of new learning—understanding the cycle of inquiry as well as working through their chosen question. The remaining time was distributed between the meetings as time allocated to complete the tasks in preparation for the next meeting. These preparatory tasks mirrored the dual focus of the inquiry program by including a series of reflective questions about the processes of teacher inquiry, as well as enabling participants to reflect on their own inquiry question.

The reflective tasks included the following prompts:

- What is my question of inquiry?
- What is the rationale for my choice of question?
- How does the question relate to the *Belonging, Being & Becoming the Early Years Learning Framework for Australia* (EYLF) (Australian Government Department of Education, Employment and Workplace Relations, 2009) and the APST? Teachers were reminded to be discerning in aligning both documents. Rather than creating a checklist of possibilities, teachers were asked to identify those points most meaningfully connected and then articulate their connections. There was opportunity to adjust these as their question developed throughout the process.
- Specific questions dependent on the stage of the process e.g., What data do I aim to collect? Why/How? What does my data tell me?

Teachers were also asked to find an academic article to support their understanding of the question and determine how this supported their changes in practice alongside the evidence they were gathering through the data. Their final meeting involved a celebration where they presented their process of inquiry to their peers and others that were invited to the celebration. As a final component of the inquiry program, teachers were asked to submit a two-page overview of their inquiry, responding to the relevant reflective tasks listed above and identifying outcomes for children as a result in their participation in the program.

The teacher inquiry program was approved through NESA to provide teachers with 17 hours of endorsed professional development on completion of the 12-month program. These hours would count towards their maintenance cycle as a proficient teacher.

Research Details

Centre directors and teachers were provided with information about the program and relationship to maintaining teacher accreditation as well as criteria for the selection of teachers to be involved in the program. These criteria included:

- ability to commit for the 12-month period (not withstanding unexpected events), to four meetings and tasks between meetings,
- currently teaching in a classroom with children, and
- ability to provide backfill to one or more teachers from the service (centre directors were able to send more than one teacher but needed to consider arrangements to replace the teacher/s when they were attending workshops).

Those meeting the above criteria were prioritised, then those not working directly with children but employed in other associated roles could be considered for selection. This possibility was included as other professional development opportunities were presented to those in leadership positions that weren't afforded to teachers working in classroom settings. Teachers in their early career stage, specifically those in their first three years after university graduation and identified as provisional teachers, were encouraged not to participate in this round of inquiry. They were advised that the likelihood of heavy dual professional learning workloads—that of the inquiry program combined with requirements for moving from provisional to proficient teacher accreditation—might be overwhelming for new teachers. Two provisional teachers chose to commence the teacher inquiry program, one stating that she, "want[ed] to be seen as a real teacher and learn from experienced teachers." Eventually she chose to withdraw after the first meeting having identified the workload as an issue. Alternative opportunities were provided for her to connect with experienced teachers. A second provisional teacher, however, was able to complete the cycle in its entirety.

Participant Teaching Experience

Following Macquarie University Human Sciences and Humanities Committee ethics approval and in consultation with the appropriate organisational representative, at the completion of the 12-month teacher inquiry program, a survey was sent to all participants regardless of whether they completed or withdrew

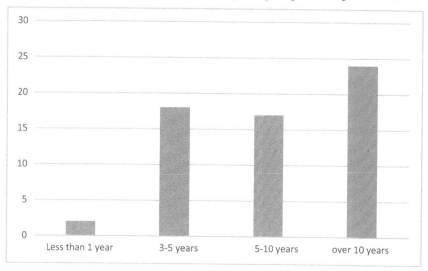

Figure 4.1 Total Years of Teaching (in a degree-qualified position)

throughout the inquiry program. Of the 107 surveys sent, 61 responses were recorded, a response rate of 57%. Figure 4.1 shows that 41% of respondents had been teaching over 5 years.

Survey Results

The survey contained 25 questions, including those relating to demographic data. Questions were a mix of free-form survey questions and Likert scales from 1–5, strongly disagree to strongly agree. Survey questions were developed to garner data in the following areas:

- definition of teacher inquiry,
- purpose for involvement,
- supports and constraints to sharing in own centre with team,
- identified question of inquiry,
- personal learning,
- practice change, and
- improved outcomes for children.

As teachers were able to identify a question that was relevant to their work, the program was not defined by an age group cohort, but rather an invitation for all teachers regardless of the age group they were working with. Although there was representation across all age groups, the majority of teachers who responded to this survey worked with children aged 3–5 years (see Figure 4.2).

Figure 4.2 Age Group Assigned to Teachers

Reasons for Involvement in the Inquiry Program

Teachers were provided with an opportunity to rate the following statements on a Likert scale 1–5, with 1 being strongly disagree and 5 being strongly agree.

I was involved in the teacher inquiry program because:

- I was curious about the process
- My centre director told me I needed to be involved
- I knew I would get NESA endorsed hours
- I thought it would help my career
- I thought it would help me be a better teacher

Of the 61 survey participants, 46 responded to this question. Figure 4.3 shows ratings for each of the statements.

Overall, teachers reported they 'strongly agreed' with all statements, except for the statement "My centre director told me to be involved in the inquiry program". The greatest number of teachers, 29 teachers (64%) assigned a 5 (strongly agree) to the statement, "I thought it would help me to be a better teacher" showing that opportunities to be involved in professional learning to improve practice were quite important to these respondents.

The second highest statement attributed a score of 5, 'strongly agree' related to supporting teaching careers, as rated by 23 respondents. Thirty five of the forty-six respondents 'agreed' or 'strongly agreed' that they chose to participate in the inquiry program as they knew they would receive NESA endorsed hours to support them in maintaining accreditation. Only three disagreed or strongly disagreed that this was their reason for being involved in the inquiry program.

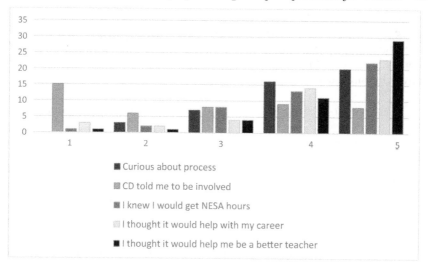

Figure 4.3 Teacher Responses (rated 1–5) to Identified Statements re: Why They Became Involved in the Inquiry Professional Learning

Interestingly, teacher accreditation was quite new in the early childhood sector in NSW at this time, and whilst anecdotally there was acknowledgement that teachers were quite unfamiliar with the process and requirements, this demonstrated that 35 of the 46 respondents had a working knowledge of accreditation and could see value in this program to support the process.

Professional and Personal Learning

Within the survey, teachers were provided with an opportunity to answer three open-ended questions that specifically related to:

- improving outcomes for children,
- what they had learned about their own pedagogical practices, and
- what they had learned about themselves.

At first glance, there may seem to be a blurring between the categories, but the context of their cycle of inquiry, the participants' intentions were clearly aligned within the category the response has been placed. Further, whilst not explicitly worded or representative of the APST, findings show a relationship between the three domains of teaching: professional knowledge, professional practice, and professional engagement (AITSL, 2017b), and the survey questions. Findings are reported below.

Improving Outcomes for Children (Professional Knowledge)

Teachers were asked to identify how their question of inquiry improved learning and development outcomes for children. Thirty-five teachers provided responses to this question; the survey allowed for teachers to provide more than one response. All the teachers were able to provide a response which showed how their question of inquiry supported outcomes for children, both in an improved understanding how they learn, and deeper understanding of content knowledge aligned with processes for learning.

There were 64 responses coded to how children learn. For example:

- More opportunities for active play and strengthened children's relationships with each other.
- By setting achievable goals for the children for their inclusion in the daily routine.
- It has helped me to be more mindful of the children having opportunities to practise skills for themselves. They are capable and confident learners and I need to allow them opportunities to attempt things for themselves.
- It gave me a starting point—look at the children and families as true individuals—then meet their individual needs.

Within this theme, teachers also identified how they had increased their understanding of how to support children to improve their learning outcomes. For example:

- I know more about how important literacy is in the entire environment than I had known before …
- … instead, you can use the interest to create experiences that can be beneficial to child/ren's learning …
- I need to pay more attention to the shift in environment that comes with a new cohort of children and their needs. I can't lay old practices over new dynamics of children and families …

What became evident in the findings for 'improving outcomes for children', was that there was an alignment with the 'professional knowledge' domain of the APST (AITSL, 2017a). Teachers identified the importance of knowing children and families to be able to implement strategies to support learning and development. The findings also highlighted understanding of appropriate content for young children and alignment to their learning goals.

Learning about Own Teaching Practices (Professional Practice)

Teachers were also asked to identify what they learnt about their own teaching practice during the process. Thirty-six teachers provided a response to this question. Their responses were coded to the following two themes: (i) the learning environment and (ii) reflection and critical reflection as a tool to improve practice.

(i)The Learning Environment

Aligned to the EYLF (Australian Government Department of Education, Employment and Workplace Relations, 2009, p. 15), responses to this category were coded to those referring to environments where learning was supported in "vibrant and flexible spaces ... responsive to the interests and abilities of each child. These spaces for different learning capacities and learning styles and invite children and families to contribute ideas, interests and questions."

Eleven responses were coded to *the learning environment*. Teachers acknowledged the importance of all facets of the learning environment; for example, the relationships, physical layout and strategies they employed with children.

Comments included:

- ... visually and verbally present expectations.
- The most amazing learning moments take place within the ordinary commonplace routines.
- My inquiry touched on other areas of concern, that I didn't realise was an issue, like the setup of the learning environment [this was in relation to a teacher's question of inquiry about children's behaviour].
- I involve children's ideas and thoughts a lot more in the process, I have discussions with them that are more meaningful now.

(ii)Reflection and Critical Reflection as a Tool to Improve Practice

This category relates to the importance of reflection and critical reflection as a process to improve practice for individual teachers. There were 25 responses coded to this category. For example,

- That reflection is an important skill that helps improve my practices, the more I reflect, the more I learn.
- I have learnt to be a more flexible teacher.
- That learning is continuous, and teaching needs to be purposeful.
- There is always room for improvement and not to be scared to try something new or different.

The 'learning about own teaching practices' findings align with the 'professional practice' domain (AITSL, 2017a). This domain highlights the learning environment, and teaching strategies used within the environment. It also identifies focus areas that relate to teachers 'evaluating' their own teaching practices to meet the learning needs of children.

Learning about Self (Professional Engagement)

Teachers were asked to identify what they had learnt about themselves during the teacher inquiry program. Responses to this question were coded to the following theme of personal growth, relationship to self and feelings of self-worth.

Eleven of the thirty-six responses were coded to 'personal growth'. Teachers spoke about what they had personally achieved and used words that demonstrated their change and pride in their achievements. For example:

- … when I brought it back to the team to implement, it made me feel a sense of achievement which made me want to continue researching and implementing strategies within the centre.
- I gained confidence when working and leading the team in an area I initially wasn't very confident in.
- To always remember we are unique and learn in different ways.

Through 'learning about self', these findings identify a link with the 'professional engagement' domain within the Australian Professional Standards for Teachers (AITSL, 2017a). Teachers were able to articulate their own learning throughout the inquiry program, show understanding of the importance of modelling and sharing their learning with others, both within their own classroom and with the broader team.

What Drives Participation in Professional Learning?

Ideally, the drivers for participation in professional learning should not be determined by regulatory requirements. Instead, we would like to think that opportunities for professional learning are strengthened through a supportive infrastructure. In this teacher inquiry program, these factors included attendance during usual work hours, backfill-funding available to replace participants, and project support from centre leadership and wider state organisational leadership. Supportive conditions such as these provide opportunities to increase teacher capabilities that are contextually relevant and lead to improved outcomes for children.

As Pelo and Carter (2018) state, "professional learning as pedagogical practice is aimed at nurturing educators to be thinkers, self-aware, reflective and responsive, creative and curious, excited by complexity, comfortable with uncertainty, energized by inquiry" (p. 72). Providing opportunities as professional provocations to re-think established ways of working, enables teachers to identify new ways of thinking and being. Practitioner inquiry (or teacher inquiry as it was framed for this organisation), provided that very opportunity. As noted in previous research by Stremmel (2012) and Fleet et al. (2016), these teachers built on their strengths, being empowered to choose a question of inquiry that was relevant to their needs and professional interests.

As the findings indicated, the opportunity to gain NESA endorsed hours may have been the initial motivational factor for teacher engagement, however, a substantial workload and commitment was required to attain those hours. It was possible for teachers to withdraw throughout: interestingly, 98 of the 107 teachers completed the inquiry and gained endorsed NESA hours. When impactful professional learning provides meaningful, contextually relevant, and professionally connected outcomes for teachers, there is an associated improved self-confidence and job satisfaction (Organisation for Economic Co-operation and Development (OECD), 2020; Jones et al., 2017). This aligns with the purpose of NESA professional development policy (2021).

When they reflected on their experiences, teachers noted what they had gained from the program rather than commenting on the required hours for accreditation. A common note was the focus on learning from each other. Teachers themselves were being providers of professional learning for their peers and within their early learning services (OECD, 2020). There were carefully considered factors to support this from the onset:

- Prior agreed commitment to attend the meetings.
- Group sizes conducive to small group discussion.
- Clearly outlined group expectations which included completing the required work to be able to share back at meetings.
- Expectation that each person would contribute to the group.

Comments shared by teachers included, "I found I was learning beyond my own learning, by simply being in networking meetings with other teachers." And "I was inspired by other teacher's work." Another teacher shared, "Thank you for the opportunity to find a love of researching again. Knowledge is power and confidence!"

Conclusion

Although the aim of the teacher inquiry program was to provide teachers with professional learning relevant to their current contexts, while empowering them to use professional judgement and articulate their decision-making processes, the program's alignment with the NESA guidelines was central in enabling teachers to partially fulfil requirements for teacher accreditation at 'proficient' level. This motivational factor may have contributed to initial teacher engagement in the process, but opportunities for teachers to deeply engage in sustained self-inquiry and collaborative learning moved participants beyond meeting regulatory requirements towards sustained growth in professional thinking and pedagogical practices.

The vehicle for change was the teacher inquiry program, yet it was the regulatory requirements that provided the impetus for many teachers as noted in their survey responses. The component process of AITSL (2018), as part of the regular review process, identified the desire to move from registration/accreditation processes being viewed by teachers as compliance-driven, to a position where teachers recognised these processes as a chance for professional growth and a symbol of professionalism. Successful teacher inquiry programs with high levels of trust, agency and collaboration provide opportunities for professional learning that inspire and document evidence-informed change. In addition, this approach to a continuous journey of professional learning may support teachers in fundamentally reframing their views of accreditation.

Key Messages

- Whilst teachers may feel persuaded to be involved in professional learning to meet regulatory requirements, teacher inquiry in this instance afforded opportunities to engage in a process that was personally and professionally rewarding.
- Professional learning is more effective when there is scope for choice that aligns specifically to teacher needs.
- Opportunities for alignment to regulatory requirements that enable sustained, meaningful engagement in professional learning can improve outcomes for children.

Thinking Points

- What statutory requirements do I need to consider as part of the inquiry process?
- What frameworks can I use to incorporate these requirements into ways of working throughout the inquiry process?
- What opportunities do I have for articulating these relationships?

Note

1 There have been changes to the Professional Development requirements since this inquiry program was offered. To be endorsed as NESA Accredited Professional Development, one of the criteria now states that a "… course must directly address one or more aspects of a priority area that has been identified by the Minister, on advice from the NESA Board" (NESA, 2022). Prior to this change there were no identified areas to be successful for approval.

References

Australian Government Department of Education, Employment and Workplace Relations. (2009). *Belonging, being & becoming: The early years learning framework for Australia.* Commonwealth of Australia.

Australian Institute for Teaching and School Leadership (AITSL). (2017a). Introducing the standards. https://www.aitsl.edu.au/teach/standards/understand-the-teacher-standards/how-the-standards-are-organised.

Australian Institute for Teaching and School Leadership (AITSL). (2017b). Domains of teaching. https://www.aitsl.edu.au/teach/standards/understand-the-teacher-standards/domains-of-teaching.

Australian Institute for Teaching and School Leadership (AITSL). (2018). *One teaching profession: Teacher registration in Australia.* https://www.aitsl.edu.au/docs/default-source/

national-review-of-teacher-registration/report/one-teaching-profession—teacher-regis
tration-in-australia.pdf.

Call, K. (2018). Professional teaching standards: A comparative analysis of their history, implementation and efficacy. *Australian Journal of Teacher Education* 43(3), 93–108.

Fenech, M., & King, S. (2020). Problematising early childhood teacher registration as a mechanism to improve quality early childhood education and care. *Contemporary Issues in Early Childhood*. Advanced online publication. https://doi.org/10.1177/1463949119896023.

Fleet, A., De Gioia, K., & Patterson, C. (2016). *Engaging with educational change: Voices of practitioner inquiry*. Bloomsbury.

Hamre, B.K., Partee, A., & Mulcahy, C. (2017). Enhancing the impact of professional development in the context of preschool expansion. *AERA Open*. https://doi.org/10.1177/2332858417733686.

Jones, C., Hadley, F., & Johnstone, M. (2017). Retaining early childhood teachers: What factors contribute to high job satisfaction in early childhood settings in Australia? *New Zealand International Research in Early Childhood Education*, 20(2), 1–18.

New South Wales Education Standards Authority (NESA). (2015). Accreditation of early childhood teachers policy. https://educationstandards.nsw.edu.au/wps/wcm/connect/8e7c76a4-aa58-403c-b29e-0a69b5bb8fb3/Accreditation+of+Early+Childhood+Teachers+Policy.pdf?MOD=AJPERES&CVID=.

New South Wales Education Standards Authority (NESA). (2021). Accreditation of professional development courses policy. https://educationstandards.nsw.edu.au/wps/portal/nesa/teacher-accreditation/resources/policies-procedures/accreditation-of-professional-development-courses-policy.

New South Wales Education Standards Authority (NESA). (2022). *NSW teacher accreditation manual*. https://educationstandards.nsw.edu.au/wps/portal/nesa/teacher-accreditation/resources/policies-procedures/nsw-teacher-accreditation-manual-2022/maintaining-proficient-teacher-accreditation

New South Wales Government. (2013). Great teaching, inspired learning. Blueprint for action. https://educationstandards.nsw.edu.au/wps/wcm/connect/b3826a4c-7bcf-4ad1-a6c9-d7f24285b5e3/GTIL+A+Blueprint+for+Action.pdf?MOD=AJPERES&CVID=.

Organisation for Economic Co-operation and Development (OECD). (2020). *Policies to support teachers' continuing professional learning: A conceptual framework and mapping of OECD data*. OECD Education Working Paper No. 235. https://www.oecd.org/officialdocuments/publicdisplaydocumentpdf/?cote=EDU/WKP(2020)23&docLanguage=En.

Pelo, A., & Carter, M. (2018). *From teaching to thinking. A pedagogy for reimagining our work*. Exchange Press.

Stremmel, A. (2012). Reshaping the landscape of early childhood teaching through 'teacher research'. In G. Perry, B. Henderson, & D. Meier (Eds.), *Our inquiry, our practice: Undertaking, supporting and learning from early childhood teacher research(ers)* (pp. 107–116). NAEYC.

Toledo-Figueroa, D., Révai, N., & Guerriero, S. (2017). Teacher professionalism and knowledge in qualifications frameworks and professional standards. In S. Guerriero (Ed.), *Pedagogical knowledge and the changing nature of the teaching profession* (pp.73–96). OECD.

Part 1 Commentary

Supporting the Transformative Potential of Practitioner Inquiry in Early Years' Contexts

Nicole Mockler

Reading the four chapters that comprise the opening section of this book, I was reminded of Stephen Kemmis's argument that action research is a practice-changing practice. He writes:

> Action research aims to be, and for better or for worse it always is, a *practice-changing practice*. Better because it sometimes helps make better practices of education, social work, nursing or medicine; worse because it may have consequences that are unsustainable for practitioners of these practices or for the other people involved in them—students or clients or patients, for example.
>
> (Kemmis, 2009, p. 464)

While this book works with the concept of *practitioner inquiry*, an adjacent concept to action research, this question of sustainability, both for individual practitioners and the educational settings and stakeholders they work within and with, is highly germane. At a time when externally imposed accountability regimes—also for better or worse—increasingly eat away at educators' available time and headspace (Santoro, 2018), it does well for us to keep in mind that frameworks for inquiry-based professional learning need to be sustainable and generative for everyone involved. Some time ago now, Marion Dadds wrote eloquently of the power of practitioner inquiry as a force for good:

> Good practitioner research, I believe, helps to develop life for others in caring, equitable, humanising ways, be it in the microcosm of a classroom, university seminar room, hospital ward, [or] social services project.
>
> (Dadds, 1998, p. 41)

Dadds argued in the same article that there was an important role for those who work to 'facilitate' or otherwise support practitioner inquiry in mitigating some of the demands that might otherwise make it less sustainable. The four chapters that form this section of the book essentially contribute to this work in several ways.

DOI: 10.4324/9781003245827-7

First, starting with Chapter 1, the chapters collectively embrace the notion of inquiry as "messy practice" (Stacey, 2019): the idea that practitioner inquiry should not be reduced to a rigid or lockstep process, but rather leave the door open to divergent adventures along the way. While Stenhouse famously defined research as "systematic inquiry made public" (1981, p. 104), 'systematic' in this context does not imply unyielding or unwilling to respond to emerging evidence. Rather, Stenhouse's vision for practitioners as researchers (in his case, teachers) involved careful and collaborative interrogation of evidence at each step along the way, and emerging directions for practitioner researchers according to their findings. The metaphor of 'messy practice' is apt here (noting that 'messy practice' and 'sloppy practice' are not one and the same!): embracing practitioner inquiry as 'messy practice' is to foreground its complexity, to commit to not 'jumping ahead in the story', and to be open to the learning from the messiness.

Second, and related to this notion of messiness, the chapters in this section, and particularly Chapter 2, point to the need for practitioner inquiry to focus on problematising practice rather than problem-solving. In their now-classic work on *inquiry as stance*, Marilyn Cochran-Smith and Susan Lytle forge a powerful argument on the relationship between inquiry and problematisation:

> Working from and with an inquiry stance, then, involves a continual process of making current arrangements problematic; questioning the ways knowledge and practice are constructed, evaluated and used; and assuming that part of the work of practitioners individually and collectively is to participate in educational and social change.
>
> (Cochran-Smith & Lytle, 2009, p. 121)

This focus engages practitioner inquiry as not only a means of professional development for practitioners but also as a part of the process of educational and social change, and as we are reminded in Chapter 2, much of this begins with the posing of good questions at a local level. Foregrounding problematisation over problem-solving in practitioner inquiry does not mean that problems of practice do not get addressed or 'solved' along the way, but rather that practitioner inquiry becomes primarily a forum for addressing complex questions of practice, turning the ordinary and everyday into what David Tripp has called "critical incidents" of practice (Tripp, 1993). In this, practitioner inquirers engage systematically to consider the assumptions embedded in their practice and make decisions about what evidence will support them to develop a better understanding of their practice in context.

Third, practitioner inquiry can be made more sustainable, as we are reminded in Chapter 3, by making good use of the rich sources of existing data and evidence we have available in education settings and working to supplement these judiciously with other data sources. Often this will mean thinking in new and different ways about this evidence, using our well-developed inquiry questions as a lens for this new thinking. When we do this, we essentially try to think about 'old evidence' of practice from different perspectives, before identifying new data sources that might be designed specifically for the inquiry. Working in this way supports sustainability in a number of ways, making it less likely that we will 'reinvent the wheel' and also honouring the time and energy already expended in collection of the existing data.

Finally, to return to issues of accountability regimes that have been established and grown in education, from early childhood to tertiary levels over the past decades, Chapter 4 reminds us that practitioner inquiry can be used as a framework for professional learning that satisfies but also moves beyond these performative accountability requirements. Frameworks for professional learning attached to structures such as professional standards for teachers do not always lean toward the transformative possibilities of practitioner inquiry, however, Chapter 4 provides us with examples of how practitioner inquiry can address both the requirements inherent in these systems while also demonstrating richer, more 'intelligent' (O'Neill, 2013) forms of accountability that build and sustain trust and professional judgement.

There can be no doubt that particularly in these times, the 'opportunity cost' of engaging in practitioner inquiry can be significant. The more time-poor we are in early childhood education and care contexts and schools, the more discerning we need to be about how we spend the discretionary time we have. There can also be no doubt that practitioner inquiry, done well—a 'slow' form of professional learning, perhaps—takes time. This is particularly the case at the beginning, when practitioners learn how to design inquiry, to ask good questions, to sit with and analyse data: as the chapters in this section have shown, these processes are complex and, in many cases, require the development of new skills and practices. The transformative potential of practitioner inquiry, however, on an individual and collective level, has been shown in many different contexts to well outweigh these costs. This potential transformation, extending from practitioners' orientations to their practice, to their relationships with their work and their students, to the educational experiences of the children and young people in their care, is the reason behind the longevity of practitioner inquiry in educational settings. This opening section of the book seeks to support contemporary practitioner researchers to engage with this potential in wise, pragmatic, but ultimately 'open-to-all-possibility' ways, to the benefit of themselves, their students, and our society.

References

Cochran-Smith, M., & Lytle, S. L. (2009). *Inquiry as stance: Practitioner research for the next generation*. Teachers College Press.

Dadds, M. (1998). Supporting practitioner research: A challenge. *Educational Action Research*, 6(1), 39–52.

Kemmis, S. (2009). Action research as a practice-based practice. *Educational Action Research*, 17(3), 463–474.

O'Neill, O. (2013). Intelligent accountability in education. *Oxford Review of Education,* 39(1), 4–16. https://doi.org/10.1080/03054985.2013.764761.

Santoro, D. A. (2018). *Demoralized: Why teachers leave the profession they love and how they can stay.* Harvard Education Press.

Stacey, S. (2019). *Inquiry-based early learning environments: Creating, supporting and collaborating.* Redleaf Press.

Stenhouse, L. (1981). What counts as research? *British Journal of Educational Studies,* 29(2), 103–114.

Tripp, D. (1993). *Critical incidents in teaching: Developing professional judgement.* Routledge.

Part 2
Sharing Stories of Experience

5 Unpacking Complexity in Complex Environments

Alma Fleet

Opening Thoughts

Recounting stories of experience with various forms of practitioner inquiry can enable greater clarity, understanding or possible directions for future thinking (Fleet & Patterson, 2009). Assuming that the goal of entering this space includes improvement in current practice, the processes involved in practitioner inquiry can support professional learning and have the potential to become vehicles of educational change (Fleet et al., 2016).

As was evident in Chapter 1, there are many roads into practitioner inquiry. The current chapter offers two different situations in which practitioner inquiry was chosen for further site or organisational goals for improvements in early childhood practice in Australia. Principles being illustrated here include agency for adult learners as seen through the choice of locally relevant questions of inquiry and forms of data collection, as well as the support of a local leader and an outside facilitator. As reminded by Lachuk et al. (2020, p. 111), "we have approached inquiry as a disposition, habit of mind, or stance" which appears in many guises, two of which are illustrated below.

In the extended first case, a (post)graduate approached the author to assist her in professional development at a church-sponsored early childhood site in New South Wales. In the second completely different situation, the author was approached by a Departmental manager in South Australia after her contribution to a closing panel at a large, state-sponsored seminar celebrating the work of a visiting Scandinavian scholar. In both cases, the local leader/initiator had a key role in introducing and navigating practitioner inquiry through systemic structures. Both situations incorporated teachers and educators with a range of experience from diverse cultural contexts. Also, in both cases, knowledge of and respect for the facilitator seemed to be as important as other recognised components of the inquiry process. These common threads became apparent in writing, reading, and living the stories being told. This approach to analytical reflection owes a debt to Clandinin and Connelly's influential work on narrative inquiry (2004).

DOI: 10.4324/9781003245827-9

Scenario One

Scanning emails for something manageable to deal with, I was pleasantly surprised to see the name of a former graduate student popping up, asking for a coffee chat. Akram was doing an investigation into practitioner inquiry as part of her master's degree study. She asked for assistance in developing her thinking and bringing her team along on the journey. In order to fund a consultancy relationship with me, she invited two other sites to join a three-month project involving evening workshops alongside her staff team, with homework identifying a focus question and relevant data collection strategies in order to implement a short inquiry project to be shared with the group and to help inform their practice.

Akram was keen to rethink their outdoor area and had embarked on a project soliciting ideas from children and staff about possibilities for an outdoor renovation. Some disappointment with responses from her staff team became a provocation for her to rethink ways to engage colleagues in the process and to embed inquiry processes into the employer's mandated staff development reviews. Other questions that emerged from the cross-site group related to concerns about whether 'nursery' routines were including 'meaningful' or authentic opportunities for pedagogical encounters; and also, to educators' concern with enabling inclusion of children expressing challenging behaviours.

Another question that emerged was from a room leader who wanted to pursue a parent's concern that her son was not 'learning' anything at 'kindy' because he was spending 'all' his time playing football. Coincidentally, as a team member, Shirley was listening to children's discussions and looking for opportunities to make a contribution. She joined a group with the football-playing boys and asked for their help. She said she was from 'another' country and didn't know about local football, so could the boys help her understand? Enthusiastically, these four-year-olds launched into animated discussions. Encouraged by Shirley to draw their understandings, they drew football fields, favourite players and explained who was playing/had played/made goals and other critical information (Figure 5.1 and Figure 5.2).

In the process, Shirley could have 'ticked off' achievements in oral language (vocabulary and sentence structure) or mathematical understandings (size and shapes as per drawings of goal posts and so on). Through her inquiry, however, what she was able to do with her co-worker, was assure the parents that the boys were pursuing literacy and numeracy outcomes through engagement with a topic of interest. Realistically, it was also established that the boys did not 'always' spend their time outside playing football! Data gathered became evidence-based practice, informing conversations with family and educators and strengthening the data base for reporting to assessors and the employer—demonstrating progress within an accountability agenda as well as supporting everyday decision-making.

Stepping inside this process as it unfolded, excerpts from an email trail are shared below to shine light onto details that get lost in broader summaries.

Figure 5.1 Crowd Watching Rugby League Match Between West Tigers and Parramatta Eels

Source: Image by Jayden

Figure 5.2 Benjie Marshall from the Tigers Team and Maika Sivo from Parramatta Eels

Source: Image anonymous

First Steps: Relationship Development and Project Conceptualisation

Initial enquiry and coffee: Late 2018

As Acting Director in a NSW preschool managed by a nongovernment organisation, Akram called to reconnect after earlier study in a master's degree where I had been on the teaching team. She was now curious about embedding practitioner inquiry into her workplace. We agreed to keep in touch and went our own ways.

Polite exchanges continued till the end of the year, including holiday greetings:

> I wish you a very merry and happy Christmas and wonderful holidays. Thank you for your time, guidance and feedback over the year. I am so grateful to know you and I hope that I will have the opportunity to work with you in the future.

In July 2019, I heard from Akram again.

> Hope you are well. My sincere apologies for the slow reply; I'd hoped to get back to you sooner. I was appointed as a director at the beginning of this year and transitioning into this new role has been a little overwhelming, but I'm excited.
> I would like to discuss with you about professional development. Can we meet up sometime this week or next?
> Thank you so much!
> Warmest Regards, Akram.

8th July
Goodness, what a nice surprise.

> Congratulations on your new role! It certainly can be daunting, and it's wise to go slowly, prioritising what really matters. Things like smiling! supporting success, building team culture, strengthening relationships—all have to come alongside reviews of policy and routines and so on. I'm sure you know all that! I'm quite heavily booked for the next few months, but we could probably meet in the first week of October. Were you thinking of support for yourself? Or work with your team? We could perhaps spend some time helping people review what they've been seeing/learning about the children and how they would like to extend that learning? I'm not sure what you have in mind.
> thanks for following up.
> all the best, Alma

From: Akram
Sent: Monday, 8 July 3:52pm
Subject: Re: Meeting

Hi Alma,

Thank you so much for your email! I would like to implement collective action research in my centre. I already talked with a couple of other directors, and they are very interested as well. I am thinking of you mentoring the directors in implementing action research with their team.

I am happy to meet you whenever it is convenient for you. Since it is a beginning of the financial year, and each site has a budget for PD [professional development] ... I wanted to talk to you and check if you are happy to mentor us ...

Warmest Regards, Akram

On Monday, 8 July, 5:48pm, Alma replied:

OK- interesting.

Certainly, I would be happy to work with a group of you to deepen your understanding of practitioner inquiry (the approach I use for action research), with the aim of developing the skills to lead your teams in this way of working. You could explore a range of models with other Directors, e.g., perhaps 4 sessions in October (all Long Day programs?)

We could review what people know about this way of working, purposes and processes, then trial a small investigation at each site by each of you so you're familiar with the feeling of researching your own practice! then analysing your data together and brainstorming ways of doing action plans to further your local professional development projects. If anyone wants to organise a teleconference along the way to explore questions, that could be costed in as well. How does that sound? Let me know what you think.

From: Akram
Sent: Monday, 8 July, 6:04pm
Subject: Re: Meeting

Great! The centres included are preschool and long day care. The best location will be in 'Middletown' where our head office is located. We have conference rooms, and I am happy to book one of them. In terms of the time, please allow me to talk to other directors tomorrow and I will get back to you.

Would you please let me know your cost?

Negotiating Details Through Collaborative Planning

From: Akram
Sent: Wednesday, 17 July, 11:22am
Subject: Re: Meeting

Hi Alma,

Hope you are well. I talked to two other directors, and they are so excited to meet with you and benefit from your extensive knowledge. Since they are from long daycare, the best time for them to attend the training would be 6:30 pm.

Would you please let me know what days are convenient for you to run the training?

Warmest Regards, Akram

On Wednesday, 17 July, 4:48pm, Alma replied:

Well, that's lovely.

Depends if any of you have other commitments on particular days of the week, but let's say two sessions 'early' and time to follow up/collect data etc., then two sessions to deal with issues and your findings, and a final session to celebrate achievements and brainstorm action plans for the future. How does that sound?

So perhaps, 6:30–8pm at 'Middletown':
Session 1 – Background
Session 2 – Planning [then small investigations on site]
Session 3 – Sharing progress
Session 4 – Analysis & forward thinking

thanks, Alma

Working with Contextual Factors

From: Akram
Sent: Tuesday, 13 August, 9:57pm
Subject: Re: Meeting

Hi Alma,

Hope you are well. I am so sorry for the late reply. We have received the letter for assessment and rating, and I was busy working on the QIP [Quality Improvement Plan]. I sent it last Friday.

I talked to [the other directors] and they are both happy with 29th Oct, and 4th Nov, but [one] is away during school holidays. Would you please reschedule the first and second session? Also, some educators are keen to attend your training course. I wanted to check with you if they can attend your course as well?

Warmest Regards, Akram

On Wednesday, 14 August, 1:04am, Alma replied:

Hi,

Assessment is certainly a big commitment! Hope it goes well.

Educators are welcome. What dates would your colleagues prefer? Are there any dates that suit you all?

Thanks, Alma

From: Akram
Sent: Thursday, 29 August 1:35pm
Subject: Re: Meeting

Hi Alma,

My sincere apology for the late reply. I submitted QIP to the department, and they called me the following week for a visit. They came on Monday and Tuesday and visited the preschool. I didn't expect it to happen so early. I am glad it is over. The assessor said that she knows you and she worked in the early learning setting where your children used to go...

Warmest Regards, Akram

Being Persistent and Flexible with Pragmatics

From: Akram
Sent: Wednesday, 4 September 8:16pm
Subject: Re: Meeting

Hi Alma,

We are happy with the following days, if you are fine with them:

Session 1 – Oct 29

Session 2 – Nov 4

Session 3 – Nov 25th

Session 4 – Dec 2nd

Is there anything you would like me to do before the training days?

Warmest Regards,

Akram

On Friday, September 6, 1:20am, Alma wrote:

Those dates are fine. Let's chat on the phone later in the month. Best number and times?

It would be helpful if all participants (how many??) would read *What's Pedagogy Anyway?* [Fleet et al. 2011] (It's a free download)—very accessible and a good basis for discussion.

thanks, Alma

From: Akram
Sent: Saturday, 7 September 9:26pm

Subject: Re: Meeting

Hi Alma,
After 2 pm is a better time for me.
There will be 12 participants in total. I will let them know to read *What's Pedagogy Anyway?*
Many thanks and warmest regards
Akram

On Saturday, 7 September, 11:38pm, Alma wrote:

Great- How does Fri 20th sound?
So- what's the make-up of the group? 3 Directors and are the others room leaders? Mostly ECTs or Diplomas? Are they distributed equally across the sites? just curious about peoples' experience.
What do you think people want to learn/think about? We can explore it when we talk, but I like to have a general idea!
all the best, Alma

Creating the Learning Community

On Sunday, 8 September, 7:36am, Akram replied:

Hi Alma,
I am happy with Friday 20th.
I was thinking to do a research project about the impact of practitioner inquiry/action research on educators' pedagogy. I thought to use this amazing opportunity while you kindly accepted to educate and mentor us to collect the data and write my finding. I wanted to ask your opinion?
I've already began to share some information about practitioner inquiry with my team. None of them knew about it, after I explained to them, they demonstrated interest and wanted to learn more about it. This happened with [the other directors] too.
[Our office] has a library, and I requested them to buy some of your books that educators can borrow and read. I just borrowed *Engaging with Educational Change*, and I can't wait to read it.
We are distributed equally between three centres, four people from each site, directors (ECT), educational leaders (ECT) and two interested educators (Diploma).
Thanks and warmest regards, Akram

From: Akram
Sent: Tuesday, 22 October 6:25pm
Subject: Meeting

Hi Alma,

Hope you are well. We are so excited to see you next week. As I spoke to you, I would like to do research to showcase how practitioner inquiry can improve educators' practice. I wanted to get your feedback about it.

I thought to collect some data before attending your training and collect some data after completing a practitioner inquiry. My question for this research will be: 'How can practitioner inquiry improve educators' practice'?

Also using different methods to collect data such as questionnaires and a daily journal.

For a start, I thought to ask educators:

- How much do they know about Practitioner Inquiry?
- What do they expect to achieve by attending the training?
- How can practitioner inquiry support their teaching and children's outcomes? Warmest Regards, Akram

Mon 23/12/2019 9:33pm

I would like to take this opportunity to thank you for the wonderful and stimulating workshop.

My team and I gained a lot, and we all are very excited to implement it next year.

I appreciate everything you have done for me, and I look forward to seeing you soon.

Wishing you all the joy of the season!

Time passed: *The new year arrived along with an international pandemic.*

Sat 11/07/2020 4:52pm

Hi Alma,

Hope this email finds you well, and hope you are safe and healthy during this unprecedented time.

I had to throw some of my plans out the window as a result of COVID-19 however there are some positive sides to it too. I tried to use the time for professional learning while we had fewer children at the preschool. All educators listened to your workshop "What's pedagogy anyway" on YouTube and began to implement practitioner inquiry. They all developed a researchable question based on a niggle they had. Several educators finished their first inquiry, and the rest are still working on it. The educators are developing their confidence to incorporate PI [practitioner inquiry] into their everyday practice and the positive impact of it is evident in their teaching.

I attached Shirley's work. I thought you might be interested to read it.

… thank you for all your guidance and support. Please let me know if you have time to meet up and have a coffee.
Warmest Regards, Akram

Dear Akram,
What an astounding surprise!
Shirley should be congratulated on an exceptional project/report. I'm sure you're all thrilled with this work—it's an absolute tribute to curiosity and persistence with this topic and this child. Well done all! Such a joy to be able to make such a contribution to a child's life and wellbeing.
Good timing for me too. I had been filing some of my papers from last year and was looking at our time together and wondering if there had been any follow-up. So yes! wonderful. Thanks so much for letting me know. At this rate, we should have a coffee sooner rather than later if we're all going to get closed down again!
Thanks for getting in touch—it's really made my day!
Alma

Mentoring from a distance: More time passed before the next coffee catch-up.

On December 1, 2020, 10:19 am, Alma wrote:

Hi,
Thanks so much for yesterday! delightful to be able to catch up.
Thanks also for giving me Anne★ (pseudonym) and Sara's reflections—you must be so proud to see these thoughtful questions and commitment to improving practice. I loved their concern and efforts to engage others in working together for improvements. As we discussed—building a culture of collaboration and joint engagement is at the core of this kind of work.
Do be careful to maintain a balance of suggestions and compliments in feedback! Energy and enthusiasm slow down if people feel they are 'doing it wrong'! Celebrating little successes must be included too! and of course, scheduling time together to share the questions and strategies is SO important—maybe a priority in 2021! Perhaps ask the team for ideas on how to make that happen …
thanks again and keep in touch.
All the best, Alma

Wed 2/12/2020 7:18 PM

Hi Alma,
It was so lovely to see you again and thank you so much for taking the time to read my papers …I take your feedback on board and definitely will work with my team more closely to creating a community of practice. I posed the question about mirroring indoor to outdoor during morning meeting; the educators were sharing their ideas excitedly with others. They provided diverse ideas. Bertie★ thought outdoor should be the

extension of indoor. Carlene and Sara believed that outdoor should be set up based on indoor activities however it needs to be a more natural base. Jemrica and Rashmeen stressed that all indoor activities should be set up outdoors, for example having blocks, craft, and quiet areas both indoor and outdoor. Anne was not sure as some resources cannot be taken outdoors.

I believe, mirroring doesn't mean to set up the same resources or activities outdoors, but the focus should be on developing various children's skills and dispositions by utilising nature and natural resources. For instance, problem-solving can be enhanced through risky play in the outdoor area. I am not sure what is the next step for me. Shall I reinforce my idea or continue with what we used to do (having the same resources and learning areas both indoor and outdoor)?

Thank you so much for your feedback regarding Sara and Anne's paper, and I will apply it to my practice.

Alma Fleet

Wed 2/12/2020 11:13 PM

Hi,

Good effort—generally, I would take a middle ground so that everyone feels their ideas have been listened to—e.g., "Since some want X and some prefer Y, let's try a bit of both and see how that works ... so which indoor activities are best suited to outdoors and which natural spaces can be strengthened?" that's a 'win-win' and all feel they have been listened to! carry on bravely.

Again, the year turned over: Winding down one cycle of inquiry, moving forward.

Tue 23/03/2021 7:30 PM
Attached: PI outdoor environment

Dear Alma,

Hope you are doing well and staying dry in the wet weather. I have been working on my practitioner inquiry since our last meeting. After going back and forth several times, I finalised my question, collected data, and documented some of my findings. I attached my PI to this email. I would appreciate your feedback.

Warmest Regards, Akram

By 21st July, coffee chats had become ZOOM meetings due to COVID lockdown.

In this case, educators had met at the 'lead' site in the evenings to enable 'long day care' staff to attend. Supper was provided by members of the host staff. There was strong attendance and participation at three of the four work-shops, but only the director and Shirley from the host site attended the final session. Illness, study commitments, transport issues, and family circumstances had taken their toll. Believing, however, that each growing educator brings value to children, their families, and the workplace, enabled several key outcomes. The initiating Director has completed her master's degree and moved on to a PhD program. Shirley, a keen support worker, has—during COVID lockdown—conducted an independent study into resources/research to support a child with autism.

Practitioner inquiry is now an established practice in this site, being formally embedded in expectations of staff. The professional journey is rippling outwards. Newer staff are being introduced to the ideas and others have extended their understanding. For example, with her 'study buddies', Jemrica questioned: "What do you believe children's rights are both at Preschool and the Community? How can we ensure children grow up to become active citizens who can advocate for themselves and others?" She began Term 1 with social skills for children while offering families and educators a questionnaire to explore relevant ideas. Following that analysis and further experiences, she collected data from children "on their ideas of their rights and used this information to create a 'Bill of Rights'" (in-house documentation). Shirley is complementing her overseas master's degree with enrolment in an Australian master's degree.

Four years from the original initiation, core staff are continuing to learn, promote inquiry approaches, and further their own investigations. Akram has become a leading voice in a group of Directors interested in her Practitioner Inquiry journey; she is sharing with them the sequence of processes that the author shared with her team a few years earlier. Happily, this network includes one of the original participating sites whose director had to discontinue the earlier project due to staffing and personal issues. The author's informal mentoring continues to be important for Akram, whose role as local leader has been instrumental in project initiation and development, with the newest project involving all staff at her site.

Scenario Two

Rather than being a pre-planned initiative, the second scenario emerged from serendipity, through a series of initially unrelated events. Having shared the stage with colleagues at a large professional gathering, the author was recognised by a Department for Education manager who was seeking a facilitator to lead a Professional Learning project for Family Day Care educators. The first person she asked was unavailable! So, I was approached. The request led to a workshop on pedagogy to assist educators in planning more effectively for young children in their care. Family Day Care had recently come under the umbrella of the assessment and rating scheme applied across the early childhood sector, finding many carers less well prepared than they were now expected to be.

A 'free' evening workshop session was presented in the Adelaide area and filmed for in-house use by educators distant from the city. Organisers were surprised by the popularity of the workshop and several months later, it was repeated for others keen to have the same opportunity. As part of the session, participants were introduced to examples of practitioner inquiry and pedagogical documentation (see Chapter 10). Those who were curious to follow up the ideas were invited to initiate a small practitioner inquiry project of their choice, related to their work as Family Day Care educators. The result was reported in a sector magazine to celebrate the commitment of those who pursued the opportunity out of professional interest (Fleet & Haynes, 2020/21). While related to their employment expectations, the inquiries were structured differently from what they had experienced previously, as educators were asked to identify a 'niggle', or some aspect of their work that was concerning, which was usually the behaviour or relationships of a child in their Family Day Care setting. The participants were encouraged to collect detailed observations of some particular aspect of their concern—with topics related to such things as supporting a child who was new to the service and reluctant to join others in play, or an overly rambunctious child who made it difficult for others to complete creative projects. Many of the educators had not previously seen the benefit of such focused attention to interactions or children's perspectives, as their planning tended to be more 'activity-oriented', rather than evolving around children's thinking or frustrations.

Assistance was given by regional coordinators within the Family Day Care structure, including analysis of observations and possible strategies to assist with the area of concern. Coordinators were also able to offer support with professional English or written expression as many educators had gained their certification with English as an additional language to their home language/s.

There was some confusion surrounding terminology and practices that were assumed knowledge in other parts of the sector. The steps taken were often small. Nevertheless, the excitement and satisfaction were a delight. As one educator concluded: "It made me more particular in my observation of this child and perhaps look at the issue from various dimensions rather than focus on the constant problem and sounding like a worn-out record with my approach" (Fleet & Haynes, 2020/2021, p. 43). When invited to share their thinking at a final gathering, many were shy but willing, when prompted, to offer their ideas to the group. One person who was encouraged to share has subsequently undertaken further study to support her growing knowledge and confidence. In addition to offering practitioner inquiry as a sustainable practice in educators' professional toolkits, this small initiative was a tribute to the valuing of potentials in adults as well as in children.

What Was in the Workshops?

For both scenarios in this chapter, the content sequence was framed by interpersonal relationships: trying to establish connections with unknown participants in a short period of time and enhanced through the environment—trying to create a welcoming ambience that invited participation. Opening explanations established the purpose of time together, an overview of the direction being travelled, and introduction to the purposes and processes of practitioner inquiry. Engagement was fostered through connection with participants' concerns and small group involvement in working through 'new' concepts. Sharing examples of ways of working led to more detailed consideration of components: identifying a useful question from something that is a 'niggle'—a worrying aspect of everyday practice—alongside consideration of ways to collect useful information to inform an investigation. Learning to analyse the data was often troublesome for participants. In-house videos from one presentation found their way into the public sphere and were thus available for revisiting on YouTube. Common difficulties were explored (like asking too big a question!), along with consideration of strategies to overcome them (like breaking the challenging niggle into smaller parts to investigate—see Chapter 2).

Considering What These Stories Tell Us

Although outcomes were often unexpected in these scenarios, growth of participants was always evident. An insightful local leader was key to participant engagement and project sustainability. Issues arising included the role of time and place for professional dialogue to take place, and recognition of the pressures applied by accountability agendas and uncontrollable contextual factors. Practitioner inquiry can also assist in these drastic circumstances: Akram has since pursued an inquiry framed around her educators' perceptions about the effects of the pandemic on their work, asking how she—as Director—could best support her staff in these difficult times. As an educator, Carlene commented that they would not be able to do this work as well without the background in practitioner inquiry.

Forming an extended learning community was intended to add multiple perspectives to the ensuing conversations and provide encouragement to participants to see themselves as part of a larger endeavour. An accessible welcoming venue was an enticement, particularly when travel was funded, and food provided. In a pandemic environment, on-line groups could also be productive.

Practitioner inquiry was not conceived initially as part of a change agenda from 'the employer'. An interest in promoting learning—alongside awareness of the benefits of a more knowledgeable, informed, curious workforce—was in evidence. Nevertheless, positioning within a larger accountability agenda was clearly a motivating factor.

Attempting to ensure mutual understanding of project parameters was crucial. A local leader with relationships to the focus participants was key. Interestingly, in this case, both initiators were actively pursuing further education in educational leadership at two different universities in different states. Meanwhile, although the facilitator was positioned initially as an outside 'expert' offering information, over time the consultancy relationship became collegial.

Another key ingredient which is important in these narratives, is that of time. Meaningful educational change through professional learning is a slow process.

Only small instructional tasks can be taken on board quickly; anything challenging philosophy and personal approaches to pedagogy requires deeper engagement and introspection. In group settings, there also needs to be the opportunity for 'false starts' and unexpected (out of your control!) developments. In these two examples, although practitioner inquiry was supported by multi-site employers, circumstances interfered with full engagement. These can include staff changes, organizational priority shifts, political events, and world pandemics.

'Good' intentions on their own are not enough. A combination of context, personal and professional interest, and affordances interact in often unpredictable ways. Core processes may be strengthened when there is a sense of joint endeavour, of fostering a learning community. It becomes clear that multiple approaches become relevant depending on varying circumstances; 'practitioner inquiry' is not the 'same animal' when appearing in different landscapes.

Key Messages

- Exploring diverse stories of implementation can offer possibilities for reflection and personal connection.
- Supportive infrastructure, including external facilitation, can be key to successful practitioner inquiry project initiations.
- Both short-term and longer initiatives have potential to promote professional growth and educational change, but both benefit from ongoing support.

Thinking Points

- Consider these narratives in the context of the first three chapters. Which elements of practitioner inquiry are becoming clearer to you through these examples?
- Choose one of the steps in one of the scenarios which jumped out at you. Was this due to the 'wow!' factor that caught your attention, the fact that it was unexpected, or that it had personal relevance to you? Make notes about your thinking or discuss with a colleague.

References

Clandinin, D. J., & Connelly, F. M. (2004). *Narrative inquiry: Experience and story in qualitative research.* Jossey-Bass.

Fleet, A., De Gioia, K., & Patterson, C. (2016). *Engaging with educational change: Voices of practitioner inquiry.* Bloomsbury.

Fleet, A., & Haynes, R. (2020/21). 20 women, 80 children. *Pedagogy+9*, 42–44.

Fleet, A., Honig, T., Robertson, J., Semann, A., & Shepherd, W. (2011). *What's pedagogy anyway? Using pedagogical documentation to engage with the Early Years Learning Framework.* Children's Services Central.

Fleet, A., & Patterson, C. (2009). A timescape: Personal narratives—professional spaces in S. Edwards & J. Nuttall (Eds.), *Professional learning in early childhood settings* (pp. 9–25). Sense.

Lachuk, A. J., Gisladottir, K. R., & DeGraff, T. (2020). *Collaboration, narrative, and inquiry that honor the complexity of teacher education.* IAP Inc.

6 Stories From the Classroom

School-Based Change Through an Inquiry-Based Approach

Anthony Semann and Leanne Armao

We are Keysborough Primary School.
We would like to say thank you to the traditional custodians of this land on which we live, learn, work and play.
We pay our respects to elders, past and present, and thank them for caring for their land.
We promise to look after the plants, the animals and the people too.
Hello land, hello sky, hello me, hello friends.

The narratives that form this chapter take place on the land of the Bunurong/Boon Wurrung and Wurundjeri peoples who are the traditional owners of this land in the state of Victoria, Australia. In bringing our narratives to this chapter we choose not to exclude the fact that we are located and work on colonised land and the need to acknowledge the devastating impact colonisation has and continues to have on Aboriginal people across this nation. We view education as a mechanism of healing, knowledge, and truth-telling.

Narratives can be considered a way of representing and (re)representing existing storylines which define the lived realities of individuals and groups. The narrative provides opportunities for others to enter and reinscribe these understandings back into the spaces they occupy. Undoubtedly, narratives are open to interpretations and as such we invite you, the reader, to contextualise, critique and reinscribe your understandings of the micro-narratives we offer you. In so doing, we aim to decommission strongly held ideals related to classroom pedagogies, spaces and relationships, in an attempt to recast utopian ideals related to ethical practices within the classroom. These creative endeavours are our way of reconstituting knowledges that align to what a playful classroom feels and sounds like, and the possibilities which await all classrooms and spaces in which children live and learn. This chapter invites the reader into a story of one school's inquiry-based project which aims to reimagine the role of playful, child-centred classrooms as the teachers learn from and alongside their colleagues from a local kindergarten. It provides opportunities for others who wish to engage in systems-change to explore the journey to date as well as illuminating the power of an inquiry-based approach to reimagine practice.

DOI: 10.4324/9781003245827-10

Geo-Mapping as Context

Keysborough Primary School is located in the South-Eastern suburbs of Melbourne, approximately 27 kms from the city centre. The school was formed in 2010 when two existing schools were merged. Over half the school children were born overseas which adds to the richness of the school population. Keysborough Primary School has approximately 420 students and 57 staff. The school offers education for children from their first year of schooling through the final year of primary school education. The families who access the school have a strong connection with the school and are often heavily invested in ensuring their children succeed at schooling. A disproportionate number of families experience social isolation with both generational and situational poverty experienced by a large portion of the school community. Despite this, the school is a vibrant education site with the primary goal of ensuring every child succeeds, a commitment to reimagining practice and staying abreast of contemporary ideas.

Launching Change – Where it all Started

In 2016, representatives from Keysborough Primary School participated in a three-day professional learning program delivered by Anthony Semann on behalf of the Victorian Department of Education and Training. The professional learning program aimed to support continuity of early learning between prior-to-school early childhood programs and the first years of school. In attending the professional learning program, representatives from Keysborough Primary School invited teachers from a local kindergarten (education for children aged 3–5 years) to join them in the learning opportunity. This coming-together launched both sites into a systematic assessment of current practices linked to continuity of learning. At the same time, a research project was put in place to investigate the ways in which increased collaboration supports young children's success during the transition period. Based on grounded research approaches, the study focused on the contribution of children as central protagonists while enabling professional learning opportunities for teachers. The research built on work by Boyle and Wilkinson (2018) who argued that pedagogical practices informed by ecological, socio-cultural and critical theoretical perspectives are characterised as long-term, iterative, multi-layered participatory processes involving a range of stakeholders.

The increasing dialogue between the stakeholders in this study highlighted the need for significant collaboration across the continuum of the education system. Rather than transition being seen as a one-off event predominantly viewing children as receivers of the transition processes, there was a re-shifting of processes towards enabling children to actively shape classroom pedagogy. In addition, this coming together opened up space for ongoing relationship building, understanding and collaboration between school representatives and prior-to-school educators. Research findings from transition studies highlight "the importance of program continuity and catering for individual learning strengths, resources and needs. Integral to the achievement of seamless transitions is the establishment of trusting relationships between families and teachers in early childhood services and schools" (Ashton et al., 2008). This attempt to disrupt long-held traditions related to transition to school required a form of 'active forgetfulness' (Zeynep, 2019) in which German philosopher Nietzsche calls for an abandonment of the past, in order to forecast and plan for the future. This form of active, persistent, and deliberate forgetfulness suggests that the knowledge of the past provides little benefit for the future. As such, the school held a commitment to relinquish what had been known as 'our approach' to transition to school and classroom practices and forge a new process of knowing and doing differently.

Finding an Inquiry Focus

It is inevitable that there are multiple ways to map a period of change. Finding the most suitable way to launch this change initiative required the school community to answer a simple question which was posed to them: 'What is the problem we are trying to solve here?' Numerous conversations were held to plan and re-plan the way forward to launch into a research inquiry. Gaining commitment and momentum across an entire school community is never an easy task; however, what became apparent was the need for strong leadership to reinforce the key messages related to the change. Building the architecture required for the inquiry highlighted the need for multiple strategies to ensure its effectiveness. As such, a series of whole school professional learning days were facilitated, many of which were attended by educators from prior-to-school settings. In addition, ongoing full-day meetings and professional learning for staff teaching in the first year of school occurred on a regular basis, along with mentoring and support for the school principal and the school's leadership team. It was this multifaceted approach which ensured that the learning and inquiry was tiered and that the key messages would 'stick'.

Overarching questions which formed the basis for the inquiry included:

- What are the important opportunities that await us in relation to continuity of early learning which we haven't tapped into yet?
- What are our big ambitious dreams for our work together across the education sector?

Starting With a Philosophy

Organisational philosophies provide the basis for aspirational statements to guide and reform practice. In light of the changes at hand, the staff at Keysborough Primary School identified the need to revisit the existing school philosophy and update this with an intent to align the philosophy to a new vision for the school and classroom pedagogy. This was deemed a necessary first step as part of the inquiry journey. A facilitated session provided an opportunity for the team to identify what they stood for, what they wished to be known for, and the values which underpinned their practices. After much debate, reflection and brainstorming, the following school philosophy was developed and adopted. It contains three significant statements:

- *Creativity is learning, and learning is creative*
  Our image of children views them as capable individuals who are hard-wired to be curious and creative. As such, the power of creativity is a core element of our DNA and being. This is presented through an innate love of learning and the desire to explore and make sense of the world.

- *Together we unlock the power and potential of learning*
  Teachers and children share a range of values that define the symbiotic relationship within the magical classroom. This includes a commitment to valuing trust, respect, open-mindedness and courage. It is a mindset hard-wired towards discovery and a love of learning. Through such a mindset we unlock the potential for both adult and child, that when faced with a learning challenge, remain persistent and brave.

- *We dare to be different in making a difference*
  We affirm our commitment to breaking away from educational tradi-tions through a process of collaboration, innovation and exploration. Inclusive pedagogical approaches embrace contemporary ideas derived from research and a growing evidence base. We acknowledge diversity and difference as a strength within our practices and view diverse ideas as the genesis for new ideas and creativity. Education is a site of global transformation.

The possibilities for reimagining classroom pedagogy were supported by the endorsement of this school philosophy. It became evident through this process that there was a need to understand how classroom practice could reflect the new philosophy. This challenge was not one the team wanted to shy away from; instead it was seen as an opportunity to explore how classroom practices could be interrogated as part of this new vision for practice.

"We Have so Much to Learn"

Opportunities for regular gatherings between the school and local kindergarten were critical in supporting systems change and ensuring multiple voices and perspectives were heard as part of this inquiry project. The outcomes of these gatherings were two-fold: Firstly, a deliberate vehicle to building and growing sustained relationships amongst the educators and secondly, opportunities to gain further knowledge and share insight into how these two different systems of education operate. Particular areas of interest for discussion and reflection during these gatherings included the philosophical and pragmatic approaches to planning and assessment, the challenges encountered in each of the education systems and the navigation of terminology which inevitably was used to explain the ways in which teaching and learning took place. A chance encounter with ideas related to play-based pedagogy was one such event that required the school staff to pause and reflect further on their current approaches. The interest by the school educators was based on their desire to explore more democratic and child-centred approaches to learning and to investigate the possible intersectionality between prior-to-school and school-based practices.

Consulting With Children

Reflecting the new philosophy and the desire for learning continuity across sites, staff embarked on a roadmap to consult with children in both the local early childhood centre and the school to identify how they would like to learn, and the spaces that they would like to learn in. This research consisted of two data sources: first, one-on-one interviews with children, and second, illustrations by children indicating features of their ideal classroom. Involving children as informants required the research team to ensure the engagement with children (Graham et al., 2015) was shaped by an ethical lens. As such, issues of consent, informed engagement and safety were considered in interviews. The data from the children served

Figure 6.1 My Ideal Classroom
Source: Image by Leonardo

Figure 6.2 My Ideal Classroom
Source: Image by Tamara

as rich and powerful information for teachers to reflect on and interrogate as part of the change initiative. In analysing the data, the distinction between what was currently occurring and what children thought should occur within classroom life became evident. Traditional methods of classroom design and pedagogy seemed misplaced and out-of-sync when juxtaposed against the children's desires. The data indicated a wish for a more playful approach to classroom design, a clearer link towards early childhood practice and more child-led teacher-supported learning (Figure 6.1 and Figure 6.2).

This presented a challenge for teachers as they began to identify the pedagogical gaps between their current skills, knowledges and practices and those identified and desired by children. Consulting with children was viewed as a democratic process, in which children moved from passive recipients of education to designers of classroom practices and evaluators of teacher practice. This meant that the school community was gifted with an opportunity to radically reimagine education. The risk inherent in consulting with children was to not act on these new learnings and insights and as such, consulting with children could be seen as a token gesture.

The data collected from the drawings were collated and presented back to teachers with themes identified and actions listed. The main themes identified included:

- a playful and inquiry-based learning across the school,
- a reimagining of assessment of learning and how pedagogical documentation can assist in capturing the layers of learning within the classroom,

- the inclusion of non-traditional materials for children to engage with, and
- greater alignment in practices between early childhood programs and school-based practices

From Ideas to Opportunities

Professional learning has been and continues to be seen as a critical component of the Keysborough Primary School community. As such, coming together several times a year as a school community, and bimonthly meetings for those who taught in the early years of schooling was a familiar mechanism to promote and support change. Encountering new ideas such as those gifted from the educational project of Reggio Emilia was a focus for the teachers. The aim was twofold, first to increase knowledge and second to map change based on these new learnings. Throughout the two years of this inquiry project, the focus of several full-day professional learning sessions included key concepts such as the image of the child, slow pedagogy, environments for learning, inquiry-based teaching, partnerships with families, and the rights of children.

Translating these ideas into practice was supported by smaller group coaching sessions and opportunities to engage in further readings. Drawing on a range of theoretical and philosophical perspectives was made possible by the leadership across the school. Leadership valued the multiplicity in ideas and the inherent challenges in crossing often clearly defined philosophical borders. Such challenges were seen as an asset and vehicle to revisit the school philosophy. It was essential to create a safe space for debate and dissensus by supporting the discussion of new ideas along with open explorations of the practical implications of these innovative approaches. Often viewed as a challenge in a workplace, debate in this instance was a reminder to pause, revisit and reaffirm new and existing ideas in order not to alienate those who remained on the edge of new possibilities.

Entering the Classroom

Classrooms often hold a history of ideas and practices, and to unshackle classroom pedagogy, one must first name them. Two dimensions in this inquiry project included a focus on the design of the classroom spaces and the design of classroom pedagogy. These two are inherently linked; to begin a journey of transformation with one aspect then required a transformation in the other. The overarching theme of a playful classroom was adopted as this encompassed a new way of working. The first step in this journey was to design classroom spaces which reflected less structured and more playful approaches to learning. Perhaps not a new idea to those who work in early childhood settings, but for many teachers in the school, this was a radical departure from what they knew. The reduction in the number of desks, the introduction of play-based materials and the opening-up of four classrooms into one larger space meant children were afforded with greater opportunities to use play as a means of learning,

Figure 6.3 Doorway to the Magical Classroom

rather than seeing play as a respite from learning. Art materials, blocks and imaginative play resources were introduced as everyday materials which children could encounter as they chose. In addition, a timber panelled wall was constructed across the hallway with a set of double doors built-in to create an old-fashioned wardrobe (Figure 6.3). The interior of the classroom was hidden behind the wall, and the children stepped through the wardrobe into the open learning space which they quickly named their 'magical classroom'. As one child commented: "*The magical classroom is really special to us, because we play and decorate with our minds, thinking what we can make, and all the kids like it.*"

From Magical Classroom to New Ways of Teaching

The newly designed classroom spaces raised the question as to what forms of teaching practices would support children to learn best in the 'magical classroom'. Play-based and inquiry-based teaching were seen as the new frontier for the school. A greater trust in children as well as creating time in the classroom life for children to guide their own learning was central to this approach. This development, however, raised more questions for the teachers including how assessment could be undertaken outside more traditional approaches which had historically been adopted. Many teachers were concerned about their role in using children's ideas to inform classroom content and how this way of

teaching and learning could dovetail with the state-based curriculum requirements for the school. Teachers in the early years of schooling began this journey by allowing larger blocks of time for children to engage with resources in
the magical classroom. These sessions were followed by a regular hosting of
'Parliament', where teachers and children could check in with each other,
identify the learning which had taken place, and explore how such learning
could be extended further. Planning for learning still took place; however, a
more responsive approach was adopted where outcomes were identified, but
less structured approaches defined classroom life.

Regular gatherings with local early childhood programs were coordinated
and took place several times per term. These gatherings aimed to ensure continuity of early learning between early childhood education and care settings
and schools. Evidenced through these gatherings was the need for ongoing
communication across the education systems as well as the need to better
understand the ways in which pedagogy and practice operated across sites.
Previous research in Victoria, by Semann et al. (2015) identified the need for
ongoing and regular communication between early childhood education and
care settings and school settings to strengthen respectful and professional relationships. Such networks can lead to greater levels of understanding regarding
pedagogy and ensure a smoother transition for children. Within this project,
these networking opportunities served as a critical vehicle to inform school-
based staff what their pedagogy might look like in future.

The Birth of a New Site

During this whole-of-school change initiative, the State Department of Education and Training announced the funding and building of a new kindergarten on the site of the school. This was an unexpected occurrence, but one
welcomed by the school and local community as a micro-narrative within the
larger change story. This had been a long-term vision for the school, as it was
seen as a means of ensuring closer ties between the school and early childhood
sites enabling the translation of learning from the inquiry project into daily
practice. During the early stages of planning for the kindergarten, decision-
making was informed by consultations with children, as well as the desire to
enhance the continuity of learning. The architects of the kindergarten were
invited to host children from the school to the site of the to-be-built kindergarten, to share preliminary site and building plans and to seek the children's
feedback on the suitability of the draft plans.

Children's ideas focused primarily on the building design. This included the
selection of appropriate colours for doors and walls which they believed would
increase the joy associated with learning. The children also emphasised the
importance of building a path to link the kindergarten to the school. A local
provider of early childhood programs was granted management of the on-site
kindergarten, and a range of structural and governance-related processes were
identified as critical to ensure a strong and sustained relationship between the

two sites. Regular meetings between the educators across both sites ensured ongoing reflection and dialogue remained a cornerstone of the relationship. Evidence related to the mechanisms and processes that support the continuity of early learning was leveraged to establish a relevant governance structure and a cross-site philosophy.

With the opening of the kindergarten in early 2022 it was deemed opportunistic to launch into another series of inquiry projects across the school and to include the kindergarten within this learning opportunity. Five learning communities were formed, one of which included specialist teachers such as Learning Support, Arts, Computing, and Physical Education as well as educators from kindergarten through to the first year of schooling (Foundation). At the time of writing this chapter, the participants in the inquiry projects were identifying individual or small group focus questions for their three-year-long inquiry projects. It is anticipated that the findings and discoveries resulting from these inquiry projects will continue to strengthen the school's approach to teaching and learning and ensure that inquiry-based pedagogy becomes embedded as the vehicle for learning.

Continuing the Learning

So, what has been the lesson learnt to date? Remembering the inquiry question—*What are the important opportunities that await us in relation to continuity of early learning?*—the micro-narratives shared have all played a powerful role in where the school finds itself today. They combine in a way not too dissimilar to streets on a map, offering the journey travelled thus far and proposing a journey yet to occur. In pausing to look back at where we find ourselves, it is undeniable that a move towards a more deliberate and focused culture of learning (and particularly inquiry-based learning) has been the catalyst for change. This approach confirms that as educators, we see the power in working with a questioning stance and spending time focused on solving some of the queries that exist related to the art of teaching.

Of course, the same 'story' will be experienced and can be told through the eyes of different people. Therefore, to round out this narrative, we invited perspectives from teachers who had been involved in the process. One of the teachers offered the following reflection:

> As a teacher, the Magical Classroom has encouraged me to step out of my comfort zone into a different approach to teaching and learning. It has been a learning journey for me as much as it is for the children. It has allowed me to completely take a step back and to allow the children to take agency of their own learning to be engaged, motivated, curious and creative learners all while supporting them along this journey.

She spoke with colleagues who had engaged in the inquiry and together they identified a number of steps in the process which stood out to them while developing and living in this space. They remembered that:

In 2019, the K-F PLC (Kindergarten/Foundation Professional Learning Circle) had just come together, with the focus on Continuity of Learning. Through this, play-based learning was also a focus; we created a philosophy with Anthony. He supported us in researching and learning about Continuity of Learning, including beautiful spaces, assessments, documentation, purposeful questioning, 'Image of the Child'. Our collective belief was that Continuity of Learning from Kindergarten to school is like 'walking from one room to another'.

We started designing 'the Magical Classroom'. What we thought needed to be one classroom space, turned into the whole Foundation building. The spaces were set up as fluid spaces—with two literacy rooms, a maths room and a 'parliament meeting space'. Children move to each room for the different purpose of their learning.

We invested in beautiful pieces of furniture, focusing on bringing the 'natural world' in and using wooden materials. Teachers began decluttering and letting go of things (which wasn't always easy!)

And then she commented

Early inquiry projects involved in the Magical Classroom were based on the ideas of 'belonging' (how to make the new kindergarten children feel like they belong) and experiencing the storybooks *Two Mates* and *How to Catch a Star*.

Children currently enjoy investigating in the Magical Classroom to spark their thinking and curiosities through play and exploring provocations related to their ideas in Investigation Projects. The Magical Classroom encourages children to explore, investigate, share ideas and curiosities, create, collaborate, and develop leadership skills.

The Transition Coordinator offered the following:

During the pandemic, we weren't discouraged and completed transition sessions online through WebEx. The attendance of Kindergarten (4-year-old) and Foundation (5-year-old) children was of a high standard.

In 2022, we continued the transition plan that we had organised the year before. Each week, a different group from the Kindergarten visit the school for play-based exploration, story and craft and then in the fourth week of the rotation, each Foundation class visits the Kindergarten for story and play. Our children and educator relationships are growing stronger with each visit. The conversations that happen between educators are rich, supportive and immediate. The confidence in the younger children is developing every week.

In terms of using the space, and building on the magical classroom, the Transition Coordinator cited the following benefits of the program:

- strong relationships between educators,
- improved confidence of children,
- information to support transition for each child,
- data-tracking of individual children over the years.

She also noted challenges included the impact of time on the regular Foundation and Kindergarten programs, and absences due to COVID and other sickness which resulted in cancelled sessions.

It is worth noting that whilst numerous changes across the school have been identified and trialled, a no-turning-back approach is still being consolidated. Relationships with the (on-site but separate) kindergarten are still evolving. Nevertheless, to ensure long-term changes continue to exist despite the usual challenges of staff turnover, a commitment to ongoing practitioner inquiry has been cemented into the school's professional learning agenda for the next three years. Undoubtedly a key ingredient to the success of this approach is the identification of 'a question' which is relevant to those undertaking this inquiry. While the whole school has a 'focus question', all individuals (sometimes working in pairs) are pursuing inquiries relating to their own concerns related to their responsibilities (from supporting a particular child, to teaching strategies, to ways to increase student engagement in particular aspects of the curriculum). Furthermore, the naming of challenges along the way and the cultivation of solutions enables the system to learn to adapt and gain leverage from each other's lived experience. The gathering of baseline data continues to be a challenge which enthusiastic participants are tempted to skip. Critical to this next cycle of the learning journey is an expectation for everyone to share and present ongoing findings from their inquiries to their colleagues. Such an approach builds the knowledge-base both within the school and potentially, across the education system.

The Road Ahead

This cyclical journey of learning, experimenting, trialling, and evaluating has served the school community well. Feedback from families and children continues to offer hope that such changes are necessary in a landscape of growing evidence regarding how children learn best. It can be challenging for teachers to keep pace with contemporary pedagogical understandings; nonetheless an inquiry-based approach has offered the school community an opportunity to pause and navigate these challenges collectively. Pausing in this sense is a disruptive task, one where a system consciously decides that change is necessary, and that relinquishing the known to find new ways is worthy of daring. To dare collectively offers a level of comfort in the sense that any disorientation in practice is best experienced with colleagues, and that a sense of solidarity in this journey is necessary if one is to succeed. System change takes time, and this localised project dares to dream. In doing so, we see our work as a localised project which potentially has a rippling effect within a system. The developing of trusting relationships has, of course, been crucial.

Sharing our learning is an invitation for others to dream of the possibilities which can be afforded to them when they commit to change. It is through this localised project that we see the existence of advocacy and activism. An inquiry-orientation has enabled the school to ensure that whole site learning was seen as an enabling strategy for change as well as a vehicle for strengthening the school's approach to data-informed practice. We invite you, the reader who has engaged with these micro-narratives, to bring these together, much like a patchwork quilt and view them as a whole, noting that each narrative, no matter how small they may seem, all have contributed to where we find ourselves today.

Key Messages

- Young children can be active participants in shaping classroom pedagogy and content.
- Collaboration between early childhood centres and primary school sites has the potential to lead to pedagogical transformation.
- Inquiry-based learning is a powerful tool to bring educational systems together.

Thinking Points

- How might continuity of early learning be strengthened across the education sector?
- How can children contribute to pedagogical decision-making?
- In what ways might inquiry-based learning be supported or strengthened to enhance children's learning?

References

Ashton, J., Woodrow, C., Johnston, C., Wangmann, J., Singh, L., & James, T. (2008). Partnerships in learning linking: Early childhood services, families and schools for optimal development. *Australasian Journal of Early Childhood*, 33(2), 10–16. https://doi.org/10.1177/183693910803300203.

Boyle, T., & Wilkinson, J. (2018) Two worlds, one site: Leading practices and transitions to school. *Journal of Educational Administration and History*, 50(4), 325–342. https://doi.org/10.1080/00220620.2018.1510384.

Graham, A., Powell, M., & Taylor, N. (2015). Ethical research involving children: Encouraging reflexive engagement in research with children and young people. *Children and Society*, 29(5), 331–343. https://doi.org/10.1111/chso.12089.

Semann, A., Madden, L., Sukkar, H., Walker, C., Mitchelmore, S., Fleet, A., & De Gioia, K. (2015). *Transition: A positive start to school. Consultation 2015.* Victorian Department of Education and Training. Victoria. https://www.education.vic.gov.au/Documents/about/research/finalsconstransition.pdf.

Zeynep, T. T. (2019). Nietzsche on memory and active forgetting. *The European Legacy*, 24(1), 46–58. https://doi.org/10.1080/10848770.2018.1538091.

7 'Forming' Ourselves as Teacher~Researchers

Chris Celada and Margo Hobba

We respectfully acknowledge that this project was designed and published on the traditional lands of the Kurnai and the Wadawurrung people. We pay our respects to the Elders and educators past, present and emerging.

Opening Context

It was hot! Very hot!

Few people sat in the usually busy Piazza Prampolini in Reggio Emilia. Even the pigeons seemed to have disappeared. An air-conditioned corner café became the 'office' for a group of Australian and New Zealand delegates of the third International Summer School. Discussions about professional learning were robust among group members. *We offer so much professional learning, but we are not seeing any real difference.* Over aperitifs and peanuts, we wondered how it might be possible to disrupt the traditional constructs around professional learning to enable deep thinking, particularly deep thinking that generates new theory to support new practice.

Beginnings…

Can I have a copy of the PowerPoint? Questions such as this, heard during our many years of offering professional learning for teachers, troubled us. Where was the curiosity and wonder? Was it the teachers? Was it us? Why did we feel so uncomfortable?

We began to research. Challenged, inspired, and mystified by the Reggio Emilia educational project, we asked ourselves: What is knowledge? What does it mean 'to know'? How do we construct and organise knowledge? In particular, we wondered how direct experience of the interconnectivity between mind, body and the material world might change our understandings.

By 2016, when we were invited to participate in a joint research project on the value of professional learning experiences for teachers with Reggio Emilia Aotearoa New Zealand (REANZ), we had assembled many interpretations, meanings and praxes associated with a relational epistemology and its

DOI: 10.4324/9781003245827-11

implication for professional learning for teachers. This project presented a valuable research context to investigate our research question: *How do adults change the shape of their knowing and become more sensitive to their own knowledge-building processes so they can become more sensitive to those of children?*

Underpinnings

How often do we consider the theories, presuppositions, cultural, historical, and societal forces that create our systems of education? When we ask teachers how they understand 'knowledge' for instance, they are often surprised by the question and are hazy in their response. Yet it seems logical to suggest that our presuppositions about the nature of knowledge and our processes of coming~to~know[1] form the foundation for the choices that we make about how we teach.

Writing in 1988, Malaguzzi, co-founder of the Reggio Emilia educational project observed

> we are going from a normative epistemology intended to disentangle the complexity of phenomena and arrive at laws and simplified certain orders, to an ecological epistemology [...] which requires us [...] to think without ever fencing concepts in, to break the closed circles, re-establish connections between what is (or seems) disjointed.
>
> (Cagliari et al., 2016, p. 320)

Influenced by Edgar Morin, (the French philosopher and sociologist), Malaguzzi described epistemology as "a fluid structure of relations with which the organism communicates, multiplying the intensity, variety and procedures of its adaptive solutions, and the constructive nature of its interactions" (Cagliari et al., 2016, p. 322). This has been described as a "pedagogy of relations" (Rinaldi, 2006, p. 172).

Encountering these theories during our many years of engagement with Reggio Emilia was initially confronting and disruptive for us, a couple of educators whose schooling was strongly embedded in a 'normative epistemology'. But the work of teachers and children in Reggio Emilia suggests that these theories are full of possibility. In particular, participation in ateliers in Reggio Emilia opened our eyes to the complex beauty and richness of things~objects~materials.

Trying to make sense of the Reggio Emilia educational project through reading, attending study programs and engaging in deep discussions, we realised that theoretical, conceptual research was not enough to shift our understanding. While we might value the ideas, their very nature was complex and situational, and their nuances and intricacies could only be understood through engaging in sensory experiences with an attitude of uncertainty and curiosity. So, we started to experiment with things~objects~materials as protagonists, seeking to create relations between theory and practice, mind and body.

We think it may be helpful for those reading this chapter to briefly describe some of the theories and presuppositions that we brought with us to the REANZ project.

Ways~of~Knowing

Our experience of knowing is a continual process of making meaning: a process of re-visiting, re-viewing, re-testing. Malaguzzi described knowledge as a "tangle of spaghetti" (Dahlberg & Moss, 2006, p. 7). Deleuze and Guattari imagined it as a rhizome, something that "shoots in all directions, with no beginning and no end, but always in between", (Rinaldi, 2006, p. 8). Vecchi states that we need to take a conscious position on "which knowledge" we want to promote (2010, p. xvii). The process of constructing knowledge "derives from actions, from actions upon actions, and, ultimately, from internal mental operations which are actions that have been internalised" (Gardner, 2011, p. 12).

It is essential to recognise the interconnected nature of human knowledge. When we reflect on our own processes of coming~to~know, and observe these processes in others, we notice many aspects in play: the role of emotion, empathy, imagination, memory, the sensory body, rationality, pleasure and so forth.

In Reggio Emilia, aesthetics is also seen as an activator for coming~to~know. Bateson (2002) defines aesthetics as "responsive to the pattern which connects" (p. 8). This sits comfortably within the framework of an ecological epistemology describing a universe that is a system of patterns—a metapattern. Aesthetics is often expressed in terms of empathy, beauty, harmony, unity, sensitivity and sensibility—qualities that are present when one perceives that the world is interconnected. From this point of view, uncertainty, knots and disagreement are a launching place where new knowledge can be generated and constructed.

Malaguzzi identified a strong relation between pleasure and learning and described pleasure as a "form of energy" (Cagliari et al., 2016, p. 309). He explained that,

> The pleasure of learning, of knowing, and of understanding is one of the most important and basic feelings that every child expects from the experience [...] a crucial feeling which must be reinforced so that pleasure survives even when the reality may prove that learning, knowing, and understanding involves difficulty and effort.
>
> (Malaguzzi, 1996, p. 34)

We would argue that pleasure is just as important in adult learning.

Materiality

We have become very interested in the agency of matter and the way our experience of the world is altered when we recognise the vitality of matter and its influence on us. Rather than viewing the world as a collection of separate, passive, inert objects on which humans act, Vecchi advocates for a process of empathy which relates "the Self to things and things to each other" (2010, p. 5).

Subjectivity and Intersubjectivity

Studies of the human brain reveal the unique subjectivity of each human being. Subjectivity is "a construction, both self-constructed and socially constructed within a context and a culture" (Rinaldi, 2006, p. 138). Many of the choices made in the schools in Reggio Emilia "allow the subjectivity of each child and each teacher to emerge in his or her relationships with others" (Rinaldi, 2006, p. 139).

The Sensory Body

The role of the body and the senses are fundamental in the processes of the construction of knowledge. Neurological research indicates that senses interact in the "construction and processing of knowledge and individual and group memory" (Ceppi, 1998, p. 16). Neuroscientist Andy Clark (2016) suggests that the brain does more than passively receive and interpret sensory information. Rather, incoming sensory information is met by a stream of unconscious predictions from the brain; 'guesses' about what the senses have discovered. This information is excluded from our awareness on the presumption that it is already 'understood'. This may explain why we adults tend to observe and recognise mainly what we already know compared to the child's hundred ways~of~knowing and discovering the world (Malaguzzi, 1996).

For adults the role of noticing, becoming conscious of what the senses are offering, is crucial to 'see' again what is in front of us. Bruner described this as "violating the expected" (Bruner, Personal communication, 2012). He refers to the Russian literary notion of *ostranenyi*, meaning to "alienate things that seem familiar so that we will inspect them anew and reflect upon what we are doing" (2002, p. 16).

These underpinnings have led us to 'trouble' the presuppositions about professional learning for teachers within a normative epistemology. Maccaferri (a pedagogista in Reggio Emilia) likens the act of teachers' research with professional learning describing research in this context as the act of 'forming ourselves'. "The important thing is to put ourselves in the shoes of the child; to try something out—in our own skin; it must be a lived experience" (2015). In this way, we become more sensitive to our own knowledge-building processes, so we can also become more sensitive to the knowledge-building processes of children and others.

Our intention for the project with REANZ was to design a context where we could together construct a shared, lived professional learning experience situated within the framework of an ecological epistemology. The project would be conducted over five months, consisting of just three face-to-face workshops in New Zealand and ongoing online interactions. Documentation and interpretation of teachers' research would support deeper, richer, more complex processes of coming~to~know.

How to Begin?

We decided to start by coming~to~know *'found materials'*. This decision was based on our conviction that professional learning grounded in a relational/ecological epistemology must connect the mind, heart, hands and body with the material world and our experience that things~objects~materials can be strong disrupters of our conceptual understandings. How could we expand the research time to include occasions when we were not physically together? What kind of shared experiences could we offer teacher~researchers whom we did not yet know?

We decided to 'extend' the encounter by offering a proposal prior to our first meeting together. We asked teacher~researchers to choose different man-made and natural-found things~objects~materials from their local environment and bring them to the meeting inside a paper bag (Figure 7.1).

When I Close my Eyes

We know that complex poly-sensory processes combine with individual and group memories, concepts, language and so forth to create deeper relations and knowings. In our own experimentation we noticed the dominance of our visual sense in encountering the world. We also observed this in the adults.

Figure 7.1 Examples from the Local Environment

We asked teacher~researchers to choose a thing~object~material from their bag; something that would be interesting for hands to experience, and to place it in the hands of a partner who has closed their eyes. We noticed paper bags rustling. Faces peered into them. What to choose? There were slight pauses. Some things~objects~materials were dropped back into the bags; others chosen. Then one was removed from the bag and carefully placed in the cupped hands of another teacher~researcher (Figure 7.2).

We noticed a sense of trusting anticipation as eyes were closed and hands extended.

> "I thought it was going to be something heavy and my hands were waiting for the weight to be dropped into them and then it was so light."
>
> (Teacher~researcher)[2]

We noticed that it seemed very hard not to look. Faces grimacing, heads leaning towards materials as if trying to 'look' through closed eyes.

> "I noticed her eyes moving under her eyelids like she was really looking!"
> "It is really hard to keep my eyes shut."

We noticed fingers exploring delicately, fingertips prodding, poking, rubbing over surfaces. Different fingers feeling different parts of the materials, hands working together, palms becoming supports for exploration.

> "We used all parts of our hands."

Figure 7.2 An Item is Placed in Waiting Hands

"I was amazed at how much my hands noticed when time was taken to explore."

We noticed that each finger has a repertoire of movements that modifies the way the hand encounters things~objects~materials (Figure 7.3).

We noticed arms were used to gauge dimensions (Figure 7.4).

We noticed that hands, fingers, things~objects~materials and emotions are interconnected.

"Mentally I had identified the object as a pinecone because I named them as being pinecone scales. But the little bits didn't fit into my idea of a pinecone. When I opened my eyes, there were no scales – they were ridges and I had made them into scales in mind" (Figure 7.5).

We noticed closed eyes gaze towards the ceiling as if seeking an answer to the question 'what is it'?

"The brain wanted to know an answer. It wanted to have a conclusion."

"I'm pretty sure it's a ..."

"I wanted to know what it was so badly!"

Figure 7.3 Fingertips Explore Things~Object~Materials

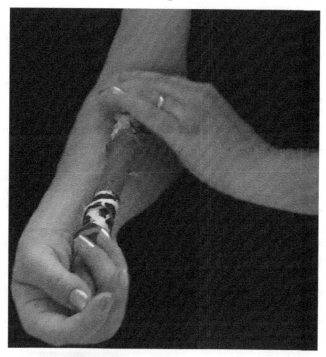

Figure 7.4 An Unexpected Use of Arms

Figure 7.5 Cedar Pinecone

"What is it?"

"Ahh! I can squeeze it, but it might fall apart. I want to work out what it is. It has a flat bottom. There is a bit of wire that is flexible. And this shape reminds me of ears, maybe a face? And a tail curling around here. But what is this? This is completely different to what I expected. I was expecting ..." (shaking head).

We noticed that persistence produced pleasure and surprise—a meeting of familiar materials as if for the first time.

"This is what it feels like inside the tube. I see this tube at work all the time, and I've never felt inside it. I assumed I know it. I thought it was 'just bamboo'. But I kept going. Now I'm glad I did" (Figure 7.6).

We noticed comments about the mental images of *things* created through the information gathered by their hands.

"In my mind it [a heart-shaped stone] was red because hearts are red, but when I imagined it as a stone, it was black" (Figure 7.7).

Figure 7.6 Fingers Explore a Tube

Figure 7.7 Hands Cradle the Stone

How to Proceed?

Malaguzzi sought an epistemology that would privilege relationships and connections. When we bring different things together, we realise that there are
connections and similarities between things that initially appear to be very different. The teacher~researchers' response to things~objects~materials had been
complex. Many were surprised by the strong emotional and imaginative reactions
experienced.

How could we create contexts where teacher~researchers, who are apparently
very familiar with the things~objects~materials brought to the workshop, see
them anew?

Things Change When They Come Together...

We noticed things~objects~materials 'escaping' from paper bags, some very
surprising: a red onion; a miniature cat holding a sign on a little spring. Small.
Large. Colourful. Monochrome. So many different shapes. Who would have
thought such a variety of things~objects~materials would have resulted from
such a simple proposal? As one teacher~researcher noted: "The more you do
this the more connections you find."

Working to explore connections, slowly and without a specific goal, the factors connecting things~objects~materials became gradually less strident and more flexible.

"They [the collection] ask to be held" (Figure 7.8).

"There is a connection between having an idea and using the material to express it and then the materials make you think differently."

Noticing an element in one thing helps teacher~researchers to see it in another—and to see how it is also different from the other. Words are never big enough to describe the actual thing and the relations between things~objects~materials.

We noticed teacher~researchers discovering unexpected connections as they explored relationships among the things~objects~materials.

"We didn't much think about the cork because it was just a cork. There was a pipe cleaner on the table. Then the cork seemed to say: 'wrap me'. And we discovered the stability of the cork. But the pipe cleaner didn't stay in place, so we noticed the slippery-ness of the cork and we also noticed that the pipe cleaner wasn't sticky" (Figure 7.9).

Investigating Shapes and Shadows

The teacher~researchers sat around the overhead projector surrounded by various objects on the floor. One by one, objects were placed on the screen

Figure 7.8 A Collection Inside a Paua Shell

Figure 7.9 Cork Wrapped in a Pipe Cleaner

with long pauses between actions. There was no conversation, everyone looked back and forth between the overhead projector and the image on wall (Figure 7.10).

The teacher~researchers noticed a figure emerging from the shadows on the screen. They began to tentatively contribute ideas.

"Her laptop. It's a girl. She's plugged in. She is a plugged-in girl."
"It's a girl with a blue laptop. But she's upside down."

Using gestures, silences, glances, and a few words, teacher~researchers carefully manipulated the things~objects~materials on the overhead screen (Figure 7.11). They were fully engaged as the "girl with the blue laptop" emerged from the collaboration of themselves, the light and shadows, and things~objects~materials

"How can she be the other way up? Everything is opposite."
"It takes so much time to think this way."

We noticed the importance of collaborative play and the way things~objects~materials changed the course of teacher~researchers' thinking in surprising and unexpected ways.

Figure 7.10 Shadows Provide New Ways to See Connections

Figure 7.11 The Figure Emerges from the Shadows

How to Proceed?

Teacher~researchers returned to their homes across New Zealand. Could the experience of researching, of growing sensitivity to knowledge-building processes within an ecological epistemology continue? What proposal might support this process?

Our experiences in Reggio Emilia ateliers prompted us to conduct our own research with things~materials~objects in our own environment, including trees. Often part of lives for years, perhaps seen but not noticed or 'known', trees offered a possibility as rich, complex subjects for research. We asked the teacher~researchers to make friends with a tree and introduce it to the group during our next face to face meeting in a few months' time.

"To Know the Tree Needs Patience"

Teacher~researchers returned to the next meeting keen to introduce 'their tree' to the group.

We noticed that sometimes the chosen tree was 'a stranger', other times 'known'—or was it?

> "The tree I see every day ... But, in 10 years, I have never come to know it closely." Diti
>
> "I planted this tree. I thought I knew it and could share much about it! I came in close contact with the trunk. My first surprise!" Katherine
>
> "An oak tree ... I never liked it. I hated it! The pondering tree. I started to notice the life forms within it ..." Leonelle (Figure 7.12)

The depth and power of emotional connections and memories was stunning: a powerful demonstration of the interconnectedness of 'ways~of~knowing'. Realising that paying attention in this way is a choice, has been a powerful experience. Having experienced this possibility with the found things~objects~materials, teachers were able to 'notice' a tree in a new way (Figure 7.13).

> "I could **smell** the earthy tones of the tree mingled with the fresh smell of the leaves as the wind blew the scent of the tree my way. When **touching** the tree with my eyes closed, I started feeling the base of the trunk and worked my way up ..." Michelle A.
>
> "She **smells** of the earth and I noticed that she has different smells depending on the weather." Katrina

We noticed teacher~researchers deliberately move past the powerful influence of vision to find the 'unexpected'... The '*I came across*' moments offered a place for curiosity, imagination, emotional connection, surprise, and wonder.

Figure 7.12 Leonelle's Tree
Source: Image by Leonelle

Figure 7.13 Kerrie's Tree
Source: Image by Kerrie

"There's a tree, it's in my garden ... My husband wanted to chop it down, "it's ugly", he said. My boys are inspired; they love to climb it, watch it; they are inspired by what it provides for us ... apples, play, wildlife, birds ... They even made a birdhouse to sit triumphantly in the middle of it ... a home for their feathered friends ... a place for them ... Can I find beauty in the ugly part of the tree?" Cindy★ pseudonym

"Slowly this tree has died. I have become inspired by imperfection, and I see beauty in this." Sue (Figure 7.14)

"I thought of the word 'heart-wood'; this made me think of the heart of this tree and the life within, and my own heart and the life within my own skin/bark." Diti

"I have been looking at the orange tree in my back yard. I see it every day from my kitchen window, but I only acknowledge it to take note of any ripe oranges on its branches. Looking at it closely, I am taken aback initially at its absolute ugliness." Angela

We noticed unexpected big questions: the apparent conflict between beauty and ugliness. What does it mean to be alive? What is the difference between 'living' and 'being alive'? What does it mean to be useful? Is it enough to be useful?

Figure 7.14 Sue's Tree
Source: Image by Sue

"I'm aware of your entangled arms, legs and limbs shooting out in all directions. I notice the graceful bend in your branches." Sheree

"When you get close up to the group [of trees], you can see how they grow very close together." Michelle B.

"I used a knob to leverage myself up into the tree, to experience the feeling of **being in the tree,** feel a different perspective from height and to look up under the leaves and around the branches." Delia★

"Over the last few weeks my ears have become more in tune with its music; its rustlings and the other sounds it brings—like bird song (Tui) and whispering winds." Helen

We noticed that teacher~researchers were using the knowledge-building strategies they had discovered in working with their things~objects~materials in building relations with their trees. They described many ways of noticing, and the interconnectedness of mind and body. They began to examine their trees more carefully to identify connections and relationships (Figure 7.15).

"A whorl pattern in the bark **reminded** me of fingerprints. The whorl has ridges that drew my eyes to follow the pattern around, and later traced it around with my finger, feeling the roughness." Delia★

Figure 7.15 Leonelle's Tree
Source: Image by Leonelle

"Battle scars
Fresh wounds bleed
In war between worlds
senseless shame …" Bridgette (Figure 7.16)

"The textures of the bark remind me of elephant skin." Michelle B.
    "When I looked more closely at the bottle brush tree, I saw ants going about their work, marching in succession." Michelle C.

We were becoming more sensitive to the relations between wholes and parts in their research. In knowing the part, do I not come~to~know more of the whole and vice versa? One part makes me notice another: they are in relations with each other.

"You see my Banyan tree is of an age, similar to mine, and her stories will be rich and full of wonder and delight, pain and grief, happiness and joy, because she, unlike me, is bare to the world, an offering with no limits." Prue
    "She looks cold and old today—cold, damp and dark. Her wrinkles and stretch marks are much more prominent today—maybe the way the light

Figure 7.16 Bridgette's Tree
Source: Image by Bridgette

Figure 7.17 Angela's Tree
Source: Image by Angela

catches her trunk. Her branches are pushing up through our backyard looking for the sun, while her hair hangs drooping, unkempt, dishevelled." Maria

"Strange, distorted face shapes and puckered lips loom out at me from her trunk. Her bole curves in to a nipped in waist and then spreads out again into bustley hips. The lichen attached to her arms almost looks like popcorn or the ruffled lace of Miss Havisham's musty wedding gown." Angela (Figure 7.17)

We noticed that trees had now become subjects with identities: "*my tree*" rather than "the tree", "*you*" rather than "it".... The trees and the teacher~researchers were becoming a relationship.

How to Proceed?

Discussion with the group explored the role of aesthetics as a thread in learning processes, aesthetics as being "responsive to the patterns that connect" (Bateson, 2002, p 8). 'Patterns', more complex and subtle were becoming more and more obvious as teacher~researchers became attuned to the 'languages' of the things~objects~materials.

We prepared postcards from a selection of the tree images and invited teacher~researchers to choose one. With the postcards for inspiration, teacher~researchers created designboards using words, drawings and fabric to express patterns and qualities of 'tree-ness' (Figures 7.18 and 7.19).

Figure 7.18 Preparing Materials for a Designboard

Figure 7.19 Beginning to Illustrate 'Tree-ness'

We noticed drawing no longer generated such anxiety. Teacher~researchers calmly and intently focused on the postcards and re-interpreted what they saw.

> "I created the textures I know in the tree. I was drawn by the 'tangliness' of the branches and by the female figure in the tree. Her bust is very sensual." Leonelle (Figure 7.20)

> "It became about texture. Then it became stormy. It's about movement and looking closely." Tracey (Figure 7.21)

> [I saw] "a woman cradling a basket coming out of the dark, covered in light." Katherine (Figure 7.22)

We noticed that strong relations with *this tree* generated sensitivities to the subtle nature of *these trees* and to the relations between them and the wider domain: light and shade; moods; shapes and forms; beauty; pattern; sound and emotion. These sensitivities in turn, generated complex expressions and attention to detail.

Figure 7.20 Leonelle's Exploration of Textures

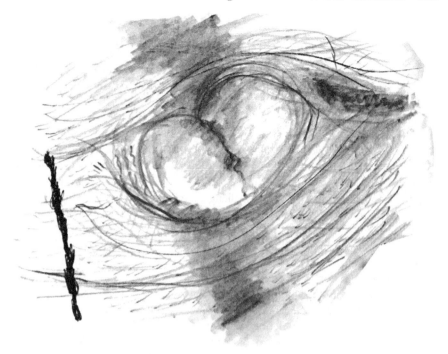

Figure 7.21 Tracey's Consideration of Movement

Figure 7.22 Katherine's Interpretation of an Emerging Shape

Considerations

Thinking About Something Carefully

It has been some years since we last met with teacher~researchers in New Zealand. Even now, re-acquainting ourselves with the project documentation filled us with emotion.

Malaguzzi reminds us that heads and hearts and hands have been separated by the school and the culture (Cagliari et al., 2016, p. 259). For both REANZ and us, the contradictions between these values and a normative epistemology have raised serious questions. How might it be possible to create a context where educators can *experience* the 'head, heart, hand' pedagogy of relations as a way to change practice? This disconnect became a challenge, a gateway to possibilities. We made a deliberate choice to place relations at the heart of this project: a choice grounded on/in our growing awareness of the interconnected nature of our world and the multiple and interrelated ways in which we respond to, interpret and create it. We designed experiences which attempted to hold the material and non-material, mind and body, theory and practice, imagination, emotion and rationality together: to create a context where subtlety and nuance are noticed and valued, and where different subjectivities and points of view are welcomed.

We were unsure about offering something as seemingly every day as 'found materials' to our teacher~researchers and wondered whether they could generate the interest necessary to sustain engagement and to give pleasure in the research. On reflection, several choices were significant. Firstly, asking teacher~researchers to choose things~objects~materials from their local environment to share, meant that these relations were already forming. The quantity and diversity of things~objects~materials invited enthusiastic participation and offered stories that helped to connect teacher~researchers who didn't know each other.

This project reinforced for us our own sense that listening, noticing and giving attention are relation building strategies. We chose the strategy of noticing as our 'way-finder': noticing as an act that seeks to give attention to both the exterior and interior worlds without expectation. We tried to create contexts for noticing allowing time, encouraging playfulness and appreciation of the elusive qualities of things~objects~materials that we often take for granted. We noticed how things~objects~materials and people are different in different relations. Working individually and in small and large groups, teacher~researchers' own coming~to~know was influenced by the noticings of those around them. Sharing noticings became a gift of an individual to the group. We observed shared pleasures when one teacher~researcher discovered different relations through listening to another. The meaning of socially constructed learning became part of the lived experience.

There are many challenges of working within a 'pedagogy of relations'. When working with large groups of adults it is impossible to notice and document the different relations being formed, especially at the beginning of the project when we were working with teacher~researchers we didn't know, and who didn't know each other or us. Group size became an important factor:

too small—and there may not be enough complexity; too big—and it becomes very difficult for relations to be formed. In the end we realised that we were only able to collect clues and traces.

The completion of each project phase presented the challenge of designing a new proposal which sought to muddle and complexify the teacher~researchers' experiences and put them in a different context. We needed to hold the project together, keep it coherent and 'safe' for the teacher~researchers and connected to our intentions. Working this way, we discovered rhythms within the project: movements backwards and forwards, between wholes and parts, subjects, and things~objects~materials, expressive languages, individuals, small groups and the whole group. Whilst each project has its own rhythm, its own song, we started to recognise the various rhythms and melody of this unique project.

We close with a great sense of gratitude to our colleagues in Reggio Emilia for welcoming us, sharing their experiences, and encouraging us to find our own questions and experience; to the New Zealand teacher~researchers who stepped into their and our unknown seeking new insights, questions and possibilities; and to REANZ for encouraging the questioning of assumptions about professional learning and backing a possibility.

Key Messages

- Traditional educational practices are predominantly grounded on an epistemology that seeks to normalise, rationalise, and standardise knowledge.
- Educational practices based on a relational/ecological epistemology recognise the complexity and interconnected nature of the world and understand knowledge as being 'in relation with' rather than 'about'.
- Rather than:

    a   ... a format that is primarily based on words, the process is experiential where body and mind and the material world are in relation.

    b   ... knowledge being something that can be 'transmitted', it is understood as making meaning and constructing understanding in collaboration with others in a place of uncertainty.

    c   ... a format that is 'time poor', research over time is fundamental in supporting the co-construction of knowledge and the 'forming' of teacher~researchers.

    d   Rather than a format that is pre-planned, decisions about 'how to proceed' come from interpretation/re-visiting of documentation making knowledge-building processes visible and prioritising 'groupness' in learning.

Thinking Points

- How could we create experiences that enable us to become sensitive to our own knowledge-building processes?

- What is the role of pleasure in learning for both children and adults?
- We invite you to research with materials.

  a   Perhaps find something on your desk, in your house, in your kitchen … that you are drawn to. Close your eyes and hold it in your hands. What do your hands notice? What images come to your mind? What memories, emotions, thoughts?

  b   Find a 'friend for it'. What do you notice?

Notes

1   In our experience, there is a strong relation between the words we use and our process of conceptualisation. The noun 'knowledge' implies a completeness and finality that misrepresents the meaning we wish to convey. We have created the word coming~to~know and use it in our work instead of the word 'knowledge'. We have also used this strategy to make relations between other words more visible, e.g., teacher~researchers and things~objects~materials.
2   These discussions and images were documented during general conversation. We are not able to attribute them to individual teacher~researchers.

References

Bateson, G. (2002). *Mind and nature: A necessary unity*. Hampton Press.

Bruner, J. (2002). 'Ostranenyi' (or: Living Dangerously). *ReChild*, 4, 16.

Bruner, J. (2012). Personal communication. Second International Summer School. Reggio Emilia.

Cagliari, P., Castignetti, M., Giudici, C., Rinaldi, C., Vecchi, V., & Moss, P. (Eds.). (2016). *Loris Malaguzzi and the Schools of Reggio Emilia. A selection of his writings and speeches, 1945–1993*. Routledge.

Ceppi, G. Z. (1998). *Children, spaces, relations. Metaproject for an environment for young children*. Domus Academy Research Centre.

Clark, A. (2016). *Surfing uncertainty: Prediction, action and the embodied mind*. Oxford University Press.

Dahlberg, G., &. Moss, P. (2006). Introduction. In C. Rinaldi (Ed.), *In Dialogue with Reggio Emilia Listening, researching and learning* (pp. 1–22). Routledge.

Gardner, H. (2011). The wonder of learning and the construction of knowledge. In I. Cavallini, T. Filippini, V. Vecchi, & L. Trancossi (Eds.). *The wonder of learning. The Hundred Languages of Children* (pp. 12–13). [Exhibition Catalogue]. Reggio Emilia: Reggio Children.

Maccaferri, E. (2015). Resonances: Listening, productions and compositions between dance and music. *Third International Summer School*. Reggio Emilia.

Malaguzzi, M. (1996). Commentary: The hundred languages of children. In T. Filippini, & V. Vecchi (Eds.), *The Hundred Languages of Children. Narrative of the possible* (pp. 28–31). [Exhibition Catalogue]. Reggio Emilia: Reggio Children.

Rinaldi, C. (2006). *In dialogue with Reggio Emilia. Listening, researching and learning*. Routledge.

Vecchi, V. (2010). *Art and creativity in Reggio Emilia. Exploring the role and potential of ateliers in early childhood education*. Routledge.

8   What Matters

Participant Voices in a Year of Sustained
Professional Learning

Diti Hill-Denee (with and Helen Aitken)

This chapter describes how a group of early learning teachers participated in a sequence of professional learning experiences designed to motivate them to examine their learning in greater depth. Building on the experiences described in Chapter 7, this chapter presents a perspective from the New Zealand researchers participating in the joint research project. While it can be read as a stand-alone account of professional learning, it is closely linked to the previous chapter. These accounts complement each other and provide opportunities for the reader to hear perspectives from two different countries.

Background

In 2017, 40 participants (early childhood and early years primary teachers from Auckland, New Zealand) shared in an intensive professional learning experience organised by the Reggio Emilia Aotearoa New Zealand Trust (REANZ). The professional learning included three full days of workshops led by professional facilitators spread across four months, along with online engagement with facilitators between these sessions. Facilitated by Margo Hobba and Chris Celada from Australia, the professional learning was named *A Pedagogy of Relations: Seeing Things Differently*. Chris and Margo explained that a pedagogy of relations is an understanding that

> knowledge is an interconnected pattern of relations that shifts and grows in response to the material and non-material world (the world of imagination and discourse) and that learning is an increasing and changing sensitivity and awareness of these relations.
>
> (Personal Workshop Notes)

Importantly, this professional learning was to be an opportunity for adults to experience knowing as relations and coming-to-know processes that, only then, could be shared with children. It was about researching adult learning as a vital aspect of facilitating children's learning and gave rise to four key ideas as explained by Margo and Chris: (i) the Reggio idea of teacher as researcher, (ii) the idea of sustained learning, (iii) the idea of experiencing materials in a

DOI: 10.4324/9781003245827-12

structured context, and (iv) the integrated ideas of knowledge, epistemology and understanding (see Chapter 7 for more details of the project).

The REANZ trustees agreed that this 'unique' experience should be researched by me (Diti) and my colleague (Helen) in an investigation entitled '*A Pedagogy of Relations: Seeing Things Differently' Professional Learning Project: Researching the Learning Processes of Participants.* Helen and I focused our data gathering on the key idea of 'teachers as researchers'. This concept was the first of four key ideas underpinning the learning. The second idea shared by Margo and Chris was that of 'sustained learning', learning over time, with a focus on both face to face and online interactions between those 'teaching' and those 'learning'. The very terms of 'teacher' and 'learner', in the context of this professional learning, were challenged early on by Chris and Margo with a quote from Carla Rinaldi:

> There are a hundred ways of expressing the concept of teachers as researchers; it is a part of the architecture of thinking of the educational project of Reggio Emilia. Working as teachers as researchers can't be taught, it is only possible to feel it, it must be experienced, it is a real part of life.
>
> (Rinaldi, 2015)

The third idea that was key to the professional learning, was that of 'experiential learning': the idea that knowing and learning can only be understood if they are experienced by forming and re-forming relations with materials over an extended period, thus providing a grounded context for discussion and reflection.

The fourth idea was gaining an understanding of 'epistemology' and 'knowledge'. Margo and Chris explained that when Elena Giacopini visited Adelaide in 2009 for the REAIE conference, they realised that (in their own words) they "had no idea about research from a Reggio perspective". Chris and Margo were taken by Elena's claim that knowledge can never be assumed. Elena shared questions that she said guided the work of teachers as researchers in Reggio Emilia:

- What is epistemology? What is knowledge?
- How do children acquire knowledge?
- How do children process and organize knowledge?
- How do children carry out research?
- How do teachers construct their knowledge together with children?

Questions were asked: How is personal knowledge created? What is the interface between epistemology (knowledge-creation) and aesthetics (the senses)? How do ideas about personal knowledge affect the teaching-learning process in early childhood and beyond?

Research Structure

From the start, we saw the research about the professional learning and the learning itself as inextricably intertwined. The research was seen as a process for the participants; a process of constructing, testing and reconstructing theories and creating new knowledge in a context of thinking about everyday practice, thus promoting the complex and subjective relationship between theory and practice.

The open-ended research questions which informed the study were:

- What were key learning moments for the participants in this professional learning?
- Which aspects of Reggio Emilia pedagogy and principles did the participants re-visit/come to learn about and how is their learning being considered in practice?
- What were the key issues and stories of change to thinking and practice?
- What stories, reflections and/or examples of knowledge-building have emerged for the teachers in relation to their everyday work and relationships with others?

Twenty of the 40 teacher participants registered their interest in continuing research into their own learning processes. Eventually six teachers withdrew from the research, leaving 14 teachers participating in the research study. As participant-researchers, Helen and I were interested in the teachers' stories, explanations and meanings ascribed to learning (rather than causation or testing). This focus suits the methodological traditions of qualitative research (Cohen et al., 2000; Mutch, 2013). The research framework chosen for this qualitative study is interpretive and draws on the pedagogy of Reggio Emilia (often known as the Reggio Approach) as a means of understanding and analysing the participants' learning experiences. According to Mutch (2013), "qualitative research places the researchers in the world, trying to uncover the lived reality or constructed meanings of the research participants" (p. 43).

A brief outline of the intended research was shared at the beginning of the first professional learning session. Helen and I initially joined the group as observer-researchers to observe proceedings and gather data on the key idea of teachers as researchers. After recognising the depth of the teachers' involvement and discussions during the first day, we came to question and reconsider our position in light of the proposed research paradigm and our own claims regarding learning and the intrinsic relationship between theory and practice. We wondered how we could seek to understand teachers' experiences if we did not also directly experience the materials and the pedagogy of relations? Rather than being passive 'observer-researchers' we negotiated a changed role to become 'participant-researchers'. This change further complicated and deepened our ideas of assumed boundaries between teacher and learner, researcher and researched. Along with Wendy and Prue (the REANZ trustees), we four joined the teachers in the professional learning experience. In this sense we became a connected community of researchers.

In keeping with a qualitative, interpretivist approach (Silverman, 2022), multiple methods of data collection were employed to make meaning of the participants' individual and collective learning experiences. We asked participants in the research (including ourselves as participant-researchers) whether they/we would like to take part in a focus group/group interview discussion or a semi-structured individual interview. Helen and I followed the facilitators' presentations, read the facilitators' Field Guide and series of background notes, and shared in the discussions and activities. The hard-copy journals, shared artefacts, and the creative outputs of the professional learning, including photographs and videos, were viewed and discussed and provided rich points for reflection and comparison with the other participants.

The two group interviews discussions and the discussions between the two participant-researchers and the two participating trustees were a combination of a focus group and an interview, drawing on literature from both methods (Anastas, 1999; Creswell, 2003; Krueger & Casey, 2000; Mutch, 2013; Sarantakos, 2013). This approach encouraged conversation, dialogue and an exchange of ideas between and amongst the participants themselves as well as responding to our loosely structured questions. The individual interviews used the same open-ended questions as for the group interviews, while allowing for emergent dialogue and ideas to develop (Mutch, 2013).

What we Found and the Literature that Gives it Meaning

When we collated the data, we found that the participant responses to the research questions fell into five broad themes:

- professional learning as sustained learning, where *time* and *flow* are critical issues
- reflection on own learning and *coming to know*
- the place of aesthetics, creativity, environment and experiential learning
- the process of building knowledge and making learning visible
- relations, relationships and making connections.

Each of these is explained below.

Professional Learning as Sustained Learning

The structure of the professional learning as sustained learning, where time and flow are critical issues was seen as very important by participants. The series of three days over four months and online engagement with the facilitators between sessions, was seen to promote deep reflection, nurture relationships, encourage the 'slow cooking' of ideas and experiences, and offer time to listen. Participants offered the following reflections:

Slowing down was made possible by the sustained professional development; the conversations during and between sessions really worked for me.

(Michelle)

By having the time, we got involved with each other, we emailed people,
we talked to people … it takes time to build a relationship, it takes time to
get to know people.

(Jenny)

Even if it's just a little bit of thinking here and there, it's always in your
mind, so you get a deeper understanding over time. Having time to think
challenges you to think further, to view things differently, and you're
more likely to put it into your daily practice.

(Kerri)

I found the continuity really important—it was like a spiral thinking
process.

(Katrina)

The teachers were encouraged to construct new ways of understanding and
working, by taking time to think individually in continuous relation with
others, leading to a permanent state of research (Rinaldi, 2006). Throughout
the professional learning, Margo and Chris reiterated the importance of participant commitment to the process, a process which would be complex and
require the teachers to *come to know* as children do, but without being children
and without seeing children's understanding as the sole focus of their work to
the exclusion of their own understanding. It would be an intensive experience
in expanding participant/adult sensitivities to the knowledge-building processes
of children.

The REANZ trustees and participant-researchers also mentioned the aspect
of time as well as the value of having to document the research and inquiry
process:

Having time to write and think and do and come back and share was
important.

(Wendy)

Margo and Chris gave us personal feedback after the first day, and that
really got the juices flowing; I was thinking 'wow'!

(Prue)

You needed time to go back over what you had done. I can't imagine
what it would have been like with just the one day.

(Diti)

Korthagen (2017) challenges traditional didactic, instructional, often 'one-off' approaches to professional development and learning, and claims that these approaches fail in a number of ways: first, teachers are asked to 'jump' from theory to practice and from practice to theory in a way that avoids taking the person and the personal qualities of the teacher into account; second, the process of reflection is frequently presented as a series of linear steps that, if followed, are thought to result in a more reflective and thoughtful teacher which Korthagen suggests is not necessarily so (Korthagen, 2017, p. 395). The participants' views align with Korthagen's claim that effective professional development is foremost values-based, starting from what practitioners themselves value in their own work. It is also more open-ended and, to a certain degree, more unpredictable than traditional approaches as it often requires deep cultural change (Korthagen, 2017, p. 399). His shift to a values-based, 'inside-out' stance on professional development and learning can be likened to the approach that Rinaldi (2006) suggests when she writes "professional development, like education itself, should not be seen as static or unchangeable, to be achieved, but rather as a process, an ongoing journey throughout our lives" (p. 137).

Reflection and the Idea of 'Coming to Know'

The participants valued reflection on their own learning and the idea of 'coming to know'. In various ways they articulated how their own unique perspectives, backgrounds and reflective approaches influenced their teaching and their roles as *knowers* of selves and young children.

> You bring your own history and experience to the learning; children are like that too! As Margo and Chris said, learning is highly subjective.
>
> (Angela)

> I feel that what I did on the course was a lot of learning about myself … just looking at things from a different perspective.
>
> (Jenny)

> I was learning about me … when I learn things, I get inspired … when I'm inspired, I've got more energy.
>
> (Kerri)

The group conversation between the two REANZ trustees and the two participant-researchers made similar reference to reflective changes in ourselves:

> I found myself saying things that children might say like 'Holes kind of like the company of other holes.' I thought to myself that's a strange thing, I wouldn't usually say that, but I was in a different space of thinking about

what we were doing. I do have a new noticing, a new awareness of trees that is quite changed.

(Helen)

I agree. I see any tree more vividly and personally now.

(Diti)

What began as coming to know something, such as shadow-ness or a tree, became a process of coming to know one's-self. It was the internalisation of a relationship with the material world that altered and deepened the learning about self as teacher. Lenz Taguchi (2010) explains that "when we think in terms of the material being as agentic as humans" (p. 29), our thinking shifts to the "intertwined nature of the relationship between discourses, things, matter and organisms" (p. 29).

The educational thinker and theorist, John Dewey, identified three fundamental attributes of reflective individuals: open-mindedness, responsibility, and wholeheartedness (Dewey, 1933). Despite a wealth of literature on reflection and reflective practice since then, those who continue to think and write about what it means to be reflective usually return to variants of these three attributes. A reflective teacher "is able to critically examine their own practice, experiences, values and beliefs to gain insights that support, inform and enrich decision-making" (Rouse, 2015, p. 27). The importance of reflection is best understood "when structured into the teaching day; this means engaging with others in thoughtful, disciplined and sustained reflection ... the complexity of real teaching can then be grasped" (Ayers, 2010, p. 24).

Reflection lies at the interface between theory and practice, with continuous change to one's practice at its heart. This view of reflection fits well with the pedagogical thinking of the Reggio Approach. In one of his last interviews, Malaguzzi talked with Carlo Barsotti about the image of the child as gifted, as amazing, with extraordinary potential: "This is a gifted child, for whom we need a gifted teacher." "But", he continued, "the gifted teacher is not to be found. The gifted teacher is shaped only by working together with children and other adults, by building together, making mistakes together, correcting, revisiting and reflecting on work that has been done" (Barsotti, 2004, p. 13). Here, Malaguzzi is reiterating the relentless and ongoing nature of the reflective process for teachers who work daily with children.

Aesthetics, Creativity, Environment and Experiential Learning

All participants referred to the experiential learning offered by Margo and Chris from the first day, and the way in which they came to understand that aesthetics, creativity, and environment are an essential part of professional learning and, therefore, of working with children. During the 2012 Study Tour to Ligonchio, near Reggio Emilia, Claudia Giudici spoke to participants before an experiential walk into the nearby hills (Giudici, 2012). A video captured Giudici's presentation as she drew on Gregory Bateson and Vea Vecchi to emphasise the tight connection between epistemology and aesthetics. Giudici explained that the original Greek word aesthetic can be interpreted as opening up the senses, while anaesthetic has the opposite meaning as in closing down the senses. Such an interdisciplinary understanding of aesthetics moves it away from a narrow arts' focus into the arena of connected feelings, senses, emotions and the Reggio idea of the hundred languages (Vecchi, 2010).

Participants noted how much they learnt about themselves through the months of professional learning:

> I didn't quite realise to what degree I need to be connected. Whether that's an emotional connection to someone else, or to an object or to a place, I didn't realise how much of that connection I need.
>
> (Kerri)

> It took a little while to get used to it, the experiential coming to know. I wouldn't say I was uncomfortable, but it was definitely something that I hadn't practised for a while.
>
> (Lisa, pseudonym)

> I had to be far more active than I had anticipated, but I was open to that. My pedagogy has been very rational to date. This experience has helped me to broaden out my pedagogical practice.
>
> (Carlyn)

Here the participants are grappling with ideas that Margo and Chris had asked them to consider over the four months. Given time, however, they developed an awareness of self in relation to the world that is echoed in Popova's (2018) link between aesthetics and epistemology when she quotes Jane Hirshfield, an American poet exploring the nature of concentration in poetry: "In the wholeheartedness of concentration, world and self begin to cohere. With that state comes an enlarging of what may be known, what may be felt, what may be done" (para. 6).

The sustained nature of the professional learning supported the participants in moving slowly into a way of being that evokes Hirshfield's image of self and world coming together; a coming together that is so well described by Ann Pelo (2013) when she writes about the sensuality of eating a peach:

> My peach knowledge is held in my body. If you've not bitten into a round, ripe peach, not taken in its scent, its flavour, its fuzz-edged, slick-smooth flesh into your body, then words describing a peach don't mean much. Peach is body-knowledge, sense-knowledge.
>
> (p. 117)

Pelo tells the story of 20-month-old Dylan's encounters with the outdoors, saying that "she lived unabashedly in her body, all senses on call" (p. 119). Pelo's observations of Dylan's aesthetic and sensory relationship with nature helped Ann herself relax more fully into her own body.

Building Knowledge and Making Learning Visible

The art and science of building knowledge is known as epistemology. For the teachers in Reggio Emilia, professional learning is an everyday occurrence with a recognition of the inextricable links between epistemology (knowing) and ontology (being) (Lenz Taguchi, 2010) and between epistemology and aesthetics/art/ sensibility (Vecchi, 2010; Giudici, 2012). The process of building knowledge and making learning visible is something done in relation with others, "based on values that are chosen, shared and constructed together ... it means living and living ourselves in a permanent state of research" (Rinaldi, 2006, p. 137).

In the first professional learning session, Margo and Chris described their discovery of just how little they knew about knowledge and coming to know. It was this realisation that set them to discover more about knowledge as an interconnected pattern of relations, a pattern that shifts and grows in response to the material and non-material world. Learning and building knowledge are linked to an increasing sensitivity to and awareness of these relations. Over an extended period, participants were offered opportunities to form and re-form relations with material(s), and each other, providing an experiential context for gaining a deep understanding of the process of knowledge-building and understanding how this process relates to teaching, learning and making learning visible for both children and adults.

> You come to know in your own way, your own subjectivity.
>
> (Angela)

> This is what drives us—sharing our ideas and communicating with other learners; otherwise, it is just sharing with yourself!
>
> (Katrina)

> Their (Margo & Chris) presentation style allowed an embodiment of learning ... an embodied coming to know.
>
> (Bridgette)

> I surprised myself about some of the things I was able to do. The professional development pushed me to push myself ... I look at life differently now. I have opened a window!
>
> (Kelly)

> It's definitely changed my way of thinking for primary, I guess I've had an epiphany really.
>
> (Sue)

Margo and Chris referred frequently to Vecchi (2010) who stated that knowledge needed to be defined in "deeper ways" (p. 17). The participants' comments and reflections resonated with Vecchi's explanation of how rationality, imagination, emotion, and aesthetics are all part of human knowledge. "Rationality without feeling and empathy, like imagination without cognition and rationality, builds up partial, incomplete human knowledge" (p. 6). Vecchi (2010) warns that our western ways of thinking, based on narrowly defined disciplines, work against seeing knowledge-building as trans-disciplinary, leading to a desire for connections and dialogue with other areas of knowledge.

During the group discussion between the two REANZ trustees and the two participant-researchers, Diti also referred to knowing and re-knowing:

> It has made me realise how much, from day to day, we rely on the knowledge we have, and not see the potential for new knowledge. I knew that my tree was a pohutukawa tree, but it became much more than that. And that's a skill that children have—to constantly re-know. It reminds me of the poem "Little Gidding" by T.S. Eliot (1943): 'We shall not cease from exploration and the end of all our exploring will be to arrive where we started and know the place for the first time'.

All research participants felt connected to their personal journals and the Field Guide that Margo and Chris had prepared for their professional learning. Participants reported that they continually re-visited their own notes, ponderings and entries. Rinaldi (2006) describes one of the purposes and intentions of documentation as "producing traces and documents that testify to and make visible the ways of learning", as well as to ensure that learners "have the possibility to observe themselves from an external point of view while they are learning" (p. 68).

> I really liked writing in my personal journal, and I still enjoy having a look through. It's like a scrap book with words and pictures. If I'd just taken notes, I wasn't likely to go back and read them again.
>
> (Lisa, pseudonym)

> The journal is something that's ours, that we could document things in, and in my reflection and review now I come up with new ideas, new thoughts…
>
> (Jenny)

> It's very different from working on a computer. I hope this doesn't stop! I hope the journey continues…
>
> (Tracey)

> I really enjoyed the journal process, almost like appraisal, documenting my evidence/journey. The articles—I revisit them almost daily.
>
> (Kelly)

Learning and coming to know were not always associated with feelings of pleasure or satisfaction. In fact, critical learning moments and reflection occurred as a result of feeling uncomfortable and disrupted. Michelle commented: "Writing down ways in which others disrupt me is good for me!"

In Reggio Emilia there is an emphasis on documentation "as an integral part of the procedures aimed at fostering learning and for modifying the learning–teaching relationship" (Rinaldi 2006, p. 63). The deliberate way in which Chris and Margo facilitated and encouraged participants to look at their own learning increased the depth and consideration of aesthetics: an awareness of being open to the senses. Consequently, this resulted in journal documentation that was aesthetic, personal and real. Vecchi (2010), taking the word 'aesthetics' into the context of research, says: "Aesthetics is not uniquely connected with art but becomes a way of researching, a key for interpretation, a place of experience" (p. 11).

Relations, Relationships and Making Connections

A focus on the nature of relations, relationships and making connections is threaded throughout the literature on the philosophy and pedagogy of Reggio Emilia. In an interview centred on the history, ideas and basic principles of the Reggio Emilia experience, Lella Gandini asked Loris Malaguzzi what kind of organisation was envisaged in realising his innovative educational ideas (Gandini, 2012). Malaguzzi replied: "We think of a school for young children as an integral living organism, as a place of shared lives and relationships among many adults and very many children" (p. 41). In the same interview, Malaguzzi stated that the children, the teachers and the parents—all three—are important, and full attention must be given to "intensifying relationships among the three central protagonists" (p. 43).

Margo and Chris explained that this same relational thinking provided the foundation for ideas behind the professional learning. The influence of this focus on relationships and connections was evident in the following participants' reflections:

> The connections made with people in this group are very different from any other professional development that I've ever done! We came to realize all these things about ourselves and each other from the items that were chosen. They were symbolizing parts of us. It was intimate—that's a good word for it.
>
> (Lisa, pseudonym)

> I learnt more how to be in tune with people, places, things, environments … And when you looked at how everyone was together, I think we learnt a lot about relationships.
>
> (Jenny)

Everything was about relationships with people and materials; it was a pedagogy of relations, every aspect of it.

(Michelle)

This notion of inter-related (entangled) notions of connection, relationship and meaning-making is the focus of Lenz Taguchi's research (2010) on intra-active pedagogy which is described as "the event of life itself as it enables and produces the connections between organisms, matter and human beings; life is an ongoing movement of living" (p. xvi). This is a view of never-ending change, where everything affects everything else all the time. Nothing is fixed or finally known; everything is "in a continuous flow of force and intensities that work in predictable and sometimes totally unpredictable ways" (p. 15).

Ritchie (2013) takes a uniquely Aotearoa New Zealand stance when she draws on the centrality of relationship to Māori concepts such as *mauri* (life force), *manākitanga* (the obligation to be generous and hospitable), and *kaitiakitanga* (the responsibility to act as guardians of our natural environment). Ritchie talks about "recognising our intersubjectivity as planetary beings" (p. 310) and asks teachers to develop "dispositions of relationality to both human and 'more-than-human' entities with whom we share our places and spaces" (p. 322). Lisa's comment about the *intimacy* of the relationship between materials and participants reflects these ideas of relationship, intersubjectivity and intra-active pedagogy.

Four Years Later: A Continuous Process of Learning

Pacini-Ketchabaw et al. (2015) take inspiration from Rinaldi's 2006 conception of relational professional development and suggest that teachers engage in asking questions about their own practices and "make sense of what teaching and learning could become" (p. 6). When we asked the participants what they could recall from their professional learning experience we received responses from four teachers (three early childhood and one primary) who were keen to share their views four years later in 2021.

Bridgette said that the notions of "interconnection and interdependence" are what she remembers as the premise of the professional learning: "This is what I personally carry forward strongly into my work and thinking today." Carlyn's predominant recall is the issue of time—time to slow down in the primary classroom and revisit new knowledge. She recalls the importance of realising the value of drawing and taking photographs "to help further thinking and discovery". Materials, especially those from the natural environment, are collected, exhibited, shared, discussed and linked to new learning with the children she teaches. Katrina says that "what bubbles up to the surface" for her is the notion of "coming to know". She goes on to explain that "various sensorial landscapes" always come to mind now when offering provocations to children. For Michelle, her key memory is exploring the pedagogy of relations in multiple ways, "highlighting the creative connections that are made when you bring disparate ideas and materials together".

The professional learning journals remain as an important resource and "trigger memories, feelings and thoughts ... these were such powerful artefacts! I also still get as much, if not more, satisfaction from seeing the journals, interpretations, artwork, thinking and experiences of my colleagues" (Bridgette). As part of the original professional learning experience, participants were asked by Margo and Chris to decide on a tree of significance to each person (see Chapter 7 for more details). As participants came to know more about their 'own' tree they were asked to give it a special gift. Carlyn's gift was a prayer, which she still remembers every time she looks at how the tree has flourished in her garden. She says: "My journal is on a shelf by my desk along with all my other current teaching resource materials; I refer to it regularly for inspiration." Katrina 'arm-knitted' a long scarf for her tree in a public space. She lives in a different part of New Zealand now but has visited the tree since moving. She explained:

> The tree is still there but not my scarf; I hope the person who took it enjoyed it as much as the tree. This professional development has led me into a different terrain of learning where I have learnt about myself as a learner, as a teacher and as a researcher. I am more creative in my thinking about materials and their relationship with each other and with me. The gift I made for the tree really helped me think outside the box!

At the start of the professional development in 2017, Chris and Margo posed the following question to participants: *At what point in time do teachers engaged in professional learning make a significant mind shift?* This chapter has explored the question of when significant mind shifts were made during the sustained professional learning. Rinaldi (2006) suggests that professional development "means living and living ourselves in a permanent state of research" (p. 137). Pacini-Ketchabaw et al. (2015) capture the intentions of Margo and Chris when they draw on Rinaldi's viewpoint: "We cannot maintain an open, dynamic practice without further theoretical insights; neither can we create theories without extending them through moments of practice" (p. 6).

This chapter challenges the widely held belief that the creation of quality learning opportunities for early learners can be achieved by simply transferring and applying knowledge through professional development. Yet, as Margo and Chris affirmed throughout this professional learning experience, when we take a relational and continuous view of practice, it becomes even more complex and exciting, opening up rich processes of discovery and of meaning-making. More is always possible.

Key Messages

- Thinking together with colleagues over time can deepen and strengthen professional learning.

- Adult engagement in learning processes enables broader understanding of children's learning processes.
- The continuous search for knowledge, relations and connections creates new and exciting ways of seeing and understanding children—and ourselves, in relationship with children.

Thinking Points

- How could professional reflection become an expected and everyday component of professional practice in your work?
- How will you make time to grow a culture of inquiry and a community of learners, where knowledge-building is an ongoing and contemplative exploration of ideas?
- How might you introduce engagement with materials as a vehicle for professional learning in your site?

References

Anastas, J. (1999). *Research design for social work and human services*. Columbia University Press.

Ayers, W. (2010). *To teach: The journey of a teacher* (3rd ed.). Teachers College Press.

Barsotti, C. (2004). 'Walking on threads of silk': Interview with Loris Malaguzzi. *Children in Europe*, 6, 10–15.

Cohen, L., Manion, L., & Morrison, K. (2000). *Research methods in education* (5th ed.). RoutledgeFalmer.

Creswell, J. W. (2003). *Research design: Qualitative, quantitative, and mixed method approaches* (2nd ed.). Sage Publications.

Dewey, J. (1933). *How we think: A restatement of the relation of reflective thinking to the educative process* (2nd ed.). D.C. Heath.

Eliot, T.S. (1943). *Four Quartets*. Harcourt.

Gandini, L. (2012). History, ideas, and basic principles: An interview with Loris Malaguzzi. In C. Edwards, L. Gandini, & G. Forman (Eds.). *The hundred languages of children: The Reggio Emilia Experience in transformation* (3rd ed., pp.27–71). Praeger.

Giudici, C. (2012). *The hundred languages and the culture of the atelier: Aesthetics and learning*. Video resource. Study Tour, June.

Korthagen, F. (2017). Inconvenient truths about teacher learning: Towards professional development 3.0. *Teachers and Teaching: Theory and Practice*, 23(4), 387–405.

Krueger, R. A., & Casey, M. A. (2000). *Focus groups: A practical guide for applied research* (3rd ed.). Sage Publications.

Lenz Taguchi, H. (2010). *Going beyond the theory/practice divide in early childhood education*. Routledge.

Mutch, C. (2013). *Doing educational research: A practitioner's guide to getting started* (2nd ed.). NZCER Press.

Pacini-Ketchabaw, V., Nxumalo, F., Kocher, L., Elliot, E., & Sanchez, A. (2015). *Journeys: Reconceptualising early childhood practices through pedagogical narration*. University of Toronto Press.

Pelo, A. (2013). *The goodness of rain: Developing an ecological identity in young children.* Exchange Press.

Popova, M. (2018). The effortless effort of creativity: Jane Hirshfield on storytelling, the art of concentration, and difficulty as a consecrating force of creative attention. https://www.brainpickings.org/2016/07/21/jane-hirshfield-concentration/.

Rinaldi, C. (2006). *In dialogue with Reggio Emilia: Listening, researching and learning.* Routledge.

Rinaldi, C. (2015). *The teacher as researcher.* Third International Summer School. Reggio Emilia.

Ritchie, J. (2013). Sustainability and relationality within early childhood care and education settings in Aotearoa New Zealand. *International Journal of Early Childhood,* 45(3), 307–326. https://doi.org/10.1007/s13158-013-0079-0.

Rouse, E. (2015). Mentoring and reflective practice: Transforming practice through reflexive thinking. In C. Murphy & K. Thornton (Eds). *Mentoring in early childhood education: A compilation of thinking, pedagogy and practice* (pp. 25–38). NZCER.

Sarantakos, S. (2013). *Social research* (4th ed.). Bloomsbury.

Silverman, D. (2022). *Doing qualitative research* (6th ed.). Sage Publishing.

Vecchi, V. (2010). *Art and creativity in Reggio Emilia: Exploring the role and potential of ateliers in early childhood education.* Routledge.

Part 2 Commentary

Experiences of Meaning-*full* Practitioner Inquiry

Maria Cooper

Practitioner inquiry that encourages individuals to stay within their comfort zones will not work. Not when we understand the need to be comfortable to move into uncomfortable spaces in order to generate shifts in thinking, knowledge, and practice. This is a key message gleaned from Part 2, which offers four unique chapters—stories of localised experiences focused on educational improvement. The authors' shared commitment to teaching and learning reverberate throughout the stories, revealed in their willingness to feed into, participate in, and learn from the cultures of inquiry and learning they helped to establish with their practitioner communities. While each story showcases unique experiences of practitioner inquiry in different contexts, altogether, they compel teachers and leaders to be more active in shaping education with children through meaning-*full* inquiry based on a dispositional mindset of *what could be.*

Experiences of open dialogue, reciprocal feedback, and mutual respect in relation to improving practice were apparent in Fleet's (Chapter 5) telling of two stories from different places. Additional insights of systems' change were highlighted in Semann and Armao's (Chapter 6) story about one school's inquiry into the role of playful, child-centred classrooms in the continuity of children's learning, with the support of kindergarten teachers. Celada and Hobba's (Chapter 7) story of becoming teacher-researchers exemplified ways traditional notions of professional learning were disrupted through interrogating knowledge-building processes to deepen thinking, develop theory, and strengthen practice. Then, the voices of early childhood and primary teachers were foregrounded in Hill-Denee's (Chapter 8) story on *What matters*, told through a 'pedagogy of relations' lens. In recognition of contextual differences, these stories suggest that de-contextualised practitioner inquiry is an ill-fated journey, perhaps even a meaning-*less* one. Instead, practitioner inquiry that has meaning for its community is context-specific, responsive to time and place, and adapts to the evolving priorities of those involved. This is an important message for the education sector, including early childhood education, and one that can sit alongside other key messages gleaned from the stories overall that now follow.

DOI: 10.4324/9781003245827-13

Experiential Learning Gives Real-life Meaning to Practitioner Inquiry

The stories show us how experiential learning can breathe life into practitioner inquiry. For example, the hands, the fingers, the senses, and the emotions can be awakened through exploring materials, nature, and their connections (Chapter 7). Undertaking cycles of experimentation, trialling, and evaluating (Chapter 6), and engaging in physical spaces for dialogue and collaboration (Chapter 5), require different modes of participation. Through embodied engagement, experiential moments like these enable practitioners to bring the whole self in harmony with their surroundings. Such moments can enhance sensitivity to the processes of knowledge-building (Chapter 7) and an alertness to the connections and relations between all living and non-living things. For me, this 'coming-to-know' (Chapter 7; Chapter 8) bodes well for experiencing anticipated outcomes of inquiry but also unanticipated epiphanies. Even years later, re-living inquiry experiences by re-visiting material prompts, such as journals and artifacts (Chapter 8), can surface understandings that have been allowed to mellow, mature, and consolidate over time as a form of knowledge-wisdom. Returning to this wisdom during inquiry dialogues offers new meanings and understandings with which to inform practice.

Meaning-*full* Practitioner Inquiry is an Ongoing Commitment, not an Overnight Fix

Also taken from these stories is that supporting meaning-*full* practitioner inquiry is meant for the hardy—those who understand its potential challenges and benefits and are in it for the long term, not an overnight fix. This commitment relies on the process going beyond a narrow transferring and translating of knowledge through professional development (Chapter 8). It also requires an understanding that establishing motivation, gaining commitment, and sustaining momentum are possible, but not easy. Indeed, reimagining practice requires us to be willing to depart from our taken-for-granted norms and practices (Chapter 6), although this can be difficult for those who are not comfortable with being uncomfortable. However, there is much for us to learn (Chapter 6), and the uncertainties and disagreements in inquiry can provide a springboard from which new knowledge can grow (Chapter 7). This message is key to 'sticking with it'.

The stories inform us that meaning-*full* practitioner inquiry requires time and space. This is for the open-ended, loosely structured questions and niggles (Chapter 5; Chapter 8) to be identified and negotiated; for appropriate courses of action to be negotiated in response to these questions and niggles; for practice to be re-calibrated and changes evaluated; and for deep reflection on the process and outcomes. The latter alone can breed excitement about *what could be*. Importantly, the stories emphasise that practitioner inquiry able to generate shifts in practice is worthy of people's time. In this regard, meaning-*full* inquiry must stimulate rather than suppress a plethora of ideas, thoughts, and feelings, including those that sit in tension with others. Seeking the perspectives of diverse voices enables practitioners to see things anew and exposes them to alternative truths, perhaps for the very first time.

Meaning-*full* Practitioner Inquiry Is Buoyed by Enduring Relationships

Underpinning the four stories is the idea that meaning-*full* practitioner inquiry is highly relational and buoyed by enduring relationships. Words commonly attributed to Aristotle tell us that "educating the mind without educating the heart is no education at all". These words point to our relationality and the value of nurturing the relationships and connections that keep us afloat during our challenges and struggles. Indeed, we live not as individuals, but as social beings connected to people and place. Moreover, learning is not a mechanical process but relies on interpretation and understanding of our realities and experiences. Sharing this learning with others who are equally devoted to the potential benefits of inquiry fosters unity and solidarity, and also invokes possibilities in others (Chapter 6).

Relationality was a shared thread in the stories. For example, relationality was apparent in the authors' opening connections to place, the reciprocal dialogues between facilitators and their practitioner communities, the fostering of a culture of collaboration and joint engagement (Chapter 5), the human engagement with materials (Chapter 7), and the emphasis on thinking with others (Chapter 8). Multiple relationships were also seen to give access to the plethora of voices and perspectives (Chapter 6) that are needed to introduce alternative truths and broaden perspectives on teaching. Also sensed in the stories was the importance of honouring relationships, people, their time and ideas, and creating space for an ongoing search for knowledge (Chapter 8). Without the open and enduring connections to others, the risk is that commitment will subside, momentum will wane, and knowledge will stale. To give meaning and an enduring quality to practitioner inquiry, the relational space needs to be seen as sacred, and protected and nurtured. This relational work will enable practitioners to embrace rather than reject the complexities of teaching and learning in generating new insights for practice, and to become more aware of how their ideas and actions might touch others. Furthermore, thinking with external facilitators, as was evident in the stories, can support momentum and keep practitioner inquiry from becoming a self-affirming process of taken-for-granted values, beliefs, and practices.

Finally, having enjoyed mulling over these unique experiences of practitioner inquiry, I encourage you to do the same and to consider what each story makes you think about in terms of your realities and experiences. As a starting point, consider what a shift in mindset from *what was* to *what could be* might mean for your practice. Then contemplate the following questions in light of your situation: *If practitioner inquiry is written into centre documentation as a formal expectation of teaching staff, how can we ensure it remains a dispositional mindset (Chapter 5) and a values-based commitment (Chapter 8), and not a perceived burden on practitioners' time? What kinds of 'experiences' would you like to have in your practitioner inquiry, and how could you make this happen? What would make your practitioner inquiry meaning-full?*

Part 3
Exploring Big Ideas

9 Unexpected Opportunities

Inquiry as Professional Learning

Catherine Patterson and Katey De Gioia

Over the decades, the practitioner inquiry movement has continued to grow and flourish, related to, although differentiated from, teacher research, action research, exploratory practice, practitioner research, practice-focused inquiry, and professional learning communities. Whatever the labels, traditions or methodologies, the concept of the teacher as a knowledge-creator rather than a knowledge-consumer remains a key characteristic. The teacher (or practitioner) as a knowledge-creator can build on engagement in practitioner-research to create knowledge through systematic inquiry into professional practice. Cochran-Smith and Lytle (2009), explain that practitioner researchers generate knowledge through "working in inquiry communities to … develop local knowledge by posing questions and gathering data" (p. 40). In researching their own professional practice, participants become more confident in their pedagogical choices and develop their professional self-image as they are empowered to articulate reasons behind their decision-making.

Although the concept of practitioner inquiry is gaining acceptance within K-12 education as integral to professional development (Kroll, 2018), Woodrow and Newman suggested in 2015 that it "may be seen as an emergent practice" (p. 1) in early childhood education. The different requirements for early childhood staff qualifications (Kroll, 2018), along with "the diverse range of job responsibilities" (Belzer, 2009, p. 138) between educators, teachers, directors and administrators may make it difficult to establish a shared basis for professional learning initiatives. At the same time, however, it could be argued that staff are accustomed to working in a team context, and the emphasis on "positive team dynamics" (Dyer, 2018, p. 354) common in early childhood sites may be advantageous in developing a collaborative atmosphere. Thus, practitioner inquiry is a 'good fit' for early childhood contexts because it encourages "ongoing, on-site professional growth for practitioners of varying personal and professional backgrounds" (Black, 2019, p. 228) offering opportunities to acknowledge "the voices and knowledge of those who participate" (Black, 2019, p. 228). The practitioner inquiry cycles of input and discussions enable participants to internalise the reflective cycle and transfer knowledge and skills to other aspects of pedagogical practice in unexpected ways. In this chapter, two real-life examples from early childhood leaders, teachers and educators are presented to highlight surprising outcomes of practitioner inquiry.

DOI: 10.4324/9781003245827-15

Stepping Out of the Centre and Into Practitioner Inquiry

As an approach to professional learning, practitioner inquiry is appropriate for early childhood staff by providing scope for individual growth and learning at all career stages. This first account of practitioner inquiry (below) explores unexpected outcomes experienced in a large-scale opportunity for 107 early childhood teachers from 100 centres in a single organisation. These teachers came together in 16 groups to participate in teacher inquiry over a twelve-month period (see Chapter 3). The professional learning was established by the organisation as part of a broader program of support offered to those with teacher qualifications. Whilst the majority of participants were in teaching positions, there were a small number of centre directors who also chose to participate. Usually only one teacher from each centre was able to attend as meetings were held during work hours and offsite (prior to COVID-19). The requirement for centres to access additional staff to backfill during these absences, and the need for teachers to commit to this twelve-month professional opportunity contributed to the limited number of teachers able to attend from each service. Unanticipated opportunities arose when these groups of teachers from diverse services came together, as they were working with relative strangers and had rarely experienced such a sustained period of time to collaborate, grow and learn together. These groups created circumstances which differed from an *in-centre* inquiry. Participant responses shared below were obtained through survey responses.

Image of Self

Teacher identity is described by Sachs (2005) as teachers "knowing 'how to be', 'how to act' and 'how to understand' their work and their place in society" (p. 15). These concepts are accumulated over time and informed through relationships, practices, knowledge, values and beliefs (Rus et al., 2013). There were two centre directors who chose to participate in this particular teacher inquiry experience and they both identified questions that related to their sense of self as teacher and how this impacted on their ways of working. Both these qualified teachers had taken on administrative roles and were classified within their centres as 'non-teaching directors'. As a result, whilst they were in and out of rooms, relieving educators and teachers, and working alongside them, they did not see themselves as teachers. They were participating in this professional learning because it was linked to teacher accreditation processes (see Chapter 4) which they needed to maintain as part of the compliance requirements in their setting.

In the excerpt below, Katey shared her response to their perspectives of themselves in the beginning of their inquiry:

> ... that is the second centre director who has now had this conversation with me! I am really surprised that their image of self does not encompass

themselves as teachers. They don't, or can't, see that they are likely often making decisions through a pedagogical lens, even those that are operationally focused. I will be really curious to hear their outcomes as a result of this process—note to self to connect the two to talk through their questions of inquiry!

(Katey De Gioia, research notes, 2018)

One of the centre directors framed her question as follows: *As a centre director, how do I contribute meaningfully to learning outcomes for children?* She chose to gather data focusing on ways she contributed to the programming in one of the rooms where she spent time relieving other educators as they took breaks. At the end of the process, she reflected that, "This opportunity gave me the chance to feel like a teacher again, not just a centre director." She also explained that it had changed the way she viewed herself and increased her confidence in being more explicit in mentoring educators in pedagogy and practice whilst in the rooms.

Engaging Others in the Cause

In this particular inquiry work, there was an expectation that teachers who attended meetings would take the information back to their centres and share their progress. There were many assumptions here that needed to be unpacked. Katey noted her concern in her reflections:

Well, that's interesting! Meeting Two and seeing some blank faces, polite smiles or lack of eye contact when I asked about how they had gone about sharing in centres. This is the third group, and I can pretty safely assume that this work is not being shared. I wonder why …

(Katey De Gioia, research notes, 2018)

Some teachers explained that they felt unsupported or not confident enough to share their learning back in the centre. Their reasons included:

• not feeling confident enough about what they were doing to talk about it with others,
• not knowing what information to share,
• not wanting to expose their own vulnerabilities in teaching or appear to not know about their chosen area of inquiry,
• not having dedicated time to share this information.

In order for teachers to feel connected to their new learning and able to share this with others, the following steps were enacted to support understanding back in their centre:

• After each meeting, an email was sent to each centre director, copied to the teacher, outlining key points from the meeting, and providing prompt questions to support the centre engaging in dialogue with the teacher about their inquiry question.

- Teachers were provided with clear directions about what they could share with their co-educator/s, the leadership team or at centre staff meetings, broken down into two components—the process they were experiencing and their specific question of inquiry.

On completion, one teacher stated: "I learnt how important it was to involve co-educators and families in the process; I felt I gained more traction when I shared what I was trying to achieve." Another shared, "I have become more confident in this area, so when I brought it back to the team ... it made me feel a sense of achievement." For some teachers, however, this continued to be an ongoing struggle for recognition of this way of working, with one teacher sharing, "I completed this without support from my centre director and used a lot of my time ... I feel I could have been far more successful if my centre director was more supportive."

Unexpected opportunities along the way—both positive and negative—inspired thoughtful reflection and in some instances, action, to support participants throughout the inquiry process. The last word belongs to a centre director who came along to hear one cohort of teachers share their learning as part of a celebration of teacher inquiry at the completion of the twelve months. Those involved in the process were encouraged to bring along one person from their centre to support them whilst they presented. After sitting through approximately eight presentations, she declared, "Where do I sign up? I have learnt more in the past two hours than I have in the last 10 years of engaging in professional development!"

Practitioner Inquiry Within a Single Centre

As Fleet et al. (2016) suggest "not all participants engage with practitioner inquiry in the same way at particular times in their professional lives. Rather, they engage in diverse ways depending on a range of professional and personal elements" (p. 22). The second example in this chapter illustrates the experiences of one educator engaged with practitioner inquiry in her own centre. Effey's story identifies the unexpected opportunities encountered by staff in her centre during their experiences with practitioner inquiry. When she began to work with practitioner inquiry, Effey was the room leader in a preschool room. Staff at her centre joined practitioners from two other centres in professional learning opportunities that would take participants through a process of practitioner inquiry over twelve months.

Focus on the Inquiry Process

The inquiry process began with an inital session introducing the concept of practitioner inquiry through inspirational accounts of practice from an influential practitioner. During the day, staff teams met in small groups to identify current strengths at their centre and note possible aspects of professional practice that might become the focus of an inquiry.

Later, Effey looked back at this initial session and wrote:

> When I attended the first meeting I was running late, and I was tired and grumpy, and I didn't really want to be there. On that day we were treated to some inspirational sessions and asked to think about how we thought about ourselves and our work and what areas we would like to improve. By the end of the day, I had mixed feelings. While I was refreshed and motivated, the idea of taking part in a research project was a bit overwhelming because we had no experience in doing this. I thought that we had no time to be involved because our centre was due for accreditation, and with everything else we were expected to do, I wondered what it was going to achieve anyway.

Following the first session, participants were expected to establish a direction for their research and state their concern as a question to be investigated. About a month later, participants met again to share updates from centres. Discussions focused on potential areas of investigation and strategies to establish a focus for their question. A number of issues were reported: (i) staff from Effey's centre reported less progress than anticipated due to recent accreditation involvement, (ii) staff at another centre were concerned about engaging colleagues who hadn't attended the first meeting, (iii) there were shared worries from most participants over how to focus a question on a useful investigation.

Effey recalled:

> We began the process of finding a question by having a few staff meetings and putting up questionnaires in our staffroom. We discussed our strengths and weaknesses and issues that staff felt were preventing some aspects of care. We had a few directions we could go, and ultimately an issue that had been bugging the staff for a while came up. It was felt that a lot of the routine tasks of the day, for example setting up, cleaning and housekeeping of all kinds were keeping staff off the floor more than we would have liked. As a result, collecting baseline data about how routines were affecting our time and interactions with children became our focus and this is how our question came to be: How can we spend more time with all children to create more meaningful connections?

Although Effey's group found these initial stages to be relatively straight-forward, others had more challenges. They reported that it was difficult to focus their attention because staff had so many ideas and it took many meetings and discussions to decide on a question. Even when the question seemed to be finalised it was found to be too broad or there wasn't enough time to reflect on the data that had been gathered. Challenges in trying to generate a focus question are quite common in practitioner inquiry. In a study of adult educators undertaking practitioner inquiry, Belzer (2009) recorded a similar slow start as participants struggled with the process in a "fairly typical way, with lots of fits and starts and uneven progress, but in a forward trajectory" (p. 146). Taking on the role of researchers along with the "already multifaceted roles they play in children's lives" (Roberts et al., 2010, p. 259) meant that progress towards focus questions took participants longer than anticipated.

Focus on Baseline Data

Having attempted to establish a focus question, workshop participants met again six weeks later to discuss the role of baseline data in sharpening the focus of their research. They shared ideas about progress and raised questions about concerns or worries. Staff across workplaces were facing challenges in (i) finding time for discussions, (ii) freeing up staff to observe each other, and (iii) trying to 'get everyone on board'. These shared concerns highlight common issues faced by early childhood staff working eight hour shifts with limited time to meet to discuss common concerns. While many participants felt frustrated with the slow progress, they were reassured that all services seemed to be in a similar situation. In response to these concerns, time was spent during the workshop session to investigate practical strategies that might deal with these worries. Having found that staff meetings were not necessarily the best way to engage staff (difficult to arrange in working hours, planned meetings 'hijacked' by items demanding immediate attention), new ideas highlighted the possibilities of shared staff folders, personal journals, staff room wall posters, sticky post-it notes and so on.

These early stages of the inquiry reveal challenges with 'getting started' in a practitioner inquiry investigation and illustrates the pull of daily responsibilities in a busy early learning service. Similarly, Belzer (2009) found it was common for some participants to still be seeking clarity or needing more focus in the first few months. This description reflects the experience of Effey's colleagues caught up in the reality of learning new skills as practitioner-researchers while continuing with their daily work.

Over time, however, staff in Effey's room developed their own observation schedule and supported this with photographs of adults going about their daily work. They initially decided to track one another every 15 minutes (which later became every 30 minutes as the challenge of the shorter time span became evident) during morning and afternoon sessions. They noted what the adult was doing, investigated why they were doing it and recorded the number of children involved.

Effey reported:

> While the process of working out what we wanted our research question to be went reasonably smoothly, it took us a while to finally come to a decision. We had quite a few ups and downs deciding how we were going

to collect baseline data. It was really only once we were well into the process that we realized that in fact we were achieving what we had set out to do.

Gathering baseline data is a key aspect of practitioner inquiry as it has three significant roles. First, gathering and analysing data on the current reality of professional practice provides confirmation (or rejection) of the initial concern. "Baseline data provides the groundwork from which teachers are able to make sense of their problem" (Fleet et al , 2016, p. 33). Such data can help to re-focus the investigation onto the 'actual' problem, which may (or may not) support the initial concerns or niggles identified by staff. Second, baseline data can then be used as motivation for staff during the investigation, perhaps 'look at how far we've come' or maybe 'we need to improve our game'. Finally, baseline data is a valuable resource late in an inquiry to illustrate progress to compare the initial situation with the results of the changes that have been made.

Focus on Data Management

A month later, Effey attended a half-day workshop focused on issues arising from the management of the increasing amount of data that were being collected at each centre. Updates from centres revealed a variety of data-gathering approaches. These included brainstorming ideas, observations of staff, photographic evidence over time, staff surveys, discussions at staff meetings, video recordings, transcripts of responses by staff to photos, documentation of individual children and small groups, and diary entries.

Effey revealed her experiences with data collection:

> Asking questions and collecting data calls for honesty and trust. You have to be honest with yourselves about what is happening on a daily basis, and it is not always what you would like to see. There was a great need for trust amongst the staff to allow this process to unfold. Being watched is very uncomfortable and it took a while to get used to, and not to be worried about what others might think. It also took courage to share our findings with staff from different rooms in our own centre and even more so with other centres.

This emphasis on honesty and trust reveals unexpected insight into the nature of practitioner inquiry. Encouraging practitioners to be comfortable in revealing their uncertainties and sharing professional practice calls for sensitivity in building an environment of trust. Schachter et al. (2019) suggest that the core of professional learning is the "development of trusting relationships that provide space to be vulnerable and encourage teachers to try new practices" (p. 402). Effey's experience highlights the importance of "relational trust" (Cranston, 2011) in inquiry processes.

Given the different levels of individual expertise and knowledge among participants, if practitioners are to be "agentic risk-takers" (Charteris & Smith, 2017), then courage and confidence within a safe environment are needed to develop new thinking.

Focus on Working with Data

Six weeks later another half-day workshop was arranged for staff to report back on progress and work through issues of data analysis. Participants reported diverse approaches to organising their data. These included writing observations recorded in each room and filed in shared folders, creating graphs, charts, and mind-maps, recording transcripts of conversations, making diary entries, writing up observations from photos, and writing up questions from video and staff observations.

Effey reported that staff had begun to look at their data to see if they could detect patterns in their observations. They identified three categories to describe staff involvement. There seemed to be a pattern of staff involved in routine tasks, such as setting-up experiences, nappy changes and so on. There was also a pattern of staff supervising or monitoring, checking that everything was all right but not actually interacting with children, and finally there were staff engaging with children. This analysis or looking for patterns continued to confirm their initial idea that many of their daily routines were actually opportunities for interactions with the children. As a result, staff decided they would involve the children in all they were doing as far as possible. If a staff member went out to collect the mail, two or three children went along to see what the postie had left; when lunch trolleys had to be collected, two or three children went along to help; when setting the tables, laying out bibs, or hanging artwork, children were invited to assist. These initiatives led to opportunities for authentic conversations and more meaningful relationships. Effey noted that she had learned how much children valued her attention and how much they learned through her interaction with them. She commented that she had become "more patient and now provided children more time to problem-solve instead of doing things for them".

Effey's increased understanding of research grew through her relationship with staff as they were "talking, thinking, listening, pausing, imagining possibilities, and reflecting" (Fleet & Patterson, 2009, p. 17). Their work in gathering and analysing real-life data as the inquiry progressed echoed the description provided by Hargreaves (2007) who described "trusted colleagues who value each other personally and professionally" and are "willing to discuss and disagree about evidence and data that can inform them about how to improve their practices" (p. 188).

Over the next few months, centres were supported by a visit from the workshop facilitators, and staff from each centre met locally to plan the final presentation evening. Meanwhile, data continued to be gathered and analysed to identify changes that were occurring. Staff in Effey's room worked on new ideas to engage children in routines and share responsibilities across the day. She noted that "the children are more settled and calmer now because they have the opportunity to be involved". During this time, families were invited to a parent evening at Effey's centre where staff explained the progress that had been made through the practitioner inquiry project. The director commented that the parents had been "very impressed"; they had noticed the changes and they "respected the commitment of the staff". With the concluding celebration high on everyone's minds, the final few weeks meant staff spent time reflecting on their progress, preparing storyboards, and organising presentations.

A Celebration of Progress

A final evening session enabled staff to celebrate their experiences of practitioner inquiry. Guests were welcomed into a beautifully arranged space with an atmosphere provided by carefully chosen table arrangements and subdued lighting. Attractive storyboard displays summarised the key points of investigations and guests were keen to discuss the exhibitions. As not all participants were able to be present, a sequence of photographs and quotes was shown to guests. In this way, all participants had their voice acknowledged in the celebrations. During the evening, staff made formal presentations to the guests. When discussing the effect of the practitioner inquiry project, Effey's director noted:

> I have seen tremendous thought and commitment from our staff. Outcomes for the children have been significant. Not a moment is lost in dreary routines. Staff now make use of every moment and every situation to engage with children and develop more responsive bonds with them. Now there is less stress, more time and a sense of greater depth in our days. I believe our childcare workers have now become childcare professionals.

In her presentation Effey explained:

> Practitioner inquiry gave us the opportunity to grow in different ways. Even though the process seemed long and overwhelming at first, all our effort and ideas have been really beneficial in having more meaningful interactions with children. Just by taking time to think about what we were doing we could learn so much.
>
> Practitioner inquiry gave us confidence in many different areas, such as public speaking and sharing knowledge, within our own centre and with others. It has improved communication between staff members and lifted morale and changed our perception of ourselves and what we can do. This has made me able to step outside the square and try new and challenging experiences. The inspiration continues as we look at new questions and ways to keep a fresh approach to care and learning.

Spreading the Word

Early the following year, Effey along with representatives from the two other centres presented the findings of their investigations at a national conference for early childhood researchers. She reported on her experiences with practitioner inquiry, shared her research question and reflected on the outcomes of the inquiry. Effey said that she would never have imagined herself in front of an audience when she began to work with practitioner inquiry. She explained: "A year ago I would never have thought I'd be involved in research and stand in front of an audience talking about my work. But here I am and the things we have learned are very clear in our minds."

It has been suggested that early childhood practitioners may be reluctant to share results of their research for several reasons including "thoughts that the results may not be important enough to share, a lack of confidence, or a feeling that colleagues may not be receptive" (Castle, 2012, p. 133). Overcoming this reluctance and realising that others might be interested in the study and may benefit from the learning may help a less confident presenter find a way to share results (Castle, 2012). As well as presentations in front of an audience like Effey's, it is also possible to share information in a range of ways, including casual conversations, meeting reports, websites, and journal publications.

Effey's Learning

This account of Effey's learning through her experience with practitioner inquiry highlighted a number of unexpected outcomes. First, was her increased understanding of the processes of practitioner inquiry including how to write a meaningful question, how to select appropriate data-gathering strategies, how to analyse the data, and how to present the results of her inquiry. Second, was the growth in her personal capabilities such as increased confidence to share her knowledge in public, and improved skills in problem-solving. Third, there was growth across her teaching team with increasing trust and risk-taking leading to improved team morale. A culture of ongoing collaborative professional learning appeared to be building at the centre. Finally, and perhaps most importantly, was Effey's change in her professional identity. She was seeing herself as a researcher with something important to say. She had taken ownership of her own learning and was prepared to try new and challenging experiences. Her increased sense of professional agency gave her new confidence in making choices about professional practice and prompted deeper insights into who she was as an early childhood practitioner.

Cautionary Words

Effey's positive experience, however, may not be shared by all early childhood educators embarking upon practitioner inquiry. Barron et al. (2017) explain that any research process is "likely to be messy and erratic because that is how we experience a world that defies containment" (p. 69). Several factors may influence inquiry processes. For example, given the high staff turnover in early childhood services there may be moments of vulnerability when key leaders leave. These may be identified leaders such as a director or room leader, but leadership in practitioner inquiry may come from an unexpected source and a gap becomes evident when that staff member leaves. High staff turnover rates can make it challenging to sustain efforts to implement practitioner inquiry. Alternatively, a lack of staff buy-in (Christ & Wang, 2013; Nichols & Cormack, 2016) may also derail the inquiry process as it is difficult to bring about change if staff choose not to participate.

Conclusion

The chapter has explored the development of professional agency as the result of positive outcomes when early childhood educators are given the responsibility for investigating an issue of concern. Real-life examples have shown how participants are able to establish an image of themselves as practitioner-researchers and gain new understandings of their professional roles. The time given to discussing, debating, and negotiating current practices within the early childhood centre highlights the collaborative nature of practitioner inquiry. Finally, Connelly and Clandinin (1988) provide an ultimate comment for contemplation: "After all, as John Dewey said so well, thinking is inquiry, inquiry is life and life is education. ... Living is thinking, and that, said Dewey, is what education is all about" (p. 10).

Key Messages

- The open nature of practitioner inquiry may lead to unpredictable and unexpected outcomes.
- The unexpected learning from practitioner inquiry may promote significant professional and personal development.
- Staff with different backgrounds, experiences and perspectives can work together through practitioner inquiry.

Thinking Points

- Reflect on an example of a personally powerful professional experience. Why was it particularly effective for you? What was unexpected in this experience? How can you build on this experience?
- To what extent are you aware of the skills and knowledge of your colleagues? How could you draw on these strengths in a practitioner inquiry project? How could you help your colleagues build on their pedagogical practices?
- To what extent do you think a practitioner-researcher should see their role as the 'facilitator' rather than 'investigator' when working with others? What would a role as facilitator mean for your professional practice with adults?

References

Barron, I., Taylor, L., Nettleton, J., & Amin, S. (2017). Working with the cracks in the rigging in researching early childhood professional development. *Contemporary Issues in Early Childhood*, 18(1), 67–79. https://doi.org/10.1177/1463949117692272.

Belzer, A. (2009). Getting what you pay for: Divergent conceptions of knowledge in practitioner inquiry, *Studies in the Education of Adults*, 41(2), 138–153. https://doi.org/10.1080/02660830.2009.11661578.

Black, F. V. (2019). Collaborative inquiry as an authentic form of professional development for preschool practitioners. *Educational Action Research*, 27(2), 227–247. https://doi.org/10.1080/09650792.2018.1452770.

Castle, K. (2012). *Early childhood teacher research: From questions to results*. Routledge.

Charteris, J., & Smith, J. (2017). Sacred and secret stories in professional knowledge landscapes: Learner agency in teacher professional learning. *Reflective Practice: International and Multidisciplinary Perspectives*, 18(5), 600–612. https://doi.org/10.1080/14623943.2017.1304375.

Christ, T., & X. C. Wang (2013). Exploring a community of practice model for professional development to address challenges to classroom practices in early childhood. *Journal of Early Childhood Teacher Education*, 34(4), 350–373, https://doi.org/10.1080/10901027.2013.845630.

Cochran-Smith, M., & Lytle, S. L. (2009). *Inquiry as stance: Practitioner research for the next generation*. Teachers College Press.

Connelly, F. M., & Clandinin, D. J. (1988). *Teachers as curriculum planners: Narratives of experience*. Teachers College Press.

Cranston, J. (2011). Relational trust: The glue that binds a professional learning community together. *Alberta Journal of Educational Research*, 57(1), 59–72.

Dyer, M.A. (2018). Being a professional or practising professionally. *European Early Childhood Research Journal*, 26(3), 347–361. https://doi.org/10.1080/1350293X.2018.1462999.

Fleet, A., De Gioia, K., & Patterson, C. (2016). *Engaging with educational change: Voices of practitioner inquiry*. Bloomsbury.

Fleet, A., & Patterson, C. (2009). A timescape: Personal narratives, professional spaces. In S. Edwards & J. Nuttall (Eds.), *Professional learning in early childhood settings* (pp. 9–25). Sense.

Hargreaves, A. (2007). Sustainable professional learning communities. In L. Stoll & K. S. Louis (Eds.), *Professional learning communities: Divergence, depth and dilemmas* (pp. 181–196). McGraw Hill.

Kroll, L. R. (2018). Teacher inquiry, research and pedagogical documentation. In L. R. Kroll & D. R. Meier (Eds.), *Documentation and inquiry in the early childhood classroom: Research stories from urban centres and schools* (pp. 3–18). Routledge.

Nichols, S., & Cormack, P. (2016). *Impactful practitioner inquiry: The ripple effect on classrooms, schools and teacher professionals*. Hawker Browner Education.

Roberts, S. K., Crawford, P. A, & Hickmann, R. (2010). Teacher research as a robust and reflective path to professional development. *Journal of Early Childhood Teacher Education*, 31(3), 258–275. https://doi.org/10.1080/10901027.2010.500557.

Rus, C., Tomşa, A., Rebega, O., & Apostol, L. (2013). Teachers' professional identity: A content analysis. *Procedia – Social and Behavioural Sciences*, 78, 315–319. https://doi.org/10.1016/j.sbspro.2013.04.302.

Sachs, J. (2005). Teacher education and the development of professional identity: Learning to be a teacher. In P. Denicolo & M. Kompf (Eds.), *Connecting policy and* practice: *Challenges for teaching and learning in schools and universities* (pp. 5–21). Routledge.

Schachter, R.E., Gerde, H. K., & Hatton-Bowers, H. (2019). Guidelines for selecting professional development for early childhood teachers. *Early Childhood Education Journal*, 47(4), 395–408. https://doi.org/10.1007/s10643-019-00942-8.

Woodrow, C., & Newman, L. (2015). Recognising, valuing and celebrating practitioner research. In L. Newman & C. Woodrow (Eds.), *Practitioner research in early childhood: International issues and perspectives* (pp. 1–16). SAGE.

10 Intersections of Pedagogical Documentation and Practitioner Inquiry

Alma Fleet, Adam Christie and Jessica Dubois

Alma Opens the Musings

At face value, Practitioner Inquiry and Pedagogical Documentation are separate pedagogical processes, albeit with some shared philosophical underpinnings. Involvement with a range of professional development settings and university courses may shape the view that either you are teaching or learning about one of these 'strategies' or the other. Perhaps a personal story will help position the conversation, before unpacking component complexities, both historical and theoretical.

Every chapter has a story—at least one starting point and an evolution; this one acknowledges philosophies of narrative inquiry offered by Clandinin and Connelly (2000): "... the landscapes on which we work are storied" (p. 177). It began when I worked with a team (Semann & Slattery) engaged to improve educational outcomes in a small Australian outback mining town. From the perspectives of community engagement and individual empowerment, the practitioner inquiry component of the project was successful over several years. Time passed, and another consultancy developed focusing on pedagogical documentation, particularly as it might contribute to formative assessment in government-managed preschools in South Australia (e.g., Fleet & Semann, 2019). As the project evolved, there were mentions of the 'other' topic—that is, in practitioner inquiry sessions, there were explanations about pedagogical documentation as potentially key in recording unfolding inquiries (e.g., Fleet et al., 2017). Similarly, in sessions scaffolding pedagogical documentation, it was clear that an inquiry-orientation assisted educators pursuing co-research with children (e.g., Fleet et al., 2016). The terrain was becoming less clearly defined and intersections between these pedagogical approaches more difficult to manage in professional 'development' contexts.

My tipping point happened during a 'spin-off' opportunity from the earlier South Australian project funded to explore formative assessment strategies. I was assisting educators in a group of prior-to-school sites who had chosen to extend their understanding and use of pedagogical documentation as core practice. The key conversation emerged within a supportive learning community which encouraged discussion over time, sharing queries and seeking points

DOI: 10.4324/9781003245827-16

of clarification. In this environment, an educator who had participated in the earlier practitioner inquiry project found herself working in a highly regarded suburban Children's Centre participating in the more recent project. The site had engaged in collaborative investigations throughout several years of Education Department–sponsored professional development and was continuing commitment to facilitated learning opportunities. Being frustrated with what she perceived as her lack of progress—despite enthusiasm from others around her—Ruby raised the issue with her team: she said she was having trouble seeing differences between her earlier work with practitioner inquiry and her current work with pedagogical documentation. Her experienced Director, Jess, passed on the question and her musing:

> Alma, another question that some of the team are grappling with is the difference between practitioner inquiry and pedagogical documentation. Ruby said she's had lots of experience with educator action research but not so much with the process of pedagogical documentation, which she's finding more difficult. Can they even be separated?? We thought that they both have similar processes about identifying 'niggles'/wonderings, learning about this/research, and that by changing our actions, we are refining and revising our practice as educators—continually improving what WE do in order to improve learning for children. I'm probably not the right person to be answering this question but I thought perhaps Ped Doc is centred around children and includes analysis of children's learning while also acting as a catalyst for educator reflection on own practice.
>
> Is the balance slightly tipped towards children's learning in Ped Doc whereas practitioner inquiry is tipped towards educators' learning and practice? Look—I'm not really sure! Can they be separated? But I have found it interesting following one educator's journey this year and her choices in projects … which start from an observation of children but very much align to passions of hers. Of course, I support educators sharing their passions and working on something that excites them, and as we know this whole process/everything/teaching and learning is a subjective one … it's just made me think a little more and listen in on the language we are using when talking about teaching and learning. This is such a crude example and in no way do I think anyone is at risk of entering this space, but I have memories of previous educational experiences where 'project-based learning' was the new name for 'themes' and so if a teacher was passionate about ocean life, the class would spend the term 'doing' the theme of 'under the sea'!! I'm just rabbiting on now, sorry! But I would love to hear how, as a leader, I help educators keep their gaze on the learning analysis and potential for complicating children's thinking; the two-part title really helps with this. So maybe I've answered my own question.[1]

Anyway … my head now hurts. So I'll leave you to it. Look forward to connecting soon.

Hi Jess,

As always, a pleasure to share in your thinking.

These are such worthwhile questions that you are raising (I didn't mean that to sound judgmental ... what on earth is a 'not worthwhile' question in a learning community!) Maybe I mean something more like 'inclusive provocations' that make me think as well; (sometimes the language is really limited, don't you think??).

Let's pursue the issue of intersections between practitioner inquiry and ped doc—your thinking here makes sense to me, but could (unfortunately) also be reversed—i.e., the Reggio educators say that ped doc is about professional learning for educators and Practitioner Inquiry questions focus on what we are wondering about children, with data collection as a baseline before pondering adult scaffolding/changes in practice! A curiosity-mindset plays a key role here—but the added complication is that our context is one of 'formative assessment' (the Departmental perspective). None of this is mutually exclusive—as we are sharing and evaluating experiences with children constantly, so maybe the puzzle has to do with narrowing focus in Practitioner Inquiry and including the broadly experiential in ped doc. I'm not sure either! (not very helpful from the facilitator is it?? no wonder people get confused ...) In any case—both sets of processes include the 'niggle'/question, data collection and analysis, and sharing. I just suspect that Practitioner Inquiry is meant to be more systematic and Ped Doc is more about trying to understand what we do not yet know about children, building on noticing the unexpected rather than setting out to answer something in particular.

Subjectivity is key here, and the positionality of educator/s. Wise thinking (judgmental again?? at least it's positive) about Ruby and glad that you are supporting her in this way. I suspect that the issues of balance that you raise are also key—not quite one thing or the other, but each informing the other. Certainly, an inquiring orientation, a mindset of curiosity if you will, sits underneath both of these umbrellas. I'll keep thinking more about it too (and see what others think!)!

Theorising and definitions of these pedagogical approaches and processes emerge within applied pedagogy: in exploring ideas with this team, the similarities and overlaps became even more visible. The need for a fuller explanation led to this chapter. Before moving onto the perspectives of each of our co-authors, we orient this conversation in its historical context.

Historical Development

Relationships between practitioner inquiry and pedagogical documentation are problematic. Perceived similarities and differences may reflect lack of clarity in labelling processes. Some authors and facilitators treat these pedagogical vehicles as independent subjects; others imply intersection. Without using either the term 'Practitioner Inquiry' or 'Pedagogical Documentation', the second position is described thoughtfully by Meier and Henderson (2007). Interestingly, their book is titled "*Learning from young children in the classroom*", suggesting core links to pedagogical documentation, whereas the subtitle, "*The art and science of teacher research*" relates clearly to practitioner inquiry. These authors may be suggesting persistent intertwining of these constructs with reference to "graphic documents that teachers create as part of the inquiry process", followed by a section entitled, "Understanding your data through documentation". Meier notes that

> Graphic documentation is probably one of the most important means I've found for helping teachers see their question and simultaneously extend and better represent their project-based work with children, documentation creates graphic displays, but really it is a form of teacher research that is displayed visually and typically undertaken collaboratively by several adults working in one room. Therefore, there is more importance in the process of undertaking the documentation than in the product.
>
> (p. 44)

He references relationships between these ideas and work in Reggio Emilia, Italy, where educators are renowned for representations of children's thinking. He then describes the familiar sequence:

> What's most important to learn, and to develop strategies to support long-term, is the process itself, which includes many components. Working in spiraling ways, the teacher-researcher creating documentation must frame a question, identify data sources, collect and analyze data, collaborate with others to verify findings, recast the net of the research question in better ways, and then present the findings publicly. These elements parallel the journey of teacher research.
>
> (p. 44)

This orientation resonates with the later Canadian work reported by MacDonald and Hill (2018).

Missing from these descriptions, however, is consideration of researching 'with' or 'alongside' children. Over time, literature exploring these experiences has broadened discussions about forms that pedagogical documentation might take, including, but moving beyond, the original 'panels' from Reggio Emilia. Italian educators and international colleagues have adopted sophisticated digital media representations (Kind & Argent, 2017; Vecchi et al., 2019) as well as multiple forms of collaborative record-keeping of unfolding investigations.

The field of 'teacher research' has also evolved. Henderson et al. (2012) stated that "teacher research is intentional and systematic inquiry done by teachers with the goals of gaining insights into teaching and learning" (p. 3). Additionally, there is general agreement that 'practitioner inquiry' emerged from processes labelled 'action research'. Not precisely the same thing, but including similar strategies, the tangled relationships have been explained by authors such as Campbell and Groundwater-Smith (2007, 2009), and Kemmis et al. (2020). These latter authors note their work on 'Action Research Planners' began in 1979 and evolved into 'Critical participatory action research' (p. 1). They suggest that the processes known as 'Action Research', a term probably coined by Lewin in 1951, became well-known as a spiralling system of steps. Forward thinking brought them to propose five important aspects of this research, including factors of ownership, shared language, communities of practice, and locally relevant action. This analysis led to proposing varying kinds of action research, including 'Participatory research' ("an alternative philosophy of social research") and 'Classroom action research', which "typically involves ... qualitative, interpretive modes of enquiry and data collection by teachers (often with help from academic partners) with a view to teachers making judgments about how to improve their own practices" (Kemmis et al., 2020, p. 11).

Conceptualisations of 'inquiry' itself appear in various guises over time. In 2010, Bowne et al. explained how part of their preservice teacher education program included "curriculum focused on utilizing pedagogical documentation and collaborative dialogue as tools of inquiry" (p. 49). For a more transgressive view of children's representations, Sellars (2013) challenges potential adult authority, "leaving the children's activity to do the talking, without intervention of researcher analysis and doing away with interpretive and/or de/constructive literature" (p. 85). A fusion of these interpretations leads to practitioner inquiry in the sense investigated here. To contextualise this historical positioning, reflection from within an early childhood site is offered through our second voice, Jess—the Director we've already met.

Jess Thinks Aloud

Does Ped Doc always start with noticing something unexpected—noticing patterns in children's encounters with their world? My understanding at this point in time is that it does. But is that different from practitioner inquiry—where I would imagine you decide on an area of your own practice that you would like to improve BECAUSE of something you've noticed in children's learning and progress that you think can be enhanced/extended? The impact of my practice on children's learning outcomes would be key to developing a practitioner inquiry project I imagine—i.e., I'm seeing this (in children) ... and I hypothesise that it might be because of this (in me/my practice) ... so I think I need to change this (in my practice) ... in order to see more of or less of this (in children). That's probably very basic!

This theory is interesting to re-read and reflect on after time has passed. I remember being intrigued by Ruby's practice of following areas of interest to her which she noticed as being of interest to children (rather than developing an interest alongside a child or children). I'm still intrigued by this because it seems to be a slightly different approach to the rest of our educators, i.e., she was keen to 'do something with'/explore a noticing taken WHEN it aligned to her passion or interest. She would become fully immersed in this and I could see how much this sustained her/filled her cup with invigoration (also a great thing!). Her pieces of pedagogical documentation were worthwhile pursuits in terms of the potential they created for children, educators and families to learn from and be challenged by each other. But I wonder how I would have felt (and what I would have done?!) if I didn't see much potential in the 'topic'/focus of the research. Am I to be that judge? Or is this part of the role of an instructional leader ... to help staff draw out possibilities for complicating children's thinking ... yes. Maybe this is more about me having to get off my high horse deciding what's worth pursuing and what's not! Still a fine balance between support/guidance/being open to learning/curious to new possibilities.

I wonder if this intrigue for me was amplified because another educator, in the limitations of her role, only worked on a few Ped Doc projects over many months (she is an incredibly deep thinker, but struggled to move from thinking to writing in order to relaunch the ideas), so perhaps it felt to me like these areas were a big focus of talk/reflection/pondering/more talk for many months ... whereas our other educators had multiple projects on the go at the same time ... with 'passion' diluted across projects?

And I do find it helpful that you're not sure either because it makes me feel better about all the ... 'could it be this ... but what about this ... equally this' ... 'serve-and-return' game that happens in my head daily!

Is a question in practitioner inquiry directly focused on educator practice ... i.e., 'If we do this ... then we will see this ...' whereas in Ped Doc (in our experience here), the question is often a question children ask as the first starting point, and then after hearing/inviting children to share their theories about this question, educators develop their own questions. So the child's question comes first (often ... sometimes ... always?!) and I wonder if the next question comes from an educator but is still focused on how to extend/complicate the child's thinking ... perhaps through returning with a follow-up question ... or it might be through revising/refining our actions ... 'if I offer/propose this, will we see ...' (back to practitioner inquiry) AHHH it's a cycle!

For our third voice, we turn to Adam, a pedagogical leader who—like Jess—has taught in both remote and urban settings, engaging with these ideas for a decade.

Adam's Reflections—Pedagogical Documentation and Practitioner Inquiry: Same or Different?

In opening this chapter, Alma positions practitioner inquiry and pedagogical documentation as having shared philosophical underpinnings. This provocation invites us as educators to think deeply and discuss what these shared philosophical understandings might be and therefore how we might define these processes as being the same, different and or at times running in parallel. To begin: *I invite us to consider ideas, characteristics, or ways of being that exist as an essential part in both processes.* In the following paragraphs, I offer provocation to find shared ideas, characteristics, or ways of being that we may see as coherent and connected between the approaches. Of course, these ideas are not exhaustive, simply a snippet of evolving thinking and learning.

Curiosity is the Key: Inquiry for Learning

I invite us to consider these ideas from a philosophical way of being, suggesting that in both processes, educators are invited to be curious and explore teaching and learning with a sense of inquiry for learning. In this way, both processes involve developing new understandings, not simply documenting what we already know. This learning may involve new understandings of what children know, can do, and understand[2] (skills, knowledge, or dispositions)—or perhaps new perspectives and learnings about educator practice—both processes offering possibilities of exploring new insights and perspectives, uncovering evolving thinking. This fundamental characteristic of curiosity for learning depicts a key similarity in philosophical underpinnings. Here you may start to note that both processes are driving towards educational change, as explored more deeply in my later reflection.

It Must Include: Data and Analysis

Data collection and the future analysis of this data are both integral to the process. Documentation would not be described as pedagogical if it did not reflect the collection of data about children and their learning. Nor could any kind of Practitioner Inquiry begin. Both processes require a point of data collection to begin (recognising that in some instances this initial point may be held in one's mind, one might also describe this as baseline data, later analysed to inform next steps). Data in these processes may be defined as photographs, jottings, videos, voice-recordings, annotations, excerpts of conversations (dates, names and ages of children included). And of course, organising it systematically so that it can be used effectivity and managed by an individual or team of educators—the collection and systematic organisation being critical skills for success in either process.

Reflecting on my own leadership learning, I would suggest that this part of the process is often challenging; deciding how and what to collect is an ongoing point of reflection for early years educators. It is not always easy, yet critical (with an encouraging tone I would offer that there is no wrong way to start). Data collection and later analysis are skills that require practice and persistence and are most successful in supportive, collaborative learning environments in which leaders regularly attend to team culture. Here we are considering educators engaging in purposeful collections of data, being able to respond in the moment to listen, hear and see conversations or interactions between children, families and educators unfolding in the day to day. In both the context of pedagogical documentation and practitioner inquiry, Fleet (2020) suggests that analysis of data might include self and collaborative reflection on what children know, can do and understand with attention to current or emerging ideas/theories or perspectives, similarities and differences in thinking. Of course, all this sits within contexts: context matters, positioning analysis at the heart of your own community, place and space. Analysis in both processes sees educators considering not only children but 'self'. Self-awareness and reflection of our own teaching practice may include reflection on environment (for example, 'Did the design of the environment contribute to the learning?' or 'What intentional actions or decisions could I make in the future that may support children to revisit this idea and extend their thinking?'). Here again you may feel tones of educational change speaking to you, the idea that both processes contribute to change-thinking.

It's Cyclical: Informing Teaching and Learning

Decision-making is a critical component of both processes: educators make decisions that inform next steps for teaching and learning. These next steps are revisited several times in ongoing processes of data collection, analysis, planning and evaluation. In this way, both processes support planning for learning (intentional decision-making and provisioning for learning). This may be described as the planning-cycle-in-action. Educators who are engaging thoughtfully in either process would be making the planning cycle visible. In this way of working, we have opportunities to invite our colleagues, children, and their families into the processes, generating talk about teaching and learning.

In the above three sections, I share insights into similarities between these two processes. Both processes are grounded in shared philosophical underpinnings. For now, let's leave this discussion and consider what might be differences, then circle back to the idea of educational change.

Pedagogical Documenting and Practitioner Inquiry: Agents for Educational Change

I imagine by now you are feeling confident that both approaches enable—or at least contribute to—educational change. Both processes require educators to reflect (collaboratively where possible) on children's learning and their own teaching. This intersection creates another similarity between the two processes: Educators are learning new things about children and themselves. In evaluating either process, one would imagine educators are able to articulate the differences or changes that have occurred in children's learning and for their own practice. Perhaps I may now suggest some of the subtle differences that exist (at least in my own mind), while both are positioned as complementary (neither existing in a vacuum).

What Might Be Different?

Pedagogical documentation usually emerges from careful listening and observations of children's wondering, interests, knowledge, skills, and dispositions. For educators, it is about 'seeing' or discovering the extraordinary in the ordinary, collecting data and making decisions in the analysis phase about what might happen next. In this phase, an educator may decide that this 'moment' or 'series of moments' are important to revisit and plan for over time. Both include key characteristics such as date, title, photographs or transcripts, and analysis. Possibly pedagogical documentation could be 'completed' or 'published' for sharing with families/community, as a way of 'making learning visible' (Giudici et al., 2001).

For me, the distinguishing characteristic is that practitioner inquiry generally starts with a 'niggle' from the perspective of an educator/leader. From this 'niggle', a question about children (or practice) is formed for which educators commence data collection. Perhaps it is useful to suggest that practitioner inquiry is highly intentional in its design for educational change: We are designing for educator learning to understand something about children in new ways so that we can shift our own practice to better support children's learning. Through this process we may have a piece—or several pieces—of pedagogical documentation illustrating progress in teaching and learning (perhaps 'published'/shared at some point).

Bringing it all together? It's complex. Both processes share defining ideas, characteristics, and ways of being. As highlighted above, both contribute significantly to educational change, perhaps starting at different places.

Three Voices Combined: Theoretical Underpinnings

Continuing discussion about theoretical underpinnings of these pedagogies may highlight more similarities in their shared philosophical foundations. The question of theory rests on what we consider education to be, how we conceptualise teaching and learning, and the nature and place of children in the mix. The work of both practitioner inquiry and pedagogical documentation sits within a social-constructivist frame evolving in relationship with socio-political and socio-cultural contexts. That is: place and policy, cultures, relationships and environments are interconnected in unbounded ways, with 'knowledge' incorporated and being constructed within learning experiences. Seeing dispositions as pedagogically theoretical includes curiosity and persistence in the 'grand narrative' of these vehicles of educational change.

Practitioner inquiry and pedagogical documentation position children and educators as agentic, valuing the pedagogy of listening as celebrated by Rinaldi through the 'educational project of Reggio Emilia' (2006) and in a range of research contexts as explored by Clark (2017). From similar perspectives, in their exploration of adults and children *Unearthing why?*, Britt and McLachlan (2020) portray teachers as listeners and advocates, with teaching seen as part of "a continuing conversation" (p. 198). They share narratives of children as authors, artists, scientists, mathematicians, philosophers, and citizens. These portrayals are 'evidence-based', supporting the theoretical labelling with encounters from personal teaching experiences.

Alma Thinks Some More

Building on the notion of 'interpretive theory' as integrating thinking and actual events (Rinaldi, 2006, p. 75), I offer two more early childhood site-based examples. Sarah has been in various Directing roles (shared, acting and continuing) at a busy Australian Kindergarten (mostly four-year-olds) during the site's engagement in a pedagogical documentation project. Concern with behavioural issues evolved into a focus on 'being kind' with a practitioner inquiry question for staff related to how educators could promote 'kindness' amongst children. In an email summarising progress with their data, Sarah wrote:

> We have had a good look at our communication documentation on the wall [pedagogical documentation data] and noticed that:
>
> • We had more documented observations for confident/verbally articulate children than those who are quieter and less 'obvious'.
> • Some children who we 'thought of' as kind, caring and inclusive were hardly represented at all. Most of these children are girls.
> • Most of our observations had been categorised as 'kindness', 'empathy' or 'inclusion' with less about 'listening', 'negotiation' and 'respect'.
> • There is no observable difference in communication skills between Group A and Group B.
> • Children receiving additional support are 'seen' more as there is an educator often 1:1 or nearby.
>
> From this we determined that we needed to adjust our lens from what we could hear (children's voices) to prioritise what we could see (body language, facial expressions, groups of children interacting).
>
> We are wondering if we didn't document observations about the girls as much because of gender bias and seeing those as innate rather than learnable and teachable behaviours? We are all passionate about gender equality and yet is our behaviour revealing that our deeper perspectives still consider how boys and girls 'should' and 'do' behave and interact?

This is a rich example of practitioner inquiry emerging from a project focusing on 'being present' with children through pedagogical documentation. It draws our attention to the reverse situation as pondered by Tamara who was working on pedagogical documentation (at the site of Jess's earlier reflections):

> I'm wondering if the piece about mysterious objects really is ped doc or not, because my intentions were not so much about the mysteriousness of an object, but more about the way children share their thinking. So, my

intention was not so much to research a question or idea alongside children but simply to provide provocations, with the aim of getting children to develop their ability to form complex sentences and to use these when sharing their thinking with others.

Can I call this ped doc or is it more about my own practice? As I write I'm thinking … both go hand in hand because all the ped doc I've done, I've aimed to do this anyway, the process, and then reflecting on this always improves my practice. (Giving myself another headache here). I also need to give Jessica a BIG shout out because she helped me a lot! Best team ever!

In response, Alma wrote back:

I love your question about intentionality—I think that is key to the discussion we're all having about the relationship between pedagogical documentation and practitioner inquiry. I'm suspecting that both approaches/methodologies are stronger when they intersect—but could also exist independently, depending on intentions.

This also suggests a clear framing of the thinking of educators in Jess's team, beginning with Michelle and Georgie, followed by Tamara's example:

Michelle (4-year-olds)

Practitioner Inquiry: Where can I embed my focus on culturally responsive pedagogy?

Pedagogical Documentation: "Where do the leaves go?"

Georgie (3-year-olds in Occasional Care)

Practitioner Inquiry: What strategies can I use to help children learn to listen to each other?

Pedagogical Documentation: How are children exploring their sense of belonging?

Tamara (4-year-olds)

Practitioner Inquiry: How can I encourage children to speak in more complex sentences?

Pedagogical Documentation: What sense do children make of mysterious objects?

These examples foreground thoughtful professionals, curious about 'big' questions as well as the wellbeing and growth of individuals. Certainly, there is increasing clarity after several years of thinking! As reported by Henderson et al. (2012), while "children are at the forefront of teacher research … Teacher researchers learn about themselves as teachers as they try to understand children's learning" (p. 3).

Conclusions: So, What Do we Take Away?

Does that bring us to clearer definitions? Does it matter?

It may matter if projects are funded on the basis of either focus approach, with less interest in the other. It certainly takes more time to explore both ways of working than to concentrate on one or the other. Clarity in language and thinking processes assist in developing understanding and in written forms of sharing with others.

There may be an expectation that practitioner inquiry has more structural expectations including an 'answer' or set of strategies that seem successful in assisting with the 'question' of interest, whereas pedagogical documentation may intersect with those concerns but be more open-ended with a sense of 'wondering investigation' alongside children, extending thinking and creativity as well as companionship and collaboration. It may be possible to begin with attention to either practitioner inquiry or pedagogical documentation and find pathways intersecting as explorations continue. So perhaps what we've been sharing is greater appreciation for the rich potentials of unbounded pedagogies, where teaching teams and children can work thoughtfully with the people, materials and environments around them to pursue rich questions, deep thinking and learning, entangled with wellbeing.

All educator names are either pseudonyms, or actual names used with permission.

Key Messages

- Pedagogical documentation and practitioner inquiry share intersecting pathways and shared philosophical underpinnings, perhaps stronger when they interact.
- Pedagogical documentation may be a form of co-research which offers a focused lens on children's learning and perceptions, while practitioner inquiry may focus more on adults' learning and perceptions.
- Both processes involve discovering something new, having the power to influence educational change.

Thinking Points

- How do you/your team currently define the processes and key characteristics of pedagogical documentation and practitioner inquiry?
- Consider recent events that might be considered practitioner inquiry: What were the strengths and weaker points of your investigation?
- How might processes of practitioner inquiry enable your team to focus on a particular aspect of learning/teaching in relation to working with pieces of pedagogical documentation?
- What kinds of thinking/ways of being does the word 'inquiry' invite, particularly within pedagogical documentation or practitioner inquiry?

Notes

1 Note that pedagogical leadership is explored in Chapter 11.
2 This challenge reflects core ideas in the Australian national guidelines for early childhood services (Australian Government Department of Education, Employment and Workplace Relations, DEEWR, 2009)

References

Australian Government Department of Education, Employment and Workplace Relations. (DEEWR) (2009). *Belonging, being & becoming: The early years learning framework for Australia*. Commonwealth of Australia.

Bowne, M., Cutler, K., DeBates, D., Gilkerson, D., & Stremmel, A. (2010). Pedagogical documentation and collaborative dialogue as tools of inquiry for pre-service teachers in early childhood education: An exploratory narrative. *Journal of the Scholarship of Teaching and Learning*, 10(2), 48–59.

Britt, C., & McLachlan, J. (2020). *Unearthing why: Stories of thinking and learning with children*. The Curious Teacher.

Campbell, A., & Groundwater-Smith, S. (Eds.). (2007). *An ethical approach to practitioner research: Dealing with issues and dilemmas in action research*. Routledge.

Campbell, A., & Groundwater-Smith, S. (Eds.). (2009). *Connecting inquiry and professional learning in education: International perspectives and practical solutions*. Routledge.

Clandinin, D. J., & Connelly, F. M. (2000). *Narrative inquiry: Experience and story in qualitative research*. Jossey-Bass.

Clark, A. (2017). *Listening to young children: A guide to understanding and using the Mosaic approach*. (3rd expanded edition). Jessica Kingsley.

Fleet, A. (2020). About data analysis. In-house presentation. Department for Education, S.A.

Fleet, A., & Semann, A. (2019, August 20–23). *Formative assessment to inform learning design*. [Paper presentation]. EECERA conference, Thessaloniki, Greece.

Fleet, A., De Gioia, K., & Patterson, C. (2016). *Engaging with educational change: Voices of practitioner inquiry*. Bloomsbury.

Fleet, A., Patterson, C., & Robertson, J. (2017). *Pedagogical documentation in early years practice: Seeing through multiple perspectives*. SAGE.

Giudici, C., Rinaldi, C., Barchi, P., & Reggio Children (Eds.). (2001). *Making learning visible: Children as individual and group learners*. Project Zero, Harvard.

Henderson, B, Meier, D. R., Perry, G., & Stremmel, A. J. (2012). The nature of teacher research. In G. Perry, B. Henderson, & D. R. Meier (Eds.) *Our inquiry, our practice: Undertaking, supporting and learning from early childhood teacher research(ers)* (pp. 3–10). NAEYC.

Kemmis, S., McTaggart, R., & Nixon, R. (2020). *The action research planner: Doing critical participatory action research*. Springer.

Kind, S., & Argent, A. (2017). Using video in pedagogical documentation: Interpretive and poetic possibilities. In A. Fleet, C. Patterson, & J. Robertson (Eds.) *Pedagogical documentation in early years practice: Seeing through multiple perspectives*. SAGE.

MacDonald, M., & Hill, C. (2018). The intersection of pedagogical documentation and teaching inquiry: A living curriculum. *LEARNing Landscapes, Spring* 11(2), p. 279. https://www.learninglandscapes.ca/index.php/learnland/article/view/962/959.

Meier, D., & Henderson, B. (2007). *Learning from young children in the classroom: The art and science of teacher research*. Teachers College Record.

Rinaldi, C. (2006). *In dialogue with Reggio Emilia: Listening, researching and learning*. Routledge.

Sellars, M. (2013). *Young children becoming curriculum: Deleuze, Te Whāriki and curricular understandings*. Routledge.

Vecchi, V., Boniluari, S., Mennino, I., Tedeschi, M. (Eds.). (2019). *Bordercrossings. Encounter with living things. Digital Landscapes*. [Exhibition catalogue]. Reggio Children.

11 Effecting Positive Change

The Role of Educational Leaders

Marina Papic

Early childhood teachers in educational leadership roles have an opportunity to impact educational change in their classroom and their educational settings more broadly. Educational leaders are in powerful positions to lead positive change and bring others on a journey of continuous improvement through research, mentoring and supporting professional development.

This chapter will explore the important role educational leaders have in leading change using real life examples of three educational leaders to exemplify how they used practitioner inquiry to bring teams together to create a learning community and enhance professional learning. The chapter outlines how, through a process of critical reflection, peer support and collaboration, educators and teachers deepened their professional knowledge and refined their skills with the support of centre leaders. Critical elements of leadership that enable professional growth are explored and exemplified throughout the chapter.

Opening Thoughts

Educational leaders have an important role in effecting positive change. They lead and support their teams to provide the best education program to children and to continuously reflect on, question and enhance their practice and pedagogy. "The role is a collaborative endeavour involving inquiry and reflection" (ACECQA, 2021, para. 1). Educational leaders are pedagogical leaders. They share their knowledge about planning and resourcing, they engage with children, families and the community, and support others to "reconceptualise the ways in which they work to promote learning and professional growth" (Stamopoulos & Barblett, 2018, p. 65). Pedagogical leadership involves "coaching, mentoring, initiating professional conversations and modelling ethical practice in order to build the capacity of the staff team as curriculum decision-makers" (Waniganayake et al., 2017, p. 102) and drive better outcomes for children's learning and development.

As Cunliffe (2009) has stated, "*If we know what kind of person we want to be, then what to do falls into place*" (p. 94). Reflecting this idea, Sharnee Fancett, educational leader of a children's centre on the central coast of NSW highlights

DOI: 10.4324/9781003245827-17

the critical role educational leaders have in leading professional learning and identifies the importance of understanding yourself as a leader and engaging in distributed leadership to create change:

> It is essential to have a true understanding of yourself as a leader and director of change. Leadership is a behaviour that has impact and influence on others. As an educational leader I truly believe and understand that by authentically working in partnership with others through a distributed leadership approach, more is possible. Leading action research projects through a distributed approach ensures that collectively a sphere of influence is created that is meaningful and contextual to the project at hand. To be an influential leader of excellence and change understanding, the importance of knowing yourself as a leader first is essential.

Distributed leadership recognises the leadership of others who are not in official leadership roles. Educational leaders, through distributed leadership can tap into the varied strengths, knowledge and skills their individual team members possess, and can create a culture that invites and values inquiry, deep reflection, collaboration, and dialogue. These are powerful tools that encourage early childhood teams to engage in research that supports the improvement of practice. Understanding of research and how it can inform decisions and practice is important in building professional knowledge and ultimately supports better outcomes for children.

Effective Leadership for Professional Development

Leadership in early childhood contexts is complex; every day expectations including regulatory requirements leave little time for thoughtful, planned, educator/teacher-centred professional learning. These expectations and pressures can lead to directors/managers and education leaders "looking for 'quick-fix' professional learning measures in order to meet quality benchmarks" (Woodrow & Staples, 2020, p. 4). 'Quick-fixes' or one-off 'inspiring' workshops will not drive sustained improvements in pedagogical practices. Leading positive and sustainable change requires a commitment by leaders to professional development that provides educators and teachers time and space to question, deeply reflect, research, have conversations with their colleagues about their thinking and provide opportunities for educators and teachers "to acquire or develop new ways of thinking about learning, learners and subject matter" (Evans, 2014, p. 195). Essential for the effective leadership of professional development, according to Evans (2014), is an understanding that professional development is multidimensional.

> It is not simply or narrowly about changing people's behaviour—how they do or go about things, or how much they do or produce, or what generative effect their changed practice has—it is also about changes to their

attitudes, intellectual capacity and mindsets. Yet all too often it is behavioural change alone that is the focus of professional development efforts and initiatives.

(p. 193)

Leadership for professional development requires the leader to treat each member of their team as individuals, not as a homogenous group, allowing them to focus on an area of inquiry that is "closely tied to personal agendas, goals and priorities" (Day & Gu, 2007, p. 427). There needs to be an investment in professional learning that "incorporates action research, practitioner agency and cycles of enquiry over time" (Woodrow & Staples, 2020, p. 4).

Douglass (2019) considers leadership "one of the single most important drivers of organisational performance, quality improvement and innovation" (p. 6). When leaders commit to and support the professional learning and development of their staff, "they build organisational capacity for improvement which can result in higher quality ECEC [Early Childhood Education and Care]" (p. 19). But what does it mean on a practical level to support the professional learning and development of your staff; what specifically does a leader do not only to support but to drive change? The following examples from educational leaders working across three diverse long day care centres in New South Wales, highlights some of the strategies that support effective change in early childhood practice. These include providing release time from teaching, collaborative work on defined changes with colleagues, mentoring and coaching on the practices being examined, and opportunities for reflection (Hadley et al., 2015).

What it Takes to Lead Change Through Action Research: The Perspectives of an Educational Leader from a Service of Excellence

Educational leaders can support action research projects in their centres to promote reflection and professional learning and "to extend understandings of curriculum decisions that reflect local contexts" (Waniganayake et al., 2017, p. 102). Educational leader Sharnee Fancett shares her reflection on what it takes to lead sustainable change through action research in the complex environment of a large, early childhood centre rated "Excellent" by Australian National Quality Standard processes:

Implementing and leading meaningful action research should be regarded as an ongoing journey. Questioning, collecting, analysing, planning for change, and implementing practice in an informed manner becomes deep-rooted within a project when this cycle is authentically embedded. This must be a collaborative approach that involves children, families, educators, and the wider community to result in exceptional learning outcomes for all.

When leading this process, applying the practice of critical reflection to gain understanding of who I am as a leader is the first priority to ensure I may influence others with confidence. I strongly believe that implementing an action research project involves inspiring and making change with others. It is understanding what is important to myself and others as a common purpose and advocating for what is important with passion and certainty. When leading, it is essential that I understand my own values and standpoints, however, I am as equally open to the ideas and expertise of others to learn and grow, as feeling valued can inspire confidence in others to share their own perspectives empowering all to be involved. Leading with honesty and out of vulnerability, not fear, ensures that the learning process is authentic, and lessons can be learned along the way. When leading action research with others, it is essential to understand that new ideas can be difficult and require patience, encouragement, time, and space to reflect, as change can sometimes be the opposite of what is expected—which can be both wonderful and rewarding.

Leading and embedding these practices within my service has led to exceptional outcomes for not only children, families, and educators within my own service but also those within the wider community. This has been evident through always developing a collective desire and drive to continuously develop practices that will lead to better learning outcomes for all children within and beyond our service at the forefront of our minds.

Sharnee is committed to supporting the professional learning and development of her staff. Her example below of an inquiry research project that was developed from a shared vision and established in partnerships with not just the educators and teachers in the service but with children, families and the local community, exemplifies a critical element of leadership: Providing opportunities for educators and teachers to reflect and master skills over time, allows for consolidation of the learning (Hadley et al., 2015). In this example, leadership occurs as each staff member "interacts and influences each other while contributing to a shared vision" (Stamopoulus, 2012, p. 42).

Contributing to a Shared Vision

The project evolved when an excursion to a local farm was planned to build on children's interest in learning more about where their food came from. During the excursion the children, family members, educators and farmers openly discussed and identified a shared vision "*To develop learning environments and programs that advocate for our future generation to develop the skills to be sustainable caretakers of our land*". Taking the time for conversation, sharing of ideas and debates that identify a shared vision for learning "is crucial if early childhood educator teams are to effectively live their vision and understand the implications of their pedagogical practices" (Waniganayake et al., 2017, p. 104).

Sharnee goes on to explain:

From this shared vision an inquiry research project was established in partnership with the children, families, educators, and experts from the local community farm. Taking the lead and management of the project involved building an understanding of each stakeholder who would form the project team. This was achieved through collective discussions, formal and informal meetings to establish everyone's skills set, their understanding of our project objective and what their passion for the project was. During our meetings, the project team shared our experiences from the farm, and this inspired conversations as to how the life skills explored on the farm could be adapted to our educational program and rituals within the service.

A social-constructive approach where experiences are shared, recognises that educators and teachers bring "prior learning and experience to any 'new' learning opportunity" (Kummen & Hodgins, 2019, p. 113). As Sharnee highlights, this opportunity to share and have time for conversations shaped the direction of curriculum and practice in the service: "It was collectively decided that we wanted to engage all age groups to explore the care and nurturing of animals by setting up a chicken hatching program in our service."

In her role as an educational leader, Sharnee "supported educators to critically reflect on their current and developing knowledge" (Kummen & Hodgins, 2019, p. 113).

Educators were supported and given time to assess the data (surveys, observations, and documenting children's voices) from the chicken-hatching experience. Understandings from this data highlighted the benefits of having the chicks within the service. From this data, the team proposed to collaborate and share ideas surrounding how we could have our own chickens embedded within the learning environment to develop the children's skills to be sustainable caretakers of our land as part of our daily educational program.

Educators reflected and collaborated, reaching out to other childcare services with animals, children, families and other educators to research how we could safely include chickens within our learning environment and what would be required to care for them in a responsible way. Families supported this desire, with many agreeing that: "*It would be great to have the chickens as part of the environment providing the children with the opportunity to care and be responsible for living creatures.*"

Taking the lead, I supported the staff in writing a group proposal to the Centre Director. The outline included articles exploring the benefits and challenges of having animals in the care environment, plans for caring for the chickens including checklists and the development of a specific chicken procedure, costs for set up including ongoing costs, Risk Analysis Plans, and plans for the building of the hutch. The children's voices were captured through pictures and a brainstorming session during community time in our Kindy and Pre-School rooms as to why they wanted the chickens and how they would care for them. The children, as part of our research team, took great ownership in presenting their desire for the chickens to be within the service reporting "*We can feed them our scraps from morning tea and afternoon tea*" and a child sharing "*I have chickens at home I can give to school*". This plan was also supported by families who also offered assistance to check on the health of the chickens regularly.

As a result of the inquiry research project, the service adopted three hens from a family—with the children and educators working in partnership with the guidance of the farmer and family to care for the chickens as part of the service's daily rituals. When challenges have arisen with the chickens, such as brooding, the educators and children from the research team have used this as a learning opportunity and researched how to overcome these challenges.

Educational leader Sharnee led her team to further cycles of inquiry research where the centre implemented other sustainable practices inspired by the initial project and the connections made with the community. Informed by research, the children, families and educators at the service further enhanced the learning environment by embedding seasonal vegetable gardens and worm farms within the service. The shared inquiry took "advantage of different strengths brought by novices, experienced teachers, and teacher educators, and [created] opportunities to work toward common ends" (Rosaen & Schram, 1997, p. 277).

Sharnee concludes:

> It is evident that as a leader, by developing an understanding of everyone's skills set and how they could contribute through all parts of the project, I was able to empower the team to access resources, develop processes and review data. As a leader it was essential that there was the establishment of a well-defined plan, the delegation of roles and setting of clear measures and deliverables for the project. This ensured that our research was meaningful and significant to the participants and in return made significant change to the program and practices within the service reaching our overarching goal to develop learning environments and programs that advocate for our future generation to develop the skills to be sustainable caretakers of our land, rendering the project a success.

Elements of Leadership that Influence the Environment and Drive Change

Siraj-Blatchford and Manni (2008) identify that effective early learning settings are characterised by strong leadership where leaders and their team have a shared vision of practices, pedagogy and the curriculum. Mentors play a key role in encouraging collaborative conversation.

Marie Antuoni, educational leader at an early childhood centre in Narwee, NSW, reflects on her role as educational leader and the elements of her leadership that influenced the environment and the team around her and drove change in practice. She explains:

> Through the action research inquiry: "*In what ways can we authentically engage parents/families in the service to help inform curriculum decisions?*" I have learnt that an effective educational leader views their role as a collegial, joint endeavour, enacting their role through mentoring, guiding, and supporting educators. As an educational leader, I have realised the power of mentoring and supporting educators understanding of the importance of communication with families to enrich curriculum planning for individual children within the educational program and practice uplift through building the capacities of each educator to provide positive learning outcomes for children.

In developing safe spaces for collaborative conversations, pedagogical leaders according to Stamopoulos and Barblett (2018), "nurture attributes such as curiosity, open-mindedness and resilience" (p. 76).

As Marie continues to explain:

> Through authentic professional conversations with the team, I was able to understand and draw upon each educators' strengths and expertise to further develop their confidence and skills in collaborating with families to engage within the centre curriculum to support pedagogy and practice uplift. It was an opportunity to inspire the team, to affirm, challenge and extend the practice of educators in the service to promote effective teamwork where educators can commit to a culture of change, learning, respect, and collaboration, sharing different perspectives and ideas.
>
> It was an opportunity to learn about my qualities and values as a leader and to listen and understand others' points of views, values, knowledge, and skills and be opened to learning from each other and learning together to create a culture of change. I have learnt a great deal about myself as a teacher and the importance of my role as an educational leader to enact the role through collaboration and partnerships within a team of educators and with families to deliver a meaningful and contextual curriculum.
>
> Part of my professional journey as a teacher is to critically reflect on my current practice individually and collectively to enrich decision making and action change. Through this process it was an opportunity to seek knowledge, information, and new understandings to enhance my own professional growth.

Siraj-Blatchford and Manni's (2008) study on *Effective Leadership in the Early Years Sector* (ELEYS), indicated that "a trained and skilled leader or manager, with the capacity to reflect upon and engage with changing contexts, capable of communicating and ensuring the vision of the setting, had a direct impact on the overall quality of the setting" (Ang, 2012, p. 290).

Marie's critical reflections illustrate how effective leaders influence on the quality of the setting.

> I realised that families often face obstacles when engaging in the early years' learning experience. Through research and data collection I was able to lead the team to break down the barriers and use the information provided to demonstrate to parents that we have an invested interest in their child's early years' education, that we value their knowledge about their child, and these beliefs are the foundation of our program. Through authentic engagement and collaboration, a shared vision unites us in ensuring that parents/families can authentically support curriculum decisions, that demonstrates continuity between home and the early education service.

As demonstrated in this example, education leaders are in a unique position to support their team to reflect, rethink and reconceptualise how they work with children and families, to support learning and enhance their own professional growth (Stamopoulos & Barblett, 2018).

Educational Leader Experience: Wearing Multiple Hats

The Australian early childhood sector is complex and constantly changing, a situation that poses challenges to those in leadership roles such as centre director/managers (Alchin et al., 2019). Many of these leaders wear multiple hats—director, education leader and teacher, adding to the daily challenges and ways of working.

Lisa Emme, education leader at a long-daycare centre in Western Sydney shares her experience of wearing multiple hats when driving pedagogical goals:

> A couple of years ago I engaged in my first teacher's inquiry. At the time the concept and practice were new to me, and I was still trying to understand what it was about and how this would support my professional development, growth and teaching. Unfortunately, I did not get to finish this inquiry due to workplace commitments, which was a little disappointing as I was starting to understand and enjoy my experience.
>
> A year later, I decided to try again. This time I knew more about 'teachers' inquiries' and how I thought this process would support my teaching and the work I was doing, most importantly the work with the children in my service. Being that I am also a centre director and the educational leader, I found this inquiry challenging, to wear the hat of a teacher, gaining my own understanding about my teaching inquiry and what I felt I wanted to work on as a teacher and make changes at my service, and then also to support my team at the same time as an educational leader and a centre director.
>
> Like most early education and care services, I began to see the struggles in the outdoor learning environment. I wanted to know why our indoor

environments looked so amazing and children had high engagement levels, but I was not seeing this transferred into our outdoor environment. Our outdoor space had a very natural feel to it due to a recent upgrade yet the engagement level, between children and educators was not evident and the environment did not look inviting to me. Knowing what I wanted to work on was easy but asking myself the right questions was the most challenging part, because this sets the direction of the inquiry.

It was at this stage, after talking to my team, that I realised that throughout our work so far, we had identified the same challenges within the service. On close investigation I found that this was a larger area for improvement for the whole service. I decided that the best approach for me as a teacher and to ultimately get the desired and best outcomes for children, was to strengthen my approach by joining it together with my educational leader role and what we were working on as a whole team.

Lisa shifted her inquiry from a personal inquiry project to one that had a "shared mission and collective responsibility" (Daft & Pirola-Merlo, 2009, p. 304). As the educational leader, Lisa engaged each team member, and together the team developed a common goal. In this scenario Lisa is a team member in the inquiry where she has a responsibility *to* the team but as the educational leader, she also has the responsibility *for* the team (Jones & Pound, 2008). "Better outcomes are achieved where all staff are committed, aligned, and coordinated in what they do. Therefore, effective teams need time and effective leadership to come together, share, interact and build shared understandings and relationships" (Stamopoulos & Barblett, 2018, p. 133).

Lisa's story continues:

We started with what we knew, the outdoor environment was not very inviting. We knew we had a curriculum out each week which provided children with holistic learning and many teachable moments, but it was clear that something was missing. As we looked around, children and educators were disengaged with the environment and the resources.

We decided to survey the team and the children. This allowed us to capture the children's voices and educators' thoughts. This then allowed me to really reflect on what was going on in my service, what was happening for me as a teacher and what it was that I wanted to focus on. So once again I adjusted my question. Finding the right question is quite a challenge, what is the right question? How do I know when I find the right question? I quickly realised, that without the right question I was not going to find the right answer. The importance of this question directed my whole inquiry; I felt that the success of my inquiry largely depended on the right question. [See Chapter 2.]

So once again this led to more discussions with my colleagues, and I changed my question several times until I finally felt that it was really what I wanted to learn more about: "*What teaching strategies are evident in my weekly curriculum?"* After finally finding the right question, I was able to move forward with my inquiry. It was from here that I was able to really make progress with what the real problem was in our outdoor environment.

The inquiry led by me as educational leader allowed us to find out what children wanted, what educators wanted and what intentional teaching was planned for. In addition, my own teacher inquiry allowed me to research the 'meaning of intentional teaching—why this was not working in practice?' I came to realise very quickly that I was missing an important element to my weekly curriculum—the teaching strategies. Intentional teaching is 'the act of doing'—this is what was missing. I was planning, but as a teacher I was not explaining or role modelling what I was planning or how to implement this effectively. How can educators set up experiences or engage in intentional teaching if I as the leader was not giving clear instruction and expectations on what I was trying to teach, or how I was supporting children's growth and development? How can children have the best possible outcomes if intentional teaching was not implemented effectively?

The inquiry project led and supported by me as the educational leader along with my teacher inquiry were extremely successfully. We took two different inquiry approaches and used these inquiries simultaneously, to implement change within our practices. Working in this way I believe, gave us the greatest advantage, and guided our continuous improvement for the greater good within the service for not just children, but educators as well. I now have a greater understanding and appreciation for teacher inquiries and how as an educational leader I can lead the team to positively challenge and change practice.

Lisa's story exemplifies how an educational leader can enable professional growth of others but at the same time, through the inquiry process, grow her own professional knowledge. "Leaders epitomise a love of learning by activity and continuously engaging in self-development. By proactively facilitating and strategically investing in professional learning and development, leaders promote thinking, questioning and critical reflection" (Waniganayake et al., 2017, p. 7).

Final Comments

Educational leaders are pedagogical leaders who drive continuous improvement by setting a positive example, supporting, encouraging, affirming, and challenging curriculum, pedagogy, and practice (Waniganayake et al, 2017). They display distinct capabilities which include:

- developing a clear vision that can be easily articulated,
- harnessing strategic thinking and planning,
- creating space and time for dialogue and reflection,
- offering support and mentoring to improve practice,

- providing opportunities for professional learning through action/inquiry research,
- establishing a positive, collaborative team culture,
- being knowledgeable and innovative leaders of pedagogy, curriculum, and practice.

(Adapted from Stamopoulos & Barblett, 2018)

Educational leaders create a culture that is open to change, values relationships, and supports ongoing professional learning (Fleet et al., 2015) They encourage and support critical reflection and seek ways to create a shared vision for curriculum, pedagogy, and practice. Creating positive change involves the educational leader being actively involved in the research/inquiry project with their staff: modelling, mentoring, and coaching throughout the inquiry process.

Key Messages

- Educational leaders support their teams to provide the best education learning opportunities for children.
- Educational leaders are pedagogical leaders, who continuously reflect on, question, and enhance their own practice and pedagogy while bringing others on a journey of continuous improvement through a shared vision.
- Leading sustainable change requires a commitment by leaders to professional development that provides early childhood professionals time and space to question, reflect, research, and engage in dialogue.
- Leadership for professional development requires the pedagogical leader to identify the skills of each person in their team and treat them as individuals in the inquiry process.

Thinking Points

- As an educational leader, how can you reconceptualise the way in which you work to promote learning and professional growth of your team?
- As a pedagogical leader, what opportunities can you provide your team to reflect on the practice in their room or centre to create a shared vision and goal?
- As a pedagogical leader, reflect on the skills set of your team and how they can shape the direction of curriculum and practice in your service.
- Reflect on the list of effective pedagogical leader capabilities. Which capabilities do you value most that would support your professional learning and development? Are there additional capabilities that you or your educational leader possess that you see as important in driving changes in practice?

References

Alchin, I., Arthur, L., & Woodrow, C. (2019). Evidencing leadership and management challenges in early childhood in Australia. *Australian Journal of Early Childhood*, 44(3), 285–297.

Ang, L. (2012). Leading and managing in the early years: A study of the impact of a NCSL programme on children's centre leaders' perceptions of leadership and practice. *Educational Management Administration and Leadership*, 40(3), 289–304. https://doi.org/10.1177/1741143212436960.

ACECQA (Australian Children's Education and Care Quality Authority). (2021). *Educational Leadership*. https://www.acecqa.gov.au/resources/educational-leadership.

Cunliffe, A.L. (2009). The philosopher leader: On relationalism, ethics and reflexivity—A critical perspective to teaching leadership. *Management Learning*, 40(1), 87–101.

Daft, R.L., & Pirola-Merlo, A. (2009). *The leadership experience*. Cengage Learning Australia.

Day, C., & Gu, Q. (2007). Variations in the conditions for teachers' professional learning and development: Sustaining commitment and effectiveness over a career. *Oxford Review of Education*, 33, 423–443.

Douglass, A. (2019). Leadership for quality early childhood education and care. OECD Education Working Paper No. 211.

Evans, L. (2014). Leadership for professional development and learning: Enhancing our understanding of how teachers develop. *Cambridge Journal of Education*, 44(2), 179–198.

Fleet, A., Soper, R., Semann, A., & Madden, L. (2015). The role of the Educational Leader: Perceptions and expectations in a period of change. *Australian Journal of Early Childhood*, 40(3), 29–37.

Hadley, F., Waniganayake, M., & Shepherd, W. (2015). Contemporary practice in professional learning and development of early childhood educators in Australia: Reflections on what works and why. *Professional Development in Education*, 41(2), 187–202. https://doi.org/10.1080/19415257.2014.986818.

Jones, C., & Pound, L. (2008). *Leadership and management in the early years*. Open University Press.

Kummen, K., & Hodgins, B.D. (2019). Learning collectives with/in sites of practice: Beyond training and professional development. *Journal of Childhood Studies*, 44(1), 111–122.

Rosaen, C., & Schram, P. (1997) Professional development for beginning teachers through practical inquiry. *Educational Action Research*, 5(2), 255–281. http://dx.doi.org/10.1080/09650799700200027.

Siraj-Blatchford, I., & Manni, L. (2008) *Effective Leadership in the Early Years Sector*. The ELEYS Study. London Institute of Education.

Stamopoulus, E. (2012). Reframing early childhood leadership. *Australasian Journal of Early Childhood*, 37(2), 42–48.

Stamopoulos, E., & Barblett, L. (2018). *Early childhood leadership in action*. Allen & Unwin.

Waniganayake, M., Cheeseman, S., Fenech, M., Hadley, F., & Shepherd, W. (2017). *Leadership: Contexts and complexities in early childhood education* (2nd ed.). Oxford University Press.

Woodrow, C., & Staples, K. (2020). *Leadership: Cumberland City Council Learning and Leadership Program: Research and Evaluation Report*. https://doi.org/10.26183/6arm-6e11.

12 Practitioner Research as Sustainable Professional Practice

Christine Woodrow and Linda Newman

In this chapter the authors provide a snapshot of the growing body of research literature and share an overview of their fifteen-year history of working with practitioner researchers in Australia and internationally. Snapshots of projects they have led and collaborated on, as well as those of international colleagues will be shared. These span diverse contexts including urban and regional Australia, Sweden and regional Chile. The chapter highlights evidence collected in research, reflective interviews with colleagues, resources, practices and aspects of approaches that, from the authors' experiences, have contributed to the efficacy of the work undertaken and its sustainability as a viable and valued approach to professional development for educators, with particular reference to early childhood contexts.

Practitioner research is increasingly recognised as valuable and sustainable for educators working collaboratively in professional relationships, often with university academics. Research shows practitioners gain and apply new knowledge; engage in 'deep' thinking, critically analyse; develop researcher and leader identities; broaden study and career horizons; address contextually relevant issues and questions; and integrate regulatory requirements.

Impacts and benefits of practitioner research include enhanced professional identity and credibility, new professional relationships, strengthened curriculum, improved program quality, and enhanced career trajectories. Ultimately, the strongest evidence of the benefits and impact of practitioner research comes from participants. Some of their perspectives are presented in this chapter in vignettes from interviews in different times, places, and circumstances. These bring to life critical aspects of practitioner research from lived experience, providing a rich snapshot from a number of urban and regional locations across different countries. Each participant highlighted has continued to work within an inquiry framework—once learnt, never forgotten. These insights are supported and contextualised by providing an overview of projects led by the chapter authors, some selected literature, and a short discussion. Before continuing, we ask readers to reflect on their circumstances by considering the Thinking Points included at the end of the chapter.

DOI: 10.4324/9781003245827-18

Background and Research Context

We, the authors, are experienced teacher educators and researchers in the early childhood field, with long associations with early childhood providers, policy makers and regulators, alongside close encounters with educators and early childhood sites. We also bring extensive experience in designing, implementing, documenting, critiquing, and researching many versions of professional learning. Our professional journeys, both individually and as co-developers and co-investigators have enabled us to see from the 'long-view' that not all professional learning is equal. Rather, while some approaches are of great value, others may be necessary but insufficient, and do not always 'stick'. We now understand that effective professional learning must be 'fit-for-purpose'. We have learned that the careful consideration of intended outcomes is essential when choosing an approach to professional learning as some alternatives may be more appropriate than others. We are particularly interested in inquiry approaches that involve the participants investigating their local context, enabling them to become researchers of their own practices. We use the term 'practitioner research' here for various modes (referred to elsewhere as 'practitioner inquiry', 'teacher research', or 'participant action research'). In contrast to most professional learning on offer, practitioner research involves participants in collaborating with peers, and developing broader research and leadership skills over an extended engagement spanning several months or more, often with academic leadership and support.

Our research undertaken over many years of leading such projects has provided compelling evidence about the effectiveness of collaborative inquiry approaches in mobilising change, strengthening pedagogies and building leadership (Arthur & Woodrow, 2018; Newman & Leggett, 2019; Newman & Woodrow, 2015). More recently, we have focused our research attention on issues of sustainable practice and long-term benefits for practitioners. In this chapter we consider the relationship of practitioner research to dimensions of sustainable practices, leadership, collaboration, the production of new and deep knowledge, contribution towards regulatory requirements, and opportunities for career development.

We begin by providing a snapshot of our projects, followed by a short review of relevant literature. Following this, vignettes drawn from our most recent research are presented. They are constructed from interviews from participants in Chile, Sweden, metropolitan/urban Sydney and regional NSW. Interviewees have either previously participated in projects with us or have collaborated in leading such work. They provide a rich range of perspectives. Collectively, they highlight the sustainability of practitioner research, and provide individual perspectives on themes pertinent to our research.

Our analysis and discussion highlights interviewees' distinctive perspectives to illustrate the benefits of practitioner research. These research findings will be of interest to both potential participants and leaders as they prepare for their own learning encounters, as well as organisations interested in investing in this kind of approach to professional learning.

Previous Research

Figure 12.1. captures the ten research projects that we have led over a period of 15 years. Each project differs in some ways, reflecting collaboration in design with stakeholders. This illustrates our strong commitment to co-design, resulting in bespoke programs that reflect local context and respond to participant and organisational priorities.

The longest and largest of these projects was *Futuro Infantil Hoy* (FIH— Children's Future Today) undertaken in northern Chile over almost seven years, involving 20 early childhood centres, more than 300 educators, and impacting over 3,500 children living in communities experiencing economic and social adversity. This project involved partnerships between government agencies and the private sector, supported by a mining company foundation.

Figure 12.1 Leading Practitioner Research 2008–2021
Source: Woodrow, Newman & Arthur

Subsequent projects were developed in Chile that explored innovations in pedagogical leadership.

Other projects have involved collaboration with local service providers, (Cumberland City Council and Penrith City Council), NSW Department of Education, not for profit community-based initiatives (The Hive, Connect) and individual community-based and private services (see Figure 12.1).

Related Literature

Contemporary changes in societies, children, and families combined with evidence of the characteristics supporting high-quality early education signals the need for new knowledge and changed practices that are responsive to local contexts. External professional learning activities can contribute to acquiring new technical knowledge, but a different approach is required to understand the reality of children, family and community life to tailor teaching and learning. Educators can become researchers of their own sites by integrating skill sets not easily learned in technicist or transmission models of professional development/professional learning. Professional learning for educators is widely recommended or required (e.g., OECD, 2018; NESA, 2021), and has led to a proliferation of providers and courses with the accompanying necessity to carefully question quality. Here we begin questioning by using the term 'professional learning' (as opposed to 'professional development'), as an umbrella term for activities designed for educators to acquire new knowledge, skills, and understandings.

Grieshaber and Hamm (2021) noted the tendency for professional development/professional learning to be technicist in orientation and argued that the current neo-liberal framings of educational policy position educators as 'consumers' of particular modes of professional learning that respond primarily only to mandated frameworks and standards, thereby "limit[ing] opportunities to engage with professional development [sic] as a dialogic approach, to make meaningful connections with the world and to collaborate with the community for public good" (p. 148). They argue instead for approaches to professional learning that promote a "decolonising critical pedagogical approach" (p. 148). In an earlier period when conceptualisation of teaching as an intellectual and ethical practice flourished, practitioner research also flourished through various manifestations that closely connected educators to their own classrooms and realities. For example, action research was described as research in a social setting, 'research from inside' (Noffke & Somekh, 2005), conducted by the people inside the setting or researchers working in collaboration with them. Similarly, most forms of practitioner research incorporate an inquiry stance that acknowledges the social, cultural and historical forces that shape the context, the research and its outcomes (Cochrane-Smith & Lytle, 2009). Collaborative practice has also become a hallmark of most practitioner research, in which people researching similar problems of practice form communities of practice. Peer collaboration and/or with academic partnerships adds a social dimension to the learning encounter, building confidence to propose new ideas, facilitating risk-taking with support and making learning and achievements visible (Salamon, 2010). Practitioner research is increasingly seen as a legitimate and worthwhile investment of time and resources.

The strengthening of practice-based leadership in early childhood contexts has been significantly profiled in research about the 'middle leader' (positions between directors/principals and the staff) (Rönnerman et al., 2017). This could be likened to the Educational Leader role in Australia. These leaders play critical roles in mobilising and leading change in professional learning communities. Other research draws attention to the observed connectivity between professional learning and teacher leadership. This occurs within professional learning communities where there are regular opportunities for collaboration and an ethic of enquiry (Edwards-Groves & Rönnerman, 2013). Our own research provides rich examples of changes in perspective (Woodrow & Staples, 2019), greater reflexivity and intentionality in teaching and planning (Newman & Leggett, 2019) and teacher capacity-building (Newman, et al., 2015).

Meeting the Practitioner Researchers

In this section we introduce practitioner researchers and leaders (see Figure 12.1) who collaborated with us on practitioner research. Each of the practitioner researchers, educators and managers interviewed were first introduced to practitioner research through these projects. The Swedish university professor has worked with action research for quite some time and has collaborated with the authors.

Drawing on data we collected for this publication, we present participant perspectives in the form of six vignettes that represent portraits of practitioners. This approach was selected because the portraits "emphasize spoken words and enable community members to assume an active voice in the research, therein aligning with the intent of the project to bring forth [their] stories" (Blodgett et al., 2011, p. 525). Each vignette briefly outlines the person's professional role, the focus of the vignette, and then shares their experiences and views in the person's own words. We have selected excerpts from their interviews that highlight different themes and echo data from our many participants over the years. Our overall findings supported the proposition that practitioner research is valuable and sustainable.

The research enabled us to identify the following sustainability elements:

- applying newly learnt deep thinking and critical analysis as part of developing a researcher identity,
- broadening study and career horizons,
- identifying and enacting leadership identity,
- addressing contextual issues and questions while integrating regulatory requirements,
- working in professional collaborations within and beyond the workplace, often with university academics,
- collaboratively building and applying new knowledge.

Each of these elements is explained on the following pages.

Applying Newly Learnt Deep Thinking and Critical Analysis as Part of Developing a Researcher Identity

Participants in all our programs told us in a variety of words that their thinking has been challenged, broadened, and deepened. We have become used to responses such as "I grew brain cells" and "I thought my brain would explode". In turn, a newly developed research identity often arises. In the next vignette, one of our participants describes her experiences with practitioner research.

> Melissa Duffy-Fagan is the owner of an early childhood service that participated in the *Research Connections* project with Linda Newman in 2016/2017 (Newman & Leggett, 2019). Her research focused on team-based leadership, and she has now undertaken a PhD focused on leadership. Mel was joint winner, with the 'Research Connections' team, of the European Early Childhood Research Association's (EECERA) award for practitioner research in 2017. She reflects on how practitioner research has led her to processes for becoming a deeper thinker and her newly realised researcher identity.

Practitioner research has led me to step away and to see a broader, bigger picture and think quite deeply and slowly about things. It also helped to work out the role of 'Educational Leader'. That was the launchpad to make a massive change in our centre where I've been for 17 years. ... it was a turning point in our team development.

It absolutely made a difference to my professional identity and confidence. It changed our team dynamic, the way we communicated, and the way we worked together. It slowed our practice down. The frameworks that we built from the research have been a massive impact. They're used all the time. They're part of our orientation and continuation training. I find it bizarre that now I'm doing a PhD and I just see the inherent value in research in everything. When you've actually done research, there's a better connection to seeing what the children are giving you as data that's really valid and valuable for their learning. It's so much deeper than just doing an activity plan or something.

Generally, I feel like the rest of the early childhood world needs to connect more with practitioner research. I don't see why we just don't do it. I think if it was in the compliance and regulatory world, it would then become part of a practitioners' world; it would have more gravity. It's definitely changed my career trajectory. I now say I'm a researcher. I've co-authored a journal article (Duffy-Fagan et al., 2020) and a professional book (Newman et al., 2018). These are significant skills and achievements.

I would say, if you are thinking of doing practitioner research—do it, it's going to be really, really worth your effort. Connecting with people who have done research to that level is like the richest resource you could ever have. I don't think change comes in little bursts of professional development. I think it comes in the sustained, shared thinking that is practitioner research.

Broadening Study and Career Horizons

Silvia Rojo Ramallo is the Director of El Oro, an early childhood centre in Antofagasta Chile. She participated in *Futuro Infantil Hoy* (FIH) from 2008–2010 and went on to become a mentor for other centres when FIH was expanded to 15 other sites in Northern Chile. Silvia has since undertaken two postgraduate degrees, and co-authored a chapter called "Collaborative capacity building in early childhood communities in Chile" (Newman et al., 2015). In the excerpt below, she highlights the impact participating in the program had on changing her perspectives, supporting a bolder vision and her career development, particularly in undertaking further study.

When we started, I was in charge of a centre. My action research was based on what we were doing at the time. We didn't have a vision—now my vision is no longer static but can go beyond. I could reflect on what was being done .... It allowed me to see children in a different way. I had a '*cambiar la mirada*' [change of perspective]. When you see a child in a different way you can improve the relationship with the families. The child isn't alone. She/he is part of a whole.

It has strengthened my leadership and my practice. It brought innovation. It motivated me to study—to be on top of what is going on. It has given me a lot of learning. It has been important for me to keep practising these new elements that I learned, like action research, because it's been demonstrated to me that it's efficient, that it works. In my new role my team has strengthened critical reflections on practice.

I've now finished two master's degrees: one in Education and Management, and one in Quality Management. Because I needed to strengthen my work, I thought that adding a theoretical frame of why some decisions are made around education would help. In my personal world, I am not the same Silvia that started in FIH. The experience with FIH for me was fantastic. I've had a lot more enthusiasm in sharing this with other people. It was very inspiring to be invited by the University of Valparaíso to speak to students because it helps my professional development.

Practitioner research allows you to change the way you work. Because it will help you to have more vision, and because you will be re-re-engaged with your work.

> We hadn't been taught how to do professional research before. Learning how to do it was important because it helped us to strengthen work and our teams. It's necessary. I think there's a big gap there in early childhood education.

Identifying and Enacting Leadership Identity

Jean Villacorta entered *Collaboration for Learning* (C4L) *in* 2019 as a teacher and currently holds two leadership positions, one as Educational Leader at Tregear Early Learning Centre, and the other as Strategy Lead–Early Childhood, in a social innovation project sited in one of Sydney's most disadvantaged communities. She now convenes a network of early childhood leaders promoting professional dialogues about quality early learning and family engagement. She draws attention to her strengthening leadership identity that she attributes to her participation in C4L in 2018. Jean told us the following.

> It was like a stepping-stone for me. When I joined C4L we were supposed to do research within our own service. It changed my perspective. I feel like as a teacher sometimes I'm scared to do things, scared that it's not going to work or scared of leading change. Prior to C4L I wasn't as reflective because I was just, '*que sera sera*', whatever will be will be, but when I joined C4L I became more reflective. For me it was growth. The benefit is that we all have become more conscious and intentional in what we do because we have developed something—something for our own service in a space where we all must put the hat on and think 'What can we do better and how can we improve our practice?'
>
> It had a big impact in our service. It changed all of us. You could see that it had affected our practices because I started leading the team. But what's important is that I found I'm able to lead change. I was scared at first, then I thought, well that's my role, I'm going to do it. Seeing how it led everyone to new ways of thinking and new ways of reflecting, was a joy for me as a leader. I think it was really, really good. It led to bigger changes in the service, like it wasn't just changing the outdoor environment, it led to us working on changing a lot of our practices for the better, not just for the sake of the project.
>
> Sometimes your ideas run out. For me that aspect of teaching was brought to life—a skill that I thought I didn't have but, there's another—it's like I found that there is a treasure box in our brain, and you just keep pulling it out, pulling it out, pulling it out … you kind-of just—it pops out you know.
>
> My greatest fear was maintaining sustainable change. I still coach and mentor staff but it feels good to see them doing it on their own. My biggest take-home is that we all have our fears in leading change. But for me, just do it. Just do it, do it afraid—that's my mantra.

Addressing Contextual Issues and Questions while Integrating Regulatory Requirements

Kate Higginbottom is the Director of a community-based children's centre in regional NSW, Australia. She joined 'Research Connections' in 2016. Kate and her team have co-authored a book inspired by practitioner research (Newman et al., 2018) and a journal article (Higginbottom et al., 2022). Kate was co-winner of the 2017 EECERA Practitioner Research award and was the 2019 winner of the HESTA Award for Advancing Pedagogy and Practice. She explains how her risky-play practitioner research addressed contextual issues and integrated with regulatory requirements. Kate is a strong advocate for practitioner research as she recounts in her own words.

Our practitioner research team have become deeper, more critical, and more creative thinkers. We explored governing regulations and guidelines to see how the rules and boundaries affected children's ability to learn and play. The practitioner research project included the elevation of risky-play into the curriculum while remaining consistent with national regulations.

That's transferred into improvements in pedagogy and practice. The way that we engage in our curriculum now is much more a shared perspective, which is a huge influence of that critical reflection and talking about those things. So, I think that's probably our primary 'wow moment' from the research; we've become much more critical in our thinking about everything that we do.

It's just really refreshing to have something that is owned by us, that is of that level of academic standard to have that underpinning research. We have developed a strategy that we hope will catch on. We ask parents, why did you decide to go on our wait list? It's mostly because they want to be involved in the risk-taking pedagogy that is fused right through the service. That's 400-plus families.

Our work is contextual, about what we need to know, so really pulling apart those things, being much more critical thinkers. The end-result is, it's going to live in, and be ingrained in, your soul, and that's exactly what it has done for us. It is a hundred per cent sustainable over the long term. We came up with really wanting to have that validity from the research for our families, for our community, our colleagues, about why we engage in risky-play, because it is quite controversial. We're still struggling with particular issues, but if you really want to invest in long-term change and elevate your practice, then this is something that has to be done.

Working in Professional Collaborations Within and Beyond the Workplace, often with University Academics

In each of our programs the participants have highly valued the opportunity to work with academics. One participant described this as "uni for free". Both practitioner researchers and academics have a lot to gain such as currency (in the field or in research), collaborative knowledge building, and a strengthening of professional relationships and networks. Enduring professional friendships are forged.

Janet Keegan was Children's Services Coordinator in local government. After she joined Linda and Christine's first round of practitioner research in 2008, her team's project was extended across 39 centres. She was co-author of a chapter called "Sustaining curriculum renewal in Western Sydney" (Newman, Keegan and Heely, 2015) and presented her team's research in Barcelona in 2017. Her vignette highlights working collaboratively in professional relationships within a community of practice.

As a manager, practitioner research enabled me to be surrounded by like-minded people, strong practitioners, and we all had a dual role in terms of being managers, supervisors, then as researchers. We were very committed to advancing the practice of pedagogy through a curriculum that was ultimately driven by the educators. Sustainability was a big thing for our practice at the time because we knew we wanted this to have longevity.

One impact was the sharing of knowledge. Knowledge was shared at many different levels, especially at the centre level. We focused on curriculum. It was at the craziest time of changes in the [Australian] early childhood sector for 50 years I'd say, with the new EYLF (Early Years Learning Framework) and the NQS (National Quality Standard). Initially everybody was floundering a bit, so many changes to embrace, how on earth were we going to do that? And nobody had any greater knowledge than anybody else. It was helpful that everybody was a bit open to acquiring knowledge and then sharing it. It gave us opportunities to investigate vulnerability and helped create an environment where it was okay to be not all-knowing. Not to have all the answers, to be out of our comfort zone and to trust the process.

I think the main benefit was collaboration—within the practitioner research leadership group, and within the management group and with the broader group of early childhood practitioners. Because Penrith City Council is a big provider, it was also an opportunity for us to collaborate with other people outside of the organisation. It brought our organisation together and that included about 300 adults and 32 sites. It absolutely made a difference in our assessment and ratings. We exceeded expectations in the area related to curriculum and that was exactly what we were working on. We'd been into the research for about four years before the first children's services were accredited.

We recently celebrated our 10-year milestone. We used practitioner research to influence for our decision-making, and policy and practice and then the actions of our practitioners. It developed people's skills in reflecting, analysing and then taking informed decisions and actions. It supported the ongoing cycle of reflection and action that we brought into targeted professional development to inspire and motivate our educators. We were all so open and honest with each other even when we were having difficulties or when we didn't agree with something.

Collaboratively Building and Applying New Knowledge

A great strength of practitioner research, that we have witnessed over and over, is collaborative thinking whereby the tacit knowledge of all participants is pooled and 'put on the table'. The academics cease to be the experts when the daily workings of services are discussed. Participants take on the role of helping and supporting each other. This can cross boundaries such as organisations and private or community services.

Karin Rönnerman is Professor Emerita at the University of Gothenberg, Sweden. Her research has focussed on the professional development of teachers through action research. Karin co-presented a symposium in Barcelona with Linda and Christine (Rönnerman, 2015). She emphasises the dialectical nature of action research, both in terms of the collegiality of groups in professional relationships within a community of practice, as well as the dialectical nature of teaching and research.

Practitioner research has always shaped and influenced my practice—not just making things better but to reflect over what you're doing. It's dialectical. So, if I have a project in preschool, things happen there that make me refine things for another project. Action research goes beyond the project to promote professional learning and professional development. I started work with a centre 15 years ago and now the whole district is working in this way. It's a very sustainable method for professional quality.

When I take a research perspective, I have learnt to be very inclusive, not just reflecting and talking, but listening. I've gained understanding of the importance of meeting in groups for reflective dialogues. Participants are really, really anxious about new meetings, and then they think it's so important and it means so much just to sit down and talk.

The Nordic Network has been a very, very good help for me for seeing what you're doing and believing and getting support—to keep and see our own Nordic traditions of education, which are different from the Anglo-Saxon. We share ideas with one another in a very democratic way. These networks have helped me to stick to these values. We use the 'Bildung' process—Bildung is to grow like a human being. The process never ends.

It's not like you go for an education to learn *something*. Bildung is learning for life. If you see Bildung as [being] like a hiker, as opposed to going on a mystery destination flight where you don't know the goal. You know which hotel you are going to, and it's all set and you go, and then you return. But as a hiker, you're looking for, 'oh, here's a nice place to stop—to stay for the night', and you just camp there. Then you meet some other people, and they say, 'oh, you should go there'. 'Oh, yeah, that would be interesting.' So, you kind of follow the road by walking it. When you come back, you're not the same person. It's an education for life, not just education for the exam. So, the discussions, the conversations and sharing of ideas is an important part of Bildung and not just giving tests or competing to be heard. A dialogue is to let all voices be heard, and I think that's very important in this work.

Collegiality makes professional learning happen, not from the top. You can't demand professional learning. You have to let it grow among participants and make sure they are the only ones to decide what could happen, and they are the ones placed to understand that.

Discussion

Across these vignettes, one can see the diverse range of characteristics that have made practitioner research meaningful. Of particular note is that practitioner research is a sustainable practice that once learned, isn't easily forgotten. The diversity of benefits derived by individual actors is indeed its strength, as practitioner research can have a variety of approaches, thus responding to individual and group characteristics. As you read through the vignettes, we wonder what aspects captured your attention. Why would you be attracted to practitioner research and what would persuade you to be become involved?

Earlier in the chapter, we highlighted some of the benefits of practitioner research identified in the literature. The perspectives shown here have focused on different aspects in each story to illustrate the varied themes we saw emerging. This does not mean that there were not commonalities. Most of our participants, those in the past and those in the interviews featured here, stress the advantages of longer-term opportunities to focus on their own issues of interest. This, they emphasised, keeps them engaged, as opposed to 'one-shot' professional development that initially inspires but often does not lead to longer term changes. Another clear thread in the feedback from participants is that practitioner research shifts professional identity towards strengthened feelings of professionalism and images of 'teacher as researcher', or an inquiry stance.

Our reporting here indicates the many strengths of practitioner research. This does not mean that everybody who tries it out becomes fully engaged. There is deep thinking involved and it necessitates a willingness to embrace change.

Some may find the approach, and change, too challenging. A very small minority of people withdraw. Practitioner research also incurs financial costs so requires the support of upper management. As Mel reflects:

> You need money for significant time off the floor. We just changed everything because we saw the benefits of coming together. I mean, that's what practitioner research is, a lot of time. Just coming together and thinking and talking. You can't do that 'out of hours'.

From a management perspective, Janet thinks:

> It can be a bit confronting, and it took people out of their comfort zone. We actually had some questions in our recruitment rounds around candidates' involvement or potential involvement in practitioner research and I tell you what, we were able to recruit some people who I thought were at the leading edge. They'd become fantastic university students and then qualified, and it enabled us to onboard some contemporary forward thinking.

In conclusion, we would like to leave you with the words of Sarah McNabb, the 2018/2019 coordinator of *Collaboration for Learning* for The Hive (a community-led local organisation bringing people together to enable young children and their families to thrive). In a recent unsolicited email, she said:

> Thank you for introducing me to the social justice values of ECE when we worked together. I fortuitously have been able to embed these in my [university tutoring]. I couldn't go back to teaching without bringing those new eyes with me, and now I don't have to. So much of what we learnt together influences my practice and way of 'being' as an educator. Thanks for showing me how to hold myself well in this work, for seeing in me something ..., and to inspire the prospect of future study and hopefully one day research.
>
> (Email communication, 23/9/21)

Thinking Points

- Have you become disenchanted with professional learning and seek something that will give you more opportunities for sustained engagement and making change?
- Are you ready for intellectual stimulation? Is your career at a point where you feel the need to move forward or challenge yourself?
- Would you like to work collaboratively with your team, or educators outside your workplace, in projects of your choice?
- Are you looking for ways to help meet your regulatory requirements such as teacher accreditation or Assessment and Rating processes?

Key Messages

Practitioner research is strongly supported by those who have engaged in this form of professional learning. Advocates from our practitioner research experiences say it is a sustainable process with the potential to address the diverse professional goals and imperatives listed below:

- As a 'reusable' process, it's more valuable than the 'shot in the arm' professional development.
- It enables and embeds collaboration in professional relationships within and beyond workplaces.
- New knowledge is introduced through deep thinking and critical analysis processes.
- Regulatory requirements are integrated into daily work rather than being an additional task to be completed.
- It builds a researcher identity and 'enters the soul' for continuous improvement.
- It strengthens curriculum by enabling contextual issues and questions to be addressed.
- It raises possibilities for extended career trajectories.

References

Arthur, L., & Woodrow, C. (2018). Effective pedagogies for enhancing preschoolers' engagement with learning in disadvantaged communities. In S. Gannon, R. Hattam & W. Sawyer (Eds.), *Resisting Educational Inequality: Reframing Policy and Practice in Schools Serving Vulnerable Communities* (pp. 99–109). Routledge. https://doi.org/10.4324/9781315109268.

Blodgett, A., Schinke, R., Smith, B., Peltier, D., & Pheasant, C. (2011). In Indigenous words: Exploring vignettes as a narrative strategy for presenting the research voices of Aboriginal community members. *Qualitative Inquiry*, 17(6), 522–533. https://doi.org/10.1177/1077800411409885.

Cochrane-Smith, M., & Lytle, S. (2009). Teacher research as stance. In S. Noffke & B. Somekh (Eds.), *The SAGE handbook of educational action research* (pp. 39–49). SAGE.

Duffy-Fagan, M., Newman, L., & Leggett, N. (2020). Critically reflective mentoring within team-based leadership: 'having conversations that matter'. *International Journal of Leadership in Education*. https://doi.org/10.1080/13603124.2021.2006798.

Edwards-Groves, C., & Rönnerman, K. (2013). Generating leading practices through professional learning. *Professional Development in Education*, 39(1), 122–140.

Grieshaber, S., & Hamm, C. (2021). The depoliticisation of professional development in Australian early childhood education. In M. Vandenbroek (Ed.), *Revisiting Paulo Freire's pedagogy of the oppressed. Issues and challenges in early childhood education* (pp.148–165). Routledge.

Higginbottom, K., Newman, L., West-Sooby, K., & Wood, A. (2022). Intentional teaching for risky play: Practitioner researchers move beyond their comfort zones. *Australasian Journal of Early Childhood*. https://doi.org/10.1177/18369391221112740.

NESA (New South Wales Education Standards Authority). (2021). Maintaining proficient teacher accreditation. https://educationstandards.nsw.edu.au/wps/portal/nesa/teacher-accreditation/meeting-requirements/maintaining-accreditation/proficient-teacher.

Newman, L., & Leggett, N. (2019). Practitioner research: With intent. *European Early Childhood Education Research Association Journal*, 27(1), 120–137.

Newman, L., & Woodrow, C. (Eds.). (2015). *Practitioner research in early childhood. International issues and perspectives*. SAGE.

Newman, L., Keegan. J., & Heely, T. (2015). Sustaining curriculum renewal in Western Sydney. Three participant views. In L. Newman & C. Woodrow (Eds.), *Practitioner research in early childhood: International issues and perspectives* (pp. 105–121). SAGE.

Newman, L., Leggett, N., Duffy-Fagan, M., & Higginbottom, K. (2018). *Strengthening quality through critical reflection and action research*. Early Childhood Australia.

Newman, L., Woodrow, C., Rojo, S., & Galvez, M. (2015). Collaborative capacity building in early childhood communities in Chile. In L. Newman & C. Woodrow (Eds.), *Practitioner research in early childhood: International issues and perspectives* (pp. 17–36). SAGE.

Noffke, S., & Somekh, B. (2005). Action research. In B. Somekh & C. Lewin (Eds.), *Research in the social sciences* (pp. 89–96). SAGE.

OECD (Organisation for Economic Co-operation and Development). (2018). *Engaging young children: Lessons from research about quality in early childhood education and care. Starting Strong*. OECD Publishing.

Rönnerman, K. (2015). Developing collaboration using mind maps in practitioner research in Sweden. In Newman, L. & Woodrow, C. (Eds.), *Practitioner research in early childhood: International issues and perspectives* (pp. 70–86). SAGE.

Rönnerman, K., Grootenboer, P., & Edwards-Groves, C. (2017). The practice architectures of middle leading in early childhood education. *International Journal of Childcare and Educational Policy*, 11(8). https://doi.org/10.1186/s40723-017-0032-z.

Salamon, A. (2010). Making thinking visible through action research. *Early Childhood Education*, 39(1), 15–21.

Woodrow, C., & Staples, K. (2019). Relational approaches to supporting transitions into school: Families and early childhood educators working together in regional Chile. In A. Edwards & M. Hedegaard, (Eds.), *Supporting difficult transitions: Children, young people and their carers* (pp. 131–153). Bloomsbury.

Part 3 Commentary

Growing Professionally

Andrew Stremmel

Creating a culture of thinking and inquiry is what distinguishes teachers as professionals from teachers as technicians. Here I use the term, 'professionals' to describe the notion of teachers as members of a particular culture of thinking and practice, and to distinguish teachers from those who simply consume and transmit knowledge. Teachers, who see themselves as part of a culture of thinking and questioning, engage in inquiry every day. That is, to make sense of their experiences with children, they formulate questions in response to specific problems of practice (problems of meaning). They design and implement a plan of action, observe, reflect on, and analyze outcomes, envision, and test alternatives, reflect some more, and then modify or alter plans to better meet the needs of children. Essentially, we cannot properly see the role of teacher as one who simply dispenses knowledge; teachers construct knowledge and new understanding of their practice with the support and encouragement of educational leaders who promote reflection and professional learning. This is the view of teaching portrayed in the previous chapters.

Practitioner inquiry is a form of sustained professional self-development through systematic self-study, through the collaborative work of teachers and others, and through the testing of ideas by classroom research procedures. Educational leaders are pedagogical leaders who have an important role in establishing a culture of inquiry, deep reflection, collaboration, and dialogue, tools that encourage early childhood teachers to engage in research that supports the improvement of practice.

I believe that in many ways teaching and research are inseparable—there is no distinction between those who teach, theorize, question, and seek to discover new meaning and understanding. Teacher knowledge originates in practice—in the doing of teaching, which is much more than action, the passing on of information, or the enhancement of skills; teacher knowledge is generated in the daily experiences of teaching and learning and in reflection on those experiences. What distinguishes teaching as an act of research or inquiry is the intentional and systematic study of what one does to improve one's practice. It is intentional because the teacher chooses to pursue a particular question of interest, a question that emerges from the teacher's own wondering or nagging curiosity about some aspect of classroom life, a question grounded

DOI: 10.4324/9781003245827-19

in the context of the teacher's practice. It is systematic in that the teacher follows specific procedures and carefully documents these from the formation of a question through data collection and analysis to conclusions and outcomes.

An intriguing question posed by the authors of Chapter 10 is whether practitioner inquiry and pedagogical documentation are separate pedagogical processes. Further, they ask, does it matter? While I do not have the answer to this question, I do suggest that in practitioner inquiry it is not the specific answers that are most important but the processes that we undergo in helping us develop greater awareness, understanding, and more meaningful ways to teach. The benefits of teacher research begin with finding and enjoying the possibilities in one's questions.

Both practitioner inquiry and pedagogical documentation are cyclical processes of inquiry that involve framing questions, observing, recording, and collecting artifacts, organizing and making sense of these observations and artifacts, and using the information to make decisions, plan, or take action. Documentation is, however, an important tool of practitioner inquiry, because it helps teachers focus attention on children's plans and understandings and on their own role in children's experiences. As teachers examine the children's work and prepare the documentation of it, their own understanding of children's development and insight into their learning is deepened. Documentation provides a basis for the modification and adjustment of teaching strategies, and a source of ideas for new strategies, while deepening teachers' awareness of each child's progress. Based on the rich data made available through documentation, teachers can make informed decisions about appropriate ways to support each child's development and learning.

Practitioner inquiry has the primary aim of understanding and improving practice, and secondly, it is a way for teachers to come to know the epistemological bases of their practice—that is, it is a way for teachers to know their own knowledge and make it explicit and problematic (Lytle & Cochran-Smith, 1994). Practitioner inquiry must be seen as an orientation toward one's practice; a questioning disposition toward the teaching life, leading to inquiry conducted within the classroom, making the classroom (and the school or center) the teacher's laboratory.

Practitioner inquiry has a natural life in schools or centers because the questions that prompt inquiry emanate from neither theory nor practice alone, but from critical reflection on the intersections of the two. Thus, the questions are more appropriate, the investigations are more natural, and the findings are more credible and valid for teaching practice. Because they have significant knowledge and perspectives about the school context, teachers ultimately should decide matters of content, pedagogy, and assessment, not some pre-packaged curriculum, or some outside entity that has little knowledge about life in classrooms and schools. Teachers must think of themselves as generating knowledge, not just using it. Otherwise, we leave it to others outside the classroom to define the knowledge that is of most worth, the questions that are most worth asking, and the knowledge that forms the basis of teaching, a dilemma with which the teaching profession arduously wrestles.

Inspired by the insights of these four chapters, I conclude this commentary with some suggestions for teachers who are interested in getting involved in practitioner inquiry, and to those who would like to aid them in that process.

1   It will take time for some teachers to accept and understand both the idea of teacher as a researcher and the research process itself. Distinguishing practitioner inquiry from traditional research and from pedagogical documentation is essential to begin to look critically and systematically at teaching as an inquiry process. Educational leaders have a vital role here.

2   Practitioner inquiry is, at best, a group activity. Teachers get the most out of it when it is done collaboratively with other teachers and when they involve critical colleagues, typically fellow teachers, who participate in research to provide one another with feedback on the accuracy, trustworthiness, and depth of analysis, findings, and implications of the inquiry. And, as stated earlier, educational leaders can create or initiate sustained professional development to encourage the intentional and systematic exploration of assumptions and ideas, the careful observation and attention to evidence, and the reflective examination of alternative interpretations and possibilities. In essence, they can create a professional culture and a sense of teaching as intellectual work.

3   Research questions should be generated by teachers themselves to create a sense of autonomy and ownership, connectedness, and competence as researchers. That is, practitioner inquiry should encourage and allow for three important elements: agency, connectedness, and competence or capability. Thus, it becomes a form of meaningful, sustainable professional development.

4   The methods used by traditional or academic researchers in the sciences and social sciences are not appropriate for developmental practitioner inquiry. The former requires resources that teachers do not have, it does not satisfy their need to know, and it does not match the rhythm of teaching. The methods of practitioner inquiry must be embedded in what teachers already do daily in the classroom.

5   And finally, for teachers to engage in research, opportunities need to be created for them to have time for conversation, the sharing of ideas and perspectives, and the establishment of a common research purpose, orientation, and commitment to action.

Practitioner inquiry in many ways challenges the assumptions that define teaching in the current age of educational accountability and narrow forms of evidence-based practice. Alternatively, it offers a compelling framework for viewing the teacher as an intellectually and critically deep and creative thinker. It promotes the idea of teaching as intellectual experimental work, an idea embedded in an education for democracy framework emphasizing the need to liberate and humanize education with a pedagogy of questioning, an approach that opens opportunities for thinking, wondering, and critically examining.

Reference

Lytle, S., & Cochran-Smith, M. (1994). Inquiry, knowledge and practice. In S. Hollingsworth & H. Sockett (Eds.), *Teacher research and educational reform* (pp. 22–51). University of Chicago Press.

Conclusion

Thinking Together

Alma Fleet, Katey De Gioia, Marina Papic and Catherine Patterson

The introduction of this book invites "you to take the time to read, to question, and to be provoked as we let the production unfold". The conclusion challenges you to reflect on your reading, be it a part, chapter, section, or the book in its entirety, to understand your current practice and ways of moving into a new model of professional learning that enables and sustains change in practice over time. As the curtain falls on this production, walk with us through a conceptual framework for engaging in educational change.

As editors of this book, we were struck by the key themes identified in the chapters and commentaries. These themes elicited a rich and robust conversation associated with educational change through practitioner inquiry. Notes were hurriedly jotted, and diagrams drafted with each of us sharing, discussing, revisiting pages in the book. What emerged was our conceptual framework presented below. Three interrelated components critical to practitioner inquiry—purposes, processes and professional learning—sit as the core foundation of the framework. These components do not exist in isolation but are dependent on the context in which the practitioner inquiry is situated, and the people embedded within that context. We note that where there is success, all components are critically integrated for educational change to occur. Each of these pieces of the framework are explored further below.

Purposes

Although we have identified that practitioner inquiry is an opportunity for educational change, we can't be 'accidental' practitioner inquirers! Before embarking on a journey of inquiry, the intent, purpose, and anticipated impact of the inquiry needs to be clear for the individual to ensure buy-in and engagement, a willingness to take a risk and feel safe to try something new based on the data collected. More broadly, individuals cannot act alone. Whether the room team, service or organisation are involved in practitioner inquiry, in their own cycle, or not, ongoing communication about the purpose of and support for the inquiry will guide the individual in the change process.

We acknowledge the sustained attention and professional growth that emerges from practitioner inquiry enables teachers and educators to investigate their own pedagogical practice, where the questions worth asking are those that

DOI: 10.4324/9781003245827-20

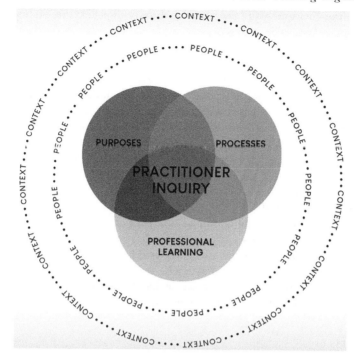

Figure 13.1 Practitioner Inquiry Framework

are meaningful to the practitioner and come from the real-world challenges in their practice. The scene is set by the context; the connection between the inquirer and the inquiry are aligned, and the meaning about the problem develops within this context.

Processes

For the novice inquirer, the process of practitioner inquiry is learnt alongside investigation of the inquiry being explored. The complex nature of these two processes running parallel should not be understated. Supportive infrastructure, including external facilitation, can be key to a successful cycle; noting that 'success' is about working effectively through the inquiry cycle. There may be points throughout the process in which the inquirer is not feeling 'success' but rather a myriad of complexities whilst continually examining, interrogating and changing practice through informed decision-making (Jhagroo et al., 2021).

Offering time for the process is critical, enabling deep connection to the problem and the ability to engage in and sustain change. Framing an inquiry question takes time and the reframing of the question often continues throughout the inquiry process as data assists in understanding not just the question, but the analysis of data provides clarity of the problem at hand. Data is a key component of the cycle of inquiry; data may exist, or methods developed to collect and triangulate data. Data gathered through a variety of means may confirm or dispel existing findings. Spirals of investigation characterise the process.

Professional Learning

Professional learning is another key component of educational change through practitioner inquiry. We have highlighted that there are many facets of professional learning that occur during the first foray into practitioner inquiry that may not be explicit. The novice inquirer tentatively steps forward, learning the craft while investigating the question of inquiry. With continuous cycles of practitioner inquiry over time, the intrepid investigator is provided with multiple opportunities to deepen professional growth and empowerment.

Gutierez (2019) reminds us of the role of organised communities of practice or networking to share learning, impact and perspectives of change and change processes. Small communities of practice, or provision for teachers and educators to share learning along the way, also enables articulation of the problem and the reasons for change, and deepens teacher reflection (Jhagroo et al., 2021). This community endeavour acts as incidental professional learning and development beyond the individual question of inquiry.

Contexts

Practitioner inquirers are embedded in the context of their teaching, their setting, and their community. These contexts drive but also support the inquiry and the ultimate change in practice. Within the context, reflection takes place, the dialogue occurs, the question emerges, the data are collected, and analysis and learning take place. Each context is different and needs to be considered in all aspects of the inquiry process. Reflection on what practitioners believe could be improved in their classroom and environment emerges in the context, foregrounding the uniqueness of the setting and the community.

Practitioner inquiry does not sit alone; it is not isolated in the classroom; it is not about gaining knowledge by one teacher. It is the theatre where the inquiry purposes, processes and professional learning take place. Both short-term and longer-term initiatives have the potential to promote professional growth and educational change, and both benefit from ongoing support within the context.

People

Children themselves, and the desire for better outcomes for children are at the centre of educational change—both playing a critical role in affecting the focus of the inquiry and the change in practice. Practitioners with different backgrounds, experiences, qualifications, and perspectives can work together through practitioner inquiry. Each bring their own strengths to the inquiry. Collaboration and engagement with colleagues, and with the children, families and the wider community support deep reflection on one's own practice and the development of an intentional inquiry question which drives the inquiry and educational change.

Leading sustainable change requires a commitment by leaders to professional development that provides early childhood practitioners time and space to question, reflect, research, and engage in dialogue. Like directors leading actors, musicians, and lighting technicians to give a quality performance, pedagogical leaders bring others on a journey of continuous improvement through a shared vision to support their teams to provide a quality learning environment and experience for children.

As the Curtain Comes Down: A Word of Warning

While many of the accounts in this book highlight positive aspects of practitioner inquiry, it is also appropriate to acknowledge there may be a 'dark side' for some participants. Practitioner inquiry may come with "ambiguities, mistakes, frustrations, tensions, conflicts and disappointment" (Bartels & Friedman, 2022, p. 99). It is not unusual to struggle with feelings of doubt and uncertainty, and as suggested by Embury et al. (2020) the uncertainty of engaging in practitioner research and "the exposure of one's professional practice" (p. 131) can be confronting. Bartels and Friedman (2022) suggest that becoming more aware of the potentially negative aspects of practitioner inquiry helps teachers be more prepared for setbacks or challenges, as focusing "only in the bright side … risks creating unrealistic expectations" (p. 100).

Chapters in this book have revealed that early childhood practitioners are often challenged by the process itself, including the identification of a focus question, gathering and analysing relevant data, and other related concerns. If this uncertainty of engagement in the research process is anticipated, then appropriate strategies may be put in place to promote professional growth and confidence. Practitioners are often more willing to persist with challenging processes when their work is "situated within trusting supportive relationships" (Fleet et al., 2016, p. 171). These relationships can be built by providing time for conversations, encouraging an understanding of diverse perspectives, and acknowledging that participants may vary in their readiness to change their pedagogical practices.

Another shadow on the 'dark side' of practitioner inquiry is presented by Mockler and Groundwater-Smith (2015) who reflect on potential shortcomings of 'celebrating' inquiry outcomes. They argue that "taking a celebratory stance … may eclipse [teachers'] capacity to confront larger and more intransigent issues" (p. 604). Mockler and Groundwater-Smith (2015) acknowledge that while inquiry celebrations are "usually highly engaging and enjoyable, [they] have rarely provided the kinds of counter narratives that might contribute to a more radical and rigorous set of possibilities for change and reform" (p. 607). Issues of social justice, accounts of failures, encounters with obstacles of power and authority are often ignored when a celebratory stance becomes the expectation for everyone. Mockler and Groundwater-Smith encourage us to move beyond celebrations to be willing to critique, to dive "beneath the surface to consider some of the messy dynamics … that are less to be celebrated and more to be problematised, re-thought and improved upon" (p. 611–612).

Thinking Forward

Reflecting on the contents of this book, we find both wide-angle and close-up versions of experiences with practitioner inquiry. These portrayals highlight what authors have chosen to notice and recognise, both the diversity of ways 'into' as well as 'the experiencing of' practitioner inquiry. Looking across the material, we find clear affirmation of the components of practitioner inquiry as previously identified in the literature as core to this way of thinking together, recognising the nature of adult learners and teachers as researchers. In addition, this focussed attention to inquiry pathways of early childhood educational change has broadened and enriched the conversation.

The authors have demonstrated:

- the importance of philosophical positioning and valuing of the potentials and agency of both adults and children,
- the relevance of context as critical to inquiry design and implementation,
- and the importance of environmental pragmatics—including avoiding simplistic interpretations and valuing unfolding complexity.

In this compilation, it is clear:

- that challenges are inevitable and may contribute to professional growth,
- that nurturing environments benefit from supportive leadership and infrastructure,
- and that approaches to accountability can be accommodated through an inquiry orientation.

Considering contributions from colleagues who have pursued these ideas for some time, it is apparent that:

- sustainability emerges from initiatives embedded and supported over time,
- collaborative, collegial relationships energise effective inquiry contexts, creating productive learning communities, and
- flexibility and willingness to work within the unknown strengthens investigations.

Finally, it is illustrated clearly that personal commitment and professional narratives bind inquiry processes together.

We have very much enjoyed working with these ideas and celebrating the professional growth in the narratives. Now, we hand them over to you, and offer them for your consideration and ongoing conversations.

Author Note: We would like to thank Anne-Marie Fernandes who interpreted our original rough sketch, and with patience and good humour created the Professional Inquiry Framework.

References

Bartels, K., & Friedman, V. (2022). Shining light on the dark side of action research: Power, relationality and transformation [Editorial]. *Action Research*, 20(2), 99–104. https://doi.org/10.1177/14767503221098033.

Embury, D. D., Parenti, M., & Childers-McKee, C. (2020). A change to educational action researchers [Editorial]. *Action Research*, 18(2). https://doi.org/10.1177/1476750320919189.

Fleet, A., De Gioia, K., & Patterson, C. (2016). *Engaging with educational change: Voices of practitioner inquiry*. Bloomsbury.

Gutierez, S.B. (2019). Teacher-practitioner research inquiry and sense making of their reflections on scaffolded collaborative lesson planning experience. *Asia Pacific Science Education*, 5(8). https://doi.org/10.1186/s41029-019-0043-x.

Jhagroo, J., Bansilal, S., & Stringer, P. (2021). Teacher learning insights from two practice-based inquiries in South Africa and New Zealand. *New Zealand Journal of Educational Studies*, 56(1), 65–81. https://doi.org/10.1007/s40841-020-00184-y.

Mockler, N., & Groundwater-Smith, S. (2015). Seeking for the unwelcome truths: Beyond celebration in inquiry-based teacher professional learning. *Teachers and Teaching*, 21(5), 603–614. https://doi.org/10.1080/13540602.2014.995480.

Index

Note: bold page numbers indicate tables; italic page numbers indicate figures; page numbers followed by n refer to notes.

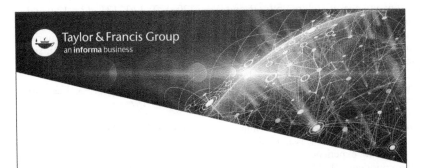

For Product Safety Concerns and Information please contact our EU
representative GPSR@taylorandfrancis.com Taylor & Francis Verlag GmbH,
Kaufingerstraße 24, 80331 München, Germany

Printed and bound by CPI Group (UK) Ltd, Croydon, CR0 4YY
08/06/2025
01896986-0008